KINGS
WITHOUT
PRIVILEGE

KINGS
WITHOUT
PRIVILEGE

David and Moses in the Story of
the Bible's Kings

A. GRAEME AULD

T&T CLARK
EDINBURGH

BS
1345.2
A95
1994

T&T CLARK LTD
59 GEORGE STREET
EDINBURGH EH2 2LQ
SCOTLAND

Copyright © T&T Clark Ltd, 1994

First published 1994

ISBN 0 567 09639 4

British Library Cataloguing-in-Publication Data
A catalogue record for this book is available from the British Library

Typeset by Type Aligne, Edinburgh
Printed and bound in Great Britain by Bookcraft, Avon

Contents

Preface

The connections between the Book of Deuteronomy and the following narrative books in the Hebrew Scriptures – and especially Joshua and Kings, the first and last of these – are clear to any attentive reader. It has become a commonplace amongst specialists to term Joshua, Judges, Samuel, and Kings 'the Deuteronomistic books'. The year 1943 saw the publication of Martin Noth's famous argument: Joshua-Kings did not just have close links with Deuteronomy; they comprised a history brought to unity out of quite disparate source-materials by an exilic scholar who had drawn his key ideas and most prominent language from the Book of Deuteronomy, or at least from the largest part of it which had been shaped towards the end of Judah's monarchy. That same 1943 publication included Noth's no less influential account of the Chronicler's History: that comprised Chronicles, Ezra, and Nehemiah, and its main source was the books of Samuel and Kings as we know them. A brief appendix suggested how Noth saw his work bearing on the vexed question of Pentateuchal origins: the sources used in Numbers had not continued into (Deuteronomy and) Joshua; it was Deuteronomy and Joshua that had influenced the composition of the final chapters of Numbers. The development of biblical thought, as Noth charted it 50 years ago, was outwards from Deuteronomy: through the Deuteronomistic History to the Chronicler's History; and through Joshua to Numbers and the final shape of the Pentateuch. Most scholarship in the last half-century has worked within Noth's conceptual structure, even where there has been vigorous debate over the details of his presentation.

This study, published in the jubilee year of Noth's Deuteronomist and Chronicler, starts by questioning Noth's assumption – and the assumption of most scholars before and since in the last two centuries – about the relationship between these two narratives. It reads them side by side and probes their common origins; and finds that it is then freed to pose new questions about the inter-connectedness of Deuteronomy and the Deuteronomistic books. Kings and Chronicles emerge from this fresh scrutiny not as history and revised history, nor as text and commentary, but as alternative or competing appropriations of an earlier story of Judah's kings. And Deuteronomy, the date of its completion pushed inexorably later, emerges as influenced by the story that follows, and not simply the source of its ideas and language.

Without a two-term sabbatical in 1992, this work would have been impossible. The several weeks I spent during May to June at the British School of Archaeology and in the École Biblique library in Jerusalem, and during November with Bentley Layton and in the library of the Yale Divinity School, were as stimulating as they were enjoyable. My Edinburgh colleague Iain Provan kindly read the whole text, and made a number of helpful suggestions. And consistent encouragement has come from the one whom an observant correspondent regularly greets as 'the other' or 'the real Dr Auld'.

New College,
University of Edinburgh

Abbreviations

AASF	Annales Academiae Scientiarum Fennicae, Helsinki: Suomalainen Tiedeakatemien
AB	Anchor Bible, New York: Doubleday
AOAT	Alter Orient und Altes Testament, Neukirchen-Vluyn: Neukirchener Verlag
AThANT	Abhandlungen zur Theologie des Alten und Neuen Testaments, Zürich: Theologischer Verlag
ATSAT	Arbeiten zu Text und Sprache im Alten Testament, St. Ottilien: Eos Verlag
BEATAJ	Beiträge zur Erforschung des Alten Testaments und des Antiken Judentums, Frankfurt am Main: Lang
Bib	*Biblica*
BIOSCS	*Bulletin of the International Organization for Septuagint and Cognate Studies*
BZAW	Beihefte zur Zeitschrift für die Alttestamentliche Wissenschaft, Berlin: de Gruyter
CBQ	*Catholic Biblical Quarterly*
DSB	Daily Study Bible, Edinburgh: St Andrews Press
EI	Eretz Israel, Jerusalem: Israel Exploration Society
FRLANT	Forschungen zur Religion und Literatur des Alten und Neuen Testaments
FS	Festschrift
HAR	*Hebrew Annual Review*
HSM	Harvard Semitic Monographs, Atlanta: Scholars Press
HUCA	*Hebrew Union College Annual*
ICC	International Critical Commentary, Edinburgh: T&T Clark
JBS	Jerusalem Biblical Studies, Tel Aviv: Simor
JSOT	*Journal for the Study of the Old Testament*

JSOTS	Journal for the Study of the Old Testament Supplements, Sheffield: JSOT Press
JTS	*Journal of Theological Study*
LXX	Septuagint
MT	Masoretic Text
NCB	New Century Bible, London: Marshall, Morgan & Scott
NPAJ	New Perspectives on Ancient Judaism
OBO	Orbis Biblicus et Orientalis, Freiburg [CH]: Universitätsverlag
OTS	Oudtestamentische Studiën, Leiden: Brill
RB	*Revue Biblique*
SBL	Society of Biblical Literature
SBT	Studies in Biblical Theology, London: SCM
SSN	Studia Semitica Neerlandica, Assen/Maastricht: Van Gorcum
SVT	Supplements to Vetus Testamentum, Leiden: Brill
ThW	Theologische Wissenschaft, Stuttgart: Kohlhammer
ThZ	*Theologische Zeitschrift*
WBC	Word Biblical Commentary, Waco, Texas: Word Publishing
WMANT	Wissenschaftliche Monographien zum Alten und Neuen Testament, Neukirchen-Vluyn: Neukirchener Verlag
ZAH	*Zeitschrift für Althebraistik*
ZAW	*Zeitschrift für die Alttestamentliche Wissenschaft*

1

Introduction

This book proposes a very simple solution to what is widely held to be a very controverted problem. Its argument, therefore, is either creatively radical or absurdly naive – I fear there is no middle way. Of course I hope for the one verdict rather than the other; but it would certainly be naive to expect it. The solution proposed has quite wide ramifications. Some of these are glimpsed in the following pages, but require much further exploration; many have not yet been dreamed of. I sketch the argument now at book-length, though far from exhaustively, because it requires more explanation than was possible either when I first advanced it (Auld 1983: 14–16, 1986: 2–3), or even where I have more recently explored more fully a fraction of the evidence (Auld, 1992, 1993). However, although I myself have no time in the immediate future to develop the issues further, I hope others will be interested to explore the issues from the perspective I am recommending. Even if they detect only rubble from yet another failed attempt, that in itself may save them from similar mistakes.

1.1 Finishing Solomon's Prayer

Solomon ends his long prayer at the dedication of the temple quite differently in Kings and Chronicles. His appeal here to Moses and there to David has suggested to me the subtitle for this book and some of the lines of enquiry which it reports. After some forty verses of petition (1 Kgs 8: 12–50a // 2 Chr 6: 1–39) in which the two books agree almost word for word, each account of the prayer moves to a brief culminating request of the deity. Kings makes a double claim on the relationship between Yahweh and

1

Israel since the deliverance from Egypt: more briefly in v. 51 and at greater length, this time mentioning Moses by name, in v. 53. Chronicles however, has Solomon request Yahweh's attention to 'a prayer of this place' (v. 40b); and in the following two verses the prayer turns out to be a version of Psalm 132: 8–10, concluding with the words 'Remember thy steadfast love for David thy servant.'

Each is a strong ending: the one appeals to divine loyalty to the founder of the dynasty, the other to a relationship between God and people as old as the separated nation liberated from Egypt. And each is typical of the book in which it is used. Chronicles makes use at other points (most extensively in 1Chr 16) of sacred poetry we also know from the book of Psalms; and that book features David as cultic organiser to an extent unparallelled in (Samuel and) Kings. Kings, on the other side, mentions the exodus from Egypt more often than the Chronicler: in other small pluses within the Solomon story (1Kgs 6: 1; 8: 21) and elsewhere (2Sam 7: 6;[1] 2Kgs 21: 15), as well as in passages relating to northern Israel (1Kgs 12: 28; 2Kgs 17: 7, 36) which are not represented at all in Chronicles.

Each of these endings is largely independent of the other, although both resume a hope from earlier in the prayer (1Kgs 8: 29 // 2Chr 6: 20) that Yahweh's eyes should remain open; and so it is not easy to argue that either has been reshaped from the other. Of course the one ending may have simply supplanted the other. However, the seventh and final petition in the preceding common text is also the most lengthy and detailed, and that may already suggest that a more original climax to the prayer has been reached there. Our preliminary conclusion is that each of Solomon's concluding requests is a secondary addition to the long prayer text which Kings and Chronicles share. The one supplement is as typical of the book in which we find it as the other.

Each new ending draws on and develops resources available within the shorter text common to both books. The exodus theme to which appeal is made so frequently in Deuteronomy may be more prominent in Samuel-Kings than in Chronicles; and

---

[1] But see also footnote 2 on p. 46 on the exodus theme in this verse.

Chronicles may make more of David and the Psalms. However, it is important to note that David and Moses are each appealed to in key verses that both books share. The common story often features the divine promises to David and his line and the conduct of David. But it is also true that references to the Moses exodus traditions in that common story, though much less frequent, are located at strategic points in the report of the dedication of the temple (1Kgs 8: 9 // 2Chr 5: 10 and 1Kgs 8: 16 //2 Chr 6: 5); and in the account of Solomon's second (Jerusalem) vision (1Kgs 9: 9 // 2Chr 7: 22).[1] And the place of Moses as classic mediator of the divine will for his people is also enshrined in material common to Kings and Chronicles.[2] The distinct conclusions to Solomon's long prayer are a part of wider patterns in Kings and Chronicles. That has been easily established in a few words. What I want to suggest in this book is that these are not simply surface or occasional patterns, but deeper structural patterns which actually indicate how the books of (Samuel-) Kings and Chronicles came to be.

1.2 Going behind W. M. L. de Wette

De Wette's judgment that the Books of Chronicles are both derived from and historically inferior to the books of Samuel-Kings has cast its shadow over biblical studies for almost two centuries. For de Wette these two claims were closely interrelated. The prevailing view before his Beiträge was that each of these biblical narratives drew on a common source. De Wette, sensing doubtless correctly the historical unreliability and artificiality of the Books of Chronicles, argued that Chronicles not only depended on Samuel-Kings (and so was even more distant than Samuel-Kings themselves from the sources these books had used), but also represented a wilful recasting of their materials.

[1] There is a reference to Egypt in each account of the oracle of Nathan, but at quite different points – 2Sam 7: 6 and 1Chr 17: 25. Chronicles also has one other Exodus, or at least desert-wandering, plus in 2Chr 20: 10 – discussed by Japhet (see p. 8 below).

[2] Moses appears ten times in 1 and 2 Kings, though only in eight passages; and twelve times in 2 Chronicles, in ten passages. However, only three of these passages are common to Kings and Chronicles; and the Kings and Chronicles pluses highlight quite different aspects of the Pentateuchal Moses.

His views were elaborated by both Wellhausen (1889) and Noth (1943). The results of these path-breakers have been developed more recently in many careful commentaries and monographs. Yet, I want to suggest anew that independent supplementation of a common inherited text may be a better model for understanding the interrelationships of Samuel-Kings and Chronicles than the dominant view since de Wette which portrays Chronicles as a substantial reshaping of Samuel-Kings – a reshaping that had involved quite as much pruning of unwanted material as encouragement of fresh growth. However, to avoid misunderstanding, I must insist at the outset on one point: In seeking to explore again the view he rejected, that the parallel biblical histories had a common source, I am in no way resiling from de Wette the modern historian's feel for the Chronicler as unreliable ancient historian. His own instincts were sound; and substantial support has been given in more recent decades by Willi (1972), Welten (1973), and Williamson (1977, 1982), to name only a few. What I am doing is opening Samuel-Kings as they stand to similarly radical literary and historical scrutiny. For I suspect that these books exemplify an appropriation of more ancient traditions of Israel and Judah that is no less partisan than the Chronicler's. Some other preliminary indicators deserve a mention.

I already offered a sketch of this proposal some years ago after comparing the very different usage in Samuel-Kings and Chronicles of the Hebrew word *nby'* always rendered 'prophet' and of the verb forms related to it (Auld 1983). The story of the Davidic line which these books share is framed by the oracles of Nathan (2Sam 7 // 1Chr 17) and Huldah (2Kgs 22 // 2Chr 34). Each book calls Nathan 'the prophet' and Huldah the 'prophetess'. And each book has a lot to say in between about other prophetic figures, some named and some anonymous, and their messages. Yet, while much of the general content is shared, they only once again use the noun 'prophet' or the related verb about the same person at the same time; and that is in the unique account, unique both in terms of length and type of subject matter, they share about Micaiah and the four hundred prophets whom Yahweh had deceived. Just as with the different endings to the Solomonic prayer, we face two critical options in this matter of prophetic language. Either, as I think, the prophetic theme in each book is the product of separate and substantial development of a much slimmer though vitally placed feature in their common source. Or Chronicles has made a series of modifications to its supposed source-book (i.e. Samuel-Kings) many of which appear quite unnecessary to its own materials and purposes.

More recently (Auld 1992, 1993) I have have provided two complementary accounts of the first element of the portraits of Solomon in Kings and Chronicles, of the rather different reports in 1Kgs3 and 2Chr 1 of Solomon's first vision – reports so divergent that at first sight they appear to have only one or two verses in common. On closer inspection, however, I have found that they share much more material: quite sufficient to reconstruct a hypothetical original vision-report whose wording could have been very lightly altered and more substantially supplemented to produce the two versions we know.

If it proves possible to generalise from the convergent results of these first scattered probes, the results for the study of Chronicles will be more modest: the Chronicler's motives for omitting great tracts of material from his principal source will simply no longer have to be explored. But the implications for our understanding of the composition of Samuel and Kings will be much more striking. For some decades we have attempted to cope with radically opposed appropriations of and modifications of Noth's account of the books of Samuel and Kings as part of a Deuteronomistic History. Something must be wrong with our appreciation of the issues at stake. Thankfully – and here the thanks are shared by author and readers – I do not require to offer yet another review of the development of the Deuteronomistic History problem. Several competent efforts have been made in that direction in very recent years, for example Provan (1988), O'Brien (1989), McKenzie (1991). Yet I suspect that none of the attached solutions has been sufficiently radical. No one doubts that Kings is part of a wider context that is in some sense Deuteronomistic. But there are irreconcileable differences between scholars when they come to pinpointing just where and how Kings is Deuteronomisitc, and just how many Deuteronomistic voices speak through its pages. If we come to feel entitled to view the material commong to Kings and Chronicles as also the source of Kings, no less than of Chronicles, then these issues will also be substantially reconfigured.

1.3 Literary History and Textual History: Julio Trebolle Barrera

Trebolle-Barrera has produces a series of path-breaking studies, mostly on Samuel and Kings, that demonstrate the very close relationship between editorial or redactional issues and text-critical issues in these books. That the various ancient witnesses to the text of Kings have a very complex relationship to each other is no new knowledge. That some of the key differences between these witnesses result from design not accident is no new knowledge. But Trebolle has argued with particular cogency that the answers to long-perceived conundrums are to be found in the Lucianic Greek tradition and in the Old Latin tradition of Samuel and Kings. As he put it once in surprising and challenging fashion: Old Latin, witness to an older Greek, witness to the oldest Hebrew. His two major studies are in Spanish, and have dealt with Solomon and Jeroboam (1980) and Jehu and Joash (1984). He has published short extracts from these books and some shorter studies in English (e.g. 1982) and French. His latest contribution (in French) is mostly concerned with Kings: it offers not only a particularly clear and authoritative restatement of his position, but interesting fresh Hebrew evidence for it from the Dead Sea Scrolls. Several details of this article (in press) will occupy us later.

Two recurring features of his work interest me here: One is the occasional important agreement between Chronicles and the Lucianic tradition in Kings. The other is that the larger part of the Kings material with which he deals is not parallelled in Chronciles. The ancient witnesses to Kings seem much less variable over the material Kings shares with Chronicles. The greatest variation between the different ancient texts of Kings is mostly within the material which I am suggesting was added to the common source of Kings and Chronicles to make the book of Kings as we know it. I suspect that, just because it was being added to an existing corpus of traditions, there were different views about where it should be placed – and these are reflected in the different ancient witnesses.

1.4 Kings and Chronicles: Steven McKenzie

McKenzie has also made a substantial start on the fresh spproach that seems to be required in two books (1985, 1991). The earlier was essentially his doctoral dissertation prepared under Cross at Harvard, and so possibly not sufficiently free from his mentor's influential model for understanding Deuteronomistic and Chronistic issues. He argued that the Samuel-Kings used by the Chronicler as his main source were not the books in the form we possess them, but an earlier edition. He was essentially seeking to use Chronicles to clarify the distinction made by Cross (1973) and elaborated by Nelson (1981) between a first (Josianic) edition of the history (Dtr 1) and a second (exilic) one (Dtr 2). In the last words of that study, McKenzie concluded: 'although C is not a completely reliable criterion for isolating Dtr 2 material, at least where C has a parallel to a K passage, one must be extremely cautious about attributing the latter to Dtr 2. There must be reason to suspect that the Chronicles passage as it stands is not from Chr 1's edition.' (1985: 206)

His more recent 'Trouble with Kings' appears to represent almost an alternative approach to the Book of Kings and its problems. There is remarkably little mention of his first book; and, where it is quoted, it is in relation to matters of detail rather than larger issues. McKenzie too has been influenced by Trebolle's insistence on the interconnection of textual and editorial issues, and commits his first main chapter to a critical review of Trebolle's presentation of the alternative LXX account of Jeroboam's emergence. From the prophetic interests in the Jeroboam story, he moves to reviews of oracles against Israelite dynasties and other prophetic additions to Kings, and then, through substantial chapters on Hezekiah and Josiah in Kings, finally to issues of dating and overall composition. In find myself in sympathy with much of the drift of this book, not least to viewing much of 1 Kgs 17–2 Kgs 10, including most of the Elijah-Elisha narratives, as not part of the original edition of Kings. But even McKenzie has been insufficiently radical.

In his first book he sought Chronicles' help in solving a particular issue of Kings criticism, and deduced rightly that important elements of what Kings now reports about Judah were not in the version of Kings known to the Chronicler.[1] Then, when facing in the second book the larger issues of Kings scholarship, he concluded that a great deal of the material in Kings about northern Israel and especially its prophets was not part of the first edition of Kings. But nowhere has he drawn these two arguments together, and gone on to pose the necessary and more radical question – whether the main source of Chronicles contained any independent material about Israel at all. Of course Chronicles too offers some information about Israel as part of Judah's story, but hardly more than it offers about others of Judah's neighbours, such as Aram or Edom or Ammon. Arising out of McKenzie's two important studies, each of Samuel-Kings and Chronicles must now have its growth measured in terms of the much shorter text common to them both. When we re-focus first on the common text and its language and attitudes, and then on the principles embodied in possibly several levels of Samuel-Kings pluses, our perception of first and second Deuteronomists, or of Dtr H – Dtr P – Dtr N, will inevitably – and perhaps beneficially – be altered.

The radical creativity of the Chronicler is not in doubt.[2] And one of the advances exemplified in studies of Chronicles in more recent decades has been positive recoginition of the Chronicler as independent commentator on the text available to him for the purposes of his own period and community – this over against the apparent historical willfulness which distressed the historian's conscience of a de Wette, or a Wellhausen, or a Noth. But what I fear is that by over-emphasising the Chronicler's radical freedom, by continuing to suppose that he not only adapted much of what he inherited and composed substantial fresh material but also deleted and even suppressed much more, we may for far too long

---

[1] McKenzie's earlier book has not generally won the recognition it deserved. But its arguments have been heeded in some significant successor studies such as Barnes (1991).

[2] Japhet (1989) has very conveniently marshalled the materials for an ideological comparison of Samuel/Kings and Chronicles. Her principal strategy for pin-pointing the ideology of Chronicles is to compare that book with what she also deems its source-material in Samuel-Kings, weighing the pluses and minuses for their tendency. Unfortunately, since she does not appear to have taken the opportunity to update what started as her dissertation, and was published in Hebrew in 1977, when issuing it in English translation, there is the drawback that this recent publication contains neither discussion with allies like Williamson nor critique of McKenzie or Trebolle.

have unwittingly prevented recognition of similar creativity in those who produced the books of Samuel and Kings. In fact, by privileging the books of Samuel and Kings as the 'text' to which Chronicles is mere 'commentary', we may have been insufficiently sensitive to the degree to which Samuel-Kings are also commentary on an earlier text.

1.5 The Books of Chronicles – Benchmark for Late Biblical Hebrew?

One well-known objection to our whole enterprise has to be mentioned and summarily answered before we go any further: that the language of Chronicles is markedly later Hebrew than the language of Samuel and Kings. The unspoken inference is that since Samuel-Kings with their earlier grammar and spelling had been completed long before Chronicles with its later forms was composed, these earlier narratives must have been familiar to – and available to – the Chronicler; and so it is idle to propose a relationship between Samuel-Kings and Chronicles other than the familiar thesis. Two recent studies with very different concerns from our own have set the often quoted evidence in a wholly new light. Verheij's close analysis (1990) of the varying use of the Hebrew verb in Samuel, Kings, and Chronicles has shown a remarkable number of examples of characteristically 'later' verb forms in Samuel-Kings. And Barr's study of variation in spelling in the Masoretic Bible (1989) has documented first that Chronicles is far from consistent in use of the fuller (*plene*) spellings, and second that Samuel-Kings have many more such spellings than is usually recognised. Barr, I think helpfully, attributes much of the variation to later copyists of these books rather than to their authors.

This is not the place for a review of these important studies. But they do encourage me to make two points. Chronicles was 'known' on historical grounds to be later than Samuel-Kings, and so its linguistic differences could also be explained in terms of historical development – both Barr and Verheij may have exposed a degree of circularity in much of the discussion of the development from earlier to later biblical Hebrew. Then, even if Masoretic Chronicles is broadly an example of somewhat later Hebrew than

Masoretic Samuel-Kings, that may tell us more about the freedom
with which one or the other was copied and less about relative
dates of composition.

I might add that the complete Isaiah scroll found at Qumran
serves as a good example of what I have in mind: the orthography
of even the most ancient copy we happen to possess of a biblical
book is far from a secure guide to the orthography of the original
composition, and so to the date of that original. If we possessed
only the ancient Qumran copies of Isaiah, and not the very much
later though more conservative Masoretic copies of that book, we
might draw quite wrong conclusions about the grammar and
spelling of Isaiah or the Isaiah school. In the case of the Qumran
text of Isaiah, nobody suggests we are dealing with different
books from the Masoretic version or of different authorship. And
so their evidence is all the more interesting of how free some
scribes could be as they copied a manuscript, whether that
freedom was exercised deliberately or in more haphazard fashion.
Proto-Masoretic Chronicles may have experienced more of their
freedom than Samuel-Kings. If it really is the case that the Books
of Chronicles were 'canonised' later – and to a lesser degree –
than the Books of Samuel and Kings, that might explain greater
flexibility in their official handling. Of course, such an explanation
would have to dismiss Qumran Isaiah as an unofficial copy of a
book from the prophetic 'canon'.

1.6 Outlook

We are playing in this enquiry for important prizes - a fresh
understanding of the development of Samuel-Kings on the one
side and Chronicles on the other. Perhaps even more fascinating:
if we can persuade readers that a text containing more or less
simply the material common to both Samuel-Kings and Chronicles
did once exist, new and more secure appreciation will be possible
of how two biblical books interpreted a now-lost book available to
them both. And furthermore, comparisons will be possible of that
long submerged text with possibly related materials within
Pentateuch, Prophets, and Psalms. In a brief radicalisation of
McKenzie's (1985) conclusion noted above: where C and K are
running in parallel, we have to have good grounds for terming

their shared material 'Deuteronomistic'. These are the goals. A brief conspectus follows immediately of the David and Solomon story common to Samuel-Kings and Chronicles, and of the further material preserved in each of the biblical books. The most extended portrayals in the common narrative, as also in the familiar biblical books, are those of David and Solomon. Then, because we have already introduced some of the issues, and also because it happens to offer in microcosm opportunities to study the problems that recur throughout any synoptic[1] analysis of the two biblical histories, we shall devote most of our next chapter to a more detailed account of the divergent portraits of David's royal son and designated heir, concluding it with a much briefer mention of the portrayal of David in Samuel and 1 Chronicles. It is not in the nature of much of the material discussed in this book to be talking about proof. If demonstration might be claimed as a better word than proof, then what is offered is the demonstration that we can have a better view if we stand and look from where I am now standing.

---

[1] In a recent review of the available Synopses of Samuel-Kings and Chronicles, Verheij (1992) has sought to distance the relationship of these books in the Hebrew Bible from the 'Synoptic Problem' in the Gospels of the New Testament. I am claiming a much closer connection between the two issues; and in fact some of my proposals for the development of Kings and Chronicles are not unlike proposals relating to Gospels origins made in O'Neill (1991).

2

Solomon and David in Biblical Narrative

2.0 Introduction

The shared account of Solomon opens with his vision at Gibeon, moves to arrangements with Hiram over practical support for the temple building in Jerusalem, and reports its construction and the making of several cultic paraphernalia. The ark is installed in the innermost sanctuary, then Solomon offers a lengthy prayer of dedication, and leads the people in large-scale sacrifice. A second vision, now in Jerusalem, follows. After miscellaneous notes the queen of Sheba's visit is reported and other details of Solomon's trade and wealth are given.

Chronicles adds only a very few typical notes to this account. However, Kings supplies several quite large additions. Its opening chapter firsts poses and then answers the question 'Who will sit on the throne of David?' The second reports the final advice of a wordly wise father to an apt learner. In the third chapter, after the vision at Gibeon, we read an example of Solomon's judicial brilliance; and summary accounts follow in chapters 4–5 of his district administration, the provisioning of his court, and his wisdom. The building of the sanctuary and the fashioning of its holy objects (chapters 6–7) are complemented in Kings by the building of the royal apartments; and the lengthy prayer is separated from the sacrifice by a royal blessing of the people (8: 54–61). A final major plus (1 Kgs 11) relates Solomon's decline to his many foreign marriages, not least to Pharaoh's daughter.

In most portions of Kings/Chronicles it is apparently easy to

12

reconstruct the text common to the two books; for, in the great majority of instances, that shared text has been modified, usually by being added to, in only one of the familiar biblical books. In such cases the 'original' can be 'restored' by simply giving preference to the shorter text, or by spotting the reason for a small change in wording. However, in an important minority of cases, both successor versions of the older story of the court of Judah have apparently made alterations to their shared 'original'. And rather closer study of these is necessary before a satisfactory reconstruction can be offered.

Solomon's great prayer, at whose end we began our first chapter, offers a microcosm of the issues. Throughout the main body of the prayer we find a typical scatter of minor divergences both between the Masoretic texts in Kings and Chronicles and within the textual witnesses to each book. The situation at the end of the prayer is different, as we already discussed. God is finally appealed to on the basis of memories of Moses and Exodus in Kings, but of David and Temple in Chronicles. In other respects too Kings and Chronicles go their own way briefly before joining again to report in almost identical terms Solomon's second vision: Kings (8: 54 –61) reports a royal blessing of the gathered people; while Chronicles (7: 1–3) records the descent of the divine fire and the arrival of the divine glory at the conclusion of the king's prayer.

Scholarship in more recent decades has seen much sensitive attention paid to the Chronicler and his special interests, as these have been detected both in his minor adjustments to his source material in Samuel-Kings and in the characer of his substantial supplements to what he inherited. And more recent voices are making us ask again just how far the Chronicler should be credited or blamed for the majority of the smaller differences between the familiar texts of Samuel-Kings and Chronicles. McKenzie (1985) in particular has noted just how many features of Chronicles in the so-called synoptic passages are shared not simply by Greek Septuagintal texts of Samuel and Kings (that has long been known) but also by texts and fragments of these books in Hebrew found at Qumran. And this demonstration that in such small matters the Chronicler was often much more faithful to his source than has been supposed, and that that source was rather different from the Masoretic text of Samuel-Kings, has led him to go on to suppose (even where no written evidence is available) that where Chronicles is substantially at variance with Kings it was following source material no longer available to us.

2.1 Overview

David	Sam + 's	Sam close to Chr		Chr + 's
Saul dead		1 S 31:1-13	1C 10:1-12	
	2 S 1-4			10: 13-14
David king		5: 1-3	11: 1-3	
	5: 4-5			
Jerusalem taken		5: 6-10	11: 4-9	
		(23: 8-39)	11: 10-47	
				12: 1-40
		(6: 1-11)	13: 1-14	
Philistines defeated	5: 11-25	14:1-17		
Ark		6: 1-11	(13: 1-14)	
	6: 12-14a			14: 1-17
to				15: 1-24
		6: 14b	(15: 27b)	
Jerusalem		6: 15	15: 25	
				15: 26-27a, 28
		6: 16-19a	15: 29-16: 3	
				16: 4-42
		6: 19b-20a	16: 43	
	6: 20b-23			
Nathan oracle		7	17	
Various victories		8	18	
	9			
Joab,		10	19	
David		11: 1	20: 1a	
	11: 2-12: 25			
and		12: 26	20: 1b	
	12: 27-29			
Ammon		12: 30-31	20: 2-3	
	13-20			
	21: 1-17			
Goliath killed		21: 18-22	20: 4-8	
	22			
	23: 1-7			
David's heroes		23: 8-39	(11: 10-47)	
David's census		24: 1-25	21: 1-27	
				22-29
				(29: 23/1 K 2: 12)

Solomon	Kgs + 's	Kgs close to Chr		Chr + 's
(succession)	1: 1–2: 46			1: 1
Vision		3: 1–15	1: 2–13	
(judge administrator provisions wisdom)	3: 16–28 4: 1–20 5: 1–8 5: 9–14 (10: 26–29)			1: 14–17
Hiram		5: 15–25	2: 1–11, 14–15	
Temple built		6: 1–28	3: 1–13	
Palace built	7: 1–12			
Hiram/artist		7: 13–14	(2: 12–13)	
Cultic objects		7: 15–51	3: 15–5: 1	
Ark installed		8: 1–11	5: 2–11a, 14b	
Solomon prayer (blessing)	8: 50b–61	8: 12–50a (8: 54a*)	(7: 1a*)	5: 11b–14a 6: 1–39 6: 40–7: 3
Sacrifice		8: 62–66	7: 4–5, 7f., 10	7: 6, 9
Second vision		9: 1–9	7: 11–22	
Miscellaneous		9: 10–28	8: 1–18	
Sheba/trade		10: 1–26 10: 27–28a	9: 1–25 9: 27–28	(1: 14–17)
(decline) End formula	10: 28b–29 11: 1–40	11: 41–43	9: 29–31	

2.2 The Vision at Gibeon

I have recently given detailed scrutiny to one of these pairs of passages, the reports of Solomon's vision at Gibeon in 1 Kgs 3: 4–15 and 2 Chr 1: 3–13; and, as a result, have come to agree with the proposal that the Chronicler was using a source other than what we read in the book of Kings. However, I have also argued that this very source available to the Chronicler was also used, and redeveloped in a different direction, by the author of Kings. In the light of what I am urging elsewhere in this chapter about the importance of the rather different text of Kings preserved in the Greek Bible, I should note that there are a few significant variants between Hebrew and Greek in their accounts of this vision at Gibeon. However, these only bear on decisions about my reconstruction of the common original in 1 Kgs 3: 8b where, as Trebolle has noted, the Lucianic text of 3: 8b attests the plus 'sand of the sea'.

2.2.1 The text

Especially since my textual reconstruction in the articles to which I am referring is presented in Hebrew (Auld 1993) or in German (Auld 1992), it may be helpful if I present the evidence in English dress in full here. In the main left- and right-hand columns below, I offer a fairly literal rendering of 1 Kgs 3: 4–15; 4: 1 and of 2 Chr 1: 3–13, beside precise verse numberings for each clause. And in the central column I present my attempt at a reconstruction of the source-text used by both Kings and Chronicles.

Kgs ref	1 Kgs 3:4-15; 4:1	Reconstructed 'source'	1 Chr 1:3-13	Chr ref
4aA	And the king	And he	And Solomon and all the congregation with him	3aA
	went	went	went	
	to Gibeon to sacrifice there	to Gibeon to sacrifice there	to the high place at Gibeon	3aB
4aB	for that was the great high place.	for that was the great high place.	for the tent of God's appointed meeting, which Moses the servant of Yahweh had made in the wilderness was there.	3b
			But the ark of God David had brought up from Kiriath-jearim to the place that David had prepared for it, for he had pitched for it a tent in Jerusalem.	4

			Moreover the bronze altar that Bezalel the son of Uri, son of Hur, had made, was there before the tabernacle of Yahweh. And Solomon and the congregation sought him.	5
			And Solomon offered up there on the bronze altar before Yahweh, which was	6
4b	A thousand holocausts did Solomon offer up on that altar.	A thousand holocausts Solomon offer up on that altar.	at the tent of meeting – he offered on it a thousand holocausts.	
			In that night	7a
5a	In Gibeon Yahweh appeared to Solomon in a dream of the night	God appeared to Solomon in the night	God appeared to Solomon	
5b	and God said Ask what I shall give you	and said: Ask what I shall give you	and said to him: Ask what I shall give you	7b
6aA	And Solomon said: You have shown great loyalty to your servant David my father,	And Solomon said: You have shown great loyalty to David my father,	And Solomon said to God: You have shown great loyalty to David my father,	8aA / 8aB
6aB	just as he walked before you in faithfulness, in righteousness, and in uprightness of heart towards you,			
6bA	and you have kept for him this great loyalty,			
6bB	and have given him a son sitting on his throne as at this day.			
7aA	Now then, Yahweh my God,			
7aB	you yourself have made your servant king in place of David my father,	and have made me king in place of him	and have made me king in place of him	8b
7b	and I am but a little lad I do not know how to go out or come in.			

8a	And your servant is in the midst of your people which you have chosen			
			Now then, God Yahweh, let your word with David my father be reliable, for you yourself have made me king over	9a / 9bA
8b	a numerous people which cannot be measured or counted for quantity.	over / a people numerous as the dust of the earth,	a people numerous as the dust of the earth.	9bB
		and I am but a little lad I do not know how to go out or come in.		
9aA	You will give your servant a hearing heart to rule this people,	Now then, wisdom give me;	Now then, wisdom and knowledge give me,	10aA
9aB	to discriminate between good and bad			
			and I shall go out before this people and come in;	10aB
9bA	for who is able to rule	for who may rule	for who may rule	10bA
9bB	this your honoured people?	this your people?	this your great people?	10bB
10a	And it was good in the Lord's eyes			
10b	that Solomon asked this thing.			
11a	and God said to him:	And God said to Solomon:	And God said to Solomon:	11aA
	Because you asked this thing, and did not ask for yourself many days,	Because this was in your heart,	Because this was in your heart,	
	and did not ask for yourself riches,	and you did not ask for riches,	and you did not ask for riches and possessions and honour,	
	and did not ask for the life of those at enmity with you	nor the life of those who hate you and even many days you did not ask	nor the life of those who hate you and even many days you did not ask for	11aB
11bA	but you asked for yourself	for but you asked for yourself	but you asked for yourself	

	discrimination	wisdom	wisdom and knowledge	11bA
1bB	for hearing cases.	to rule my people.	by which you might rule my people over which I have made you king.	11bB
2a	Look, I have acted according to your word.			
2bA	Look, I have given you a heart wise and discriminating,	Wisdom be given you;	Wisdom and knowledge be given you;	12a
2bB	such that noone has been like you before you, and after you there shall not arise one like you.			
3aA	And also what you did not ask I have given you, riches too, honour too	and riches and honour shall I give you	and riches and wealth and honour shall I give you	12bA
3aB	with no one like you among the kings all your days. And if you will walk in my	such as the kings did not have before you nor shall they have after you	such as the kings did not have before you nor shall they have after you.	12bB 12bG
14	ways, keeping my statutes and my commandments, as your father David walked, I will lengthen your days.			
15a	And Solomon woke up and found it was a dream.			
15bA	And he came

to Jerusalem and stood before the ark of the covenant of the Lord, and offered up holocausts and peace offerings | And Solomon came

to Jerusalem, | And Solomon came from the altar at Gibeon to Jerusalem from before the tent of meeting | 13aA

13aB |
| 15bB | and made a party for all his servants. | | | |
| 4:1 | And king Solomon became king over all Israel. | and ruled as king over Israel. | and ruled as king over Israel. | 13b |

2.2.2 Commentary

The reconstruction just offered has been produced in accordance with the principles mentioned at the opening of this chapter (2.0 above). Every word or phrase common to the two biblical versions of Solomon's vision has been retained. In most cases these elements appear in the same relative order in the familiar versions, and this has been retained in the reconstruction. Where the biblical versions differ in wording, but more or less mean the same, one or other version has been preferred. Only Solomon's going out and coming in is very differently placed in Kings and Chronicles; and the reconstructed 'original' has even-handedly placed this feature in a position mid-way between its rival biblical positions! One smaller, but possibly more significant transposition relates to 'the night' (K5a; C7a). I have chosen Kings' position at the end of the clause, though I have removed Kings' further specification that the vision was in fact a 'dream'. Chronicles has promoted the time phrase – I suspect to help the reader return to the main business of the story after the long detour into religious history (4–6a).

2.2.3 Chronicles

Chronicles, apart from that early historical detour, remains fairly close to the reconstructed source. In fact its only other substantial plus *vis-à-vis* Kings is in 9, where an extra appeal is made to the divine promise to David. Elsewhere it is only occasionally a little more wordy: it adds 'knowledge' to 'wisdom' in 10, 11 - using a late word found otherwise only in Daniel 1; and supplements the 'riches' in 11, 12.

2.2.4 Kings

Kings, on the other hand, has rewritten the main body of the story much more comprehensively. It has defined, quietly in 5 but more insistently in 15a, the vision as a dream. It has claimed a loyalty to Yahweh on David's side to match the divine loyalty to the former king (6). It notes that the people has been chosen (8) and not just the monarch. It replaces 'wisdom' by a hearing and discriminating heart (9, 11); and pauses (10) for Yahweh to congratulate Solomon on his choice of gift. At the end of 11 it introduces 'hearing' again in such a way that the original word, which could have meant either rule or judge (or indeed both), has been limited to the sense 'judge' in Kings new formulation 'for hearing cases'. Good conduct by Solomon (14) will secure for him long life. And final additions (15) have Solomon sacrificing again, once back in Jerusalem, and entertaining his staff.[1]

2.2.5 Connections

There are connections between several of these pluses in the Kings version of the vision at Gibeon and other sections of the opening chapters of 1 Kings which are also absent from 2 Chronicles. The staff party (15) is reminiscent of Adonijah's celebrations (1: 9–10). 'A son sitting on his throne' (6) recalls a key theme repeated throughout that opening chapter of the book. The requirement of royal obedience (6, 14) resumes part of David's deathbed advice to his son (2: 1–4). A discriminating legal mind (9, 11) is memorably illustrated in the judgment of the harlots (3: 16–28). It is clear that the Kings account of the Gibeon vision is very much at home in its wider context. One strong clue added to general probability makes it almost certain that it is not the primary account of that story. The clue is the close correspondence between the closing phrase of 2Chr 1: 13 and the wording of 1Kgs 4:1, on Solomon effectively taking up the kingship after this inaugural vision. That connection is now delayed in Kings by the insertion (3: 16–28) of the marvellous demonstration of his penetrating judgment. And the factor of general probability consists in this: that biblical editors frequently leave traces of their additions and omissions. It is just possible that the Chronicler left out of his account of Solomon the materials in chapters 1 and 2 of 1 Kings and the verdict on the harlots, but it is almost almost beyond belief that he would also have carefully weeded out of the vision report every subtle cross-reference to these discarded narratives. On the other hand, the expansive author/editor of Kings had every reason to bind his new materials more closely to the vision report in his source. He had other motives as well; but we shall explore these rather later.

[1]   In addition to the literature on 1Kgs 3: 4–15 cited in Auld (1992; 1993), see also the useful account in Brekelmans (1982) of the Deuteronomist's adaptation of his source material.

2.3 Building Temple and Palace

Translators of all periods have struggled with the building details in 1 Kings 6–7. It is generally recognised that the Hebrew materials have been supplemented and miscopied somewhat, even if there is little detailed agreement over how to restore the original. And yet, despite the uncertainties, there exists a wide consensus that it was something like the Masoretic text of those chapters, that text with which translators of all periods have struggled, which was both reshaped to produce the version we find translated in the Greek Bible and also drastically shortened to produce what we read in 2Chr 3: 1–5: 1. If the validity of that consensus view could be maintained, then – whatever its difficulties – this familiar text in Kings would have to continue to be the basis and starting point of our understanding of the (main) Jerusalem temple in the period of the Judaean monarchy.

However, in what follows, I want to question the priority of the traditional Hebrew text of 1 Kings 6–7 over these two related versions. As far as the Hebrew and Greek of Kings are concerned I am following in the footsteps of Trebolle Barrera. His detailed defence of the priority of the shape of 1 Kings 6–7 in the Greek Bible has been available in Spanish since 1980, but has been barely mentioned in subsequent English-language (or indeed any other) discussion – even though an excerpt was separately published in English in 1982. (McKenzie's 1991 critique of part of Trebolle's discussion of Jeroboam is a welcome exception.) However, I am also going beyond his lead. I suspect that if we could accustom ourselves to viewing such issues from the perspective of the briefer version in Chronicles, then we would also understand better why the longer versions in the Hebrew and Greek texts of Kings are so differently shaped. McKenzie pays little attention to these construction chapters, where Chr is often so much shorter than either version of Kings. He notes as a possibility (1985: 85) that the Chronicler was following a different source; but prefers to claim that 'C used K selectively' and that 'the omitted details of the Temple building lay somehow outside of C's interests'. Such remarks have often been made in commentaries on Chronicles, but without drawing sufficient attention to the improbability of such a view, given the close interest of Chronicles in matters religious and everything to do with them.

2.3.1 I find it significant that it is precisely over the information which is *not* also provided in Chronicles that the longer alternative construction accounts in the Hebrew and Greek versions of Kings most disagree. This is true of the short report of the palace structures: it is found *between* the reports of building and furnishing the temple in Hebrew Kings (7: 1–12), *after both* in Greek Kings (7: 38–50), and *not found at all* in Chronicles. It is true of the precise dating of the start and finish of the temple building: offered *at the end* of 1 Kgs 6 in Hebrew, *at the beginning* of that chapter in Greek, and *not at all* in Chronicles. And it is equally true of the notes about the preparation of stone and wood for the temple, reported as 1 Kgs 5: 31–32a in Hebrew, but a few clauses later after most of 1 Kgs 6: 1 in Greek, but again unreported in Chronicles. Was it precisely because these reports did not form an original part of the source document available to the Chronicler (an earlier version of the book of Kings?) that such supplements could be added to the text of Kings at different points? Alternatively, was it because there existed no sanction on the basis of an early hallowed text that editors of the different versions in which we know the Books of Kings were all the freer to relocate such secondary materials at will?

2.3.2 This situation of textual variety just sketched at the periphery is also mirrored within the various reports of the construction of the temple and its contents. At their summarising conclusions, 1 Kgs 7: 40–51 (in Hebrew and Greek) and 2 Chr 4: 11–5: 1 are all virtually identical, and join in giving credit to the Tyrian craftsman. But earlier, Kings and Chronicles, while both describe the basic dimensions of the temple (6: 2–3 // 3: 3–4a), the decoration of its interior (6: 15–18 // 3: 5–7), the dimensions of the inner sanctuary (6: 19–20 // 3: 8), the position of the cherubim within it and the gilding of the whole (6: 23–28 // 3: 10–13), the two outside pillars (7: 15–22 // 3: 15–17), the bronze sea (7: 23–26 // 4: 2–5), the lavers (7: 38–39a // 4: 6), and the position of the sea (7: 39b // 4: 10) – and deal with all of these in the same order, though Kings often in greater detail – they also each highlight different features of the building and its contents. Kings alone details the structures abutting the temple walls (6: 5–10), the interior decoration of walls and floor (6: 29–30), the wooden doors of inner sanctum and nave (6: 31–32), the bronze stands for the lavers (7: 27–37); and it deals at much greater length with the pillars Jachin and Boaz (7: 15–22, contrast 2Chr 3: 15–17). Chronicles, however, is our sole source not just for the bronze altar (4: 1), but also for lamps, tables, and basins (4: 7–8).[1]

It is important for our argument that it is again in some of these larger passages where Kings is much fuller than Chronicles that the Hebrew and Greek texts of Kings also differ most from each other, for example in 7: 30–32 within the large plus on the bronze stands and in 7: 17–22 over Jachin and Boaz: there LXX is much briefer in 7: 17-20 which are not represented at all in the much shorter text of Chronicles, and LXX like Chronicles lacks 7: 22 (MT) altogether. This book is not the place for a more detailed discussion of the temple and its construction. But I hope I have sketched sufficiently fully the complicated interrelationships of Hebrew Kings, Greek Kings, and Chronicles in their accounts of Solomon's central building operations in Jerusalem to show – at least once we have reviewed more of the neighbouring evidence – that they are not untypical of the presentations of Solomon as a whole in these three texts.

2.3.3 Yet it is one thing to detect patterns of difference between our ancient witnesses; but quite another to ascribe relative priority to them with any assurance. Commentators have long noted that the Greek order of 1 Kings 6–7 is in general tidier than that of the familiar Hebrew. The construction of the temple and the manufacture of its related paraphernalia are both reported on before the building of the palace structures. But most scholars have suggested that this Greek ordering reflects a secondary improvement of the original; and many have urged as a clinching argument that when vv. 1–12 of chapter 7 were moved to its end, v. 12b was mistakenly left in its original place and became attached to what we now read as the end of chapter 6, where in

---

[1] For a discussion of the implications for the historian seeking to reconstruct Solomon's Temple and its contents, see Auld and Steiner (1994).

the Greek we find similar though not identical content. In his substantial and authoritative review of the Hebrew and Greek versions of the stories of Solomon and Jeroboam in 1 Kings (1980 – and, excerpted in English, 1982: 24-8), Trebolle Barrera has neatly shown that this argument is readily reversible. He argues that those who promoted the account of the palace buildings to their present Hebrew position at the heart of Solomon's constructions in Jerusalem left a trace of their editorial manipulation when they inserted the relevant twelve verses half a dozen words too early, so detaching what we now read as 7:12b from its original location at the end of chapter 6, as we find it preserved in Greek. Even proponents of the common view have readily admitted that much ingenuity is required to make sense of the puzzling 1 Kgs 7: 12b in its familiar position. And Trebolle is able to interpret the parallel phrase at the end of the Greek chapter 6 with less contortion: ('After the description of the *debir* and the *hekal* with their respective doors (6: 18aB–33(6: 19–35)), we pass logically to the description of the third section of the temple: the *'ulam* or vestibule framed by its bronze pillars (7: 13– 22). Such is the sequence in the LXX where the link between the references to the vestibule and those to its two pillars is expressed by the common allusion to the "vestibule of the temple" in 6:34 (om MT) and 7: 3 (7: 15) [*to ailam tou oikou*].' (1982: 27f.)

If (as I think) he is correct about this larger tranposition of the whole palace report, then the other movement of text relating to the end of 1 Kgs 6, which he mentions but does not discuss in his English excerpt, must have happened second. Those responsible for the familiar Hebrew shape of Kings delayed until 6: 37–38 what we read in Greek near the beginning of that chapter. In the Greek, all the dating information is given together, whereas in the Hebrew it has been divided and now serves as a frame round 1 Kgs 6, with the month of Ziv of Solomon's fourth year being first mentioned in v. 2 and then resumed in v. 37.

2.3.4 Seen from a perspective sympathetic to Chronicles, the source common to Kings and Chronicles will have been a little shorter than what we read in Chronicles, and will have reported only the building and furnishing of the temple. This report had been slightly expanded to produce 2Chr 3: 1–5: 1, and more substantially expanded – including fuller dating details at the beginning and a report of palace structures at the end – to give the text translated into Greek as 3 Kingdoms 6–7. Finally, the familiar Hebrew text of 1 Kgs 6–7 was produced by moving first the new conclusion and then much of the new opening to the middle of the report (7: 1–12a and 6: 37–38). This final reshaping separates the great pillars Yachin and Boaz from the front door of their own temple! Yet the dislocation was neither isolated nor accidental, but part of a wider editorial strategy. The Hebrew text of 1 Kgs 3 opens with a report of Solomon's marriage with a daughter of Pharaoh which the Greek text mentions only much later in its account (after 5:14). Not only so; the familiar Hebrew explicitly damns their relationship by adding a note naming the union an example of that *inter*-marriage with other nations which was forbidden in Deuteronomy 7. When the editors of our Hebrew text of Kings similarly promoted the report of the king's thirteen-year palace-building operations not only to the centre of the report of his seven-year temple-building but also thereby to the very heart of the whole Solomon story, they were inviting readers to make a similar and harshly critical judgment.

2.3.5 The Hebrew book of Kings is our largest source of information on Solomon. And it contains all the primary material now available to us. But we have to read it critically and sift its information in the light of alternative sources which we have first to learn not to depreciate: Greek Kings because it is a translation, and Chronicles because much of it is manifestly unhistorical. There is no evidence that the Greek translators of Kings also re-edited the book: what they translated was already a different Hebrew edition of the book, in several respects prior to our familiar Masoretic Hebrew version.

The Solomonic building traditions as preserved in the Hebrew text of Kings were in fact developed in several stages, even where the evidence for each of these cannot be unravelled in detail. Not only were the Temple and its furnishings described first in even more summary terms than we find still in Chronicles, and then gradually more and more expanded, but an account of palace structures was only an afterthought. Indeed these notes on the apartments other than the Temple may represent only a collection and modest expansion of information found elsewhere in the text common to Kings and Chronicles. The 'House of the Forest of Lebanon' (1 Kgs 7: 2–5), which may be the same structure as is called the 'Hall of Pillars' (7: 6), is mentioned also in 1 Kgs 10: 17, 21 (cf. 2 Chr 9: 16, 20) – much gold was said to have been deposited there – and may also have been displayed there. 1 Kgs 7 mentions next a 'Hall of the Throne' or 'Hall of Judgment' (v. 7); and indeed the construction of Solomon's throne is described, in 1 Kgs 10: 18–20 (2 Chr 9: 17–19), between the references to the 'House of the Forest of Lebanon' just mentioned. In even more summary ways as well, the text common to Kings and Chronicles – *and so too perhaps their common source* – notes that Solomon's building works extended to more than the sanctuary: 1 Kgs 9: 1, 10 (2 Chr 7: 11; 8: 1) talk of the completion of 'the house of Yahweh and the king's house'.

These brief notes in 1 Kgs 7: 1–12 have received a lot of attention because, with other brief portions of Kings, they have been claimed to be summary notes from an archive of the early monarchical period. My remarks, together with the very sketchy nature of the notes about these non-religious structures, in fact suggest a date in the Second Temple period for their incorporation in Kings – and also perhaps for their first drafting. Their brevity may have less to do with terse drafting by a Solomonic secretary, and more to do with the paucity of information in the Persian period about structures that either no longer stood, or were no longer used for royal or state purposes. I suggest that what we see in the Greek text of Kings is how a short report of a separate building operation was first created out of scattered information about Solomon already elsewhere in the source text, and then placed at the end of the report of the building and furnishing of the temple. And what we find in the changed order of contents preserved in the Hebrew text of Kings is polemical use of that new report to dent Solomon's reputation. The material in 1 Kgs 7: 1–12 was never an extract from the royal archives; and in its present (Hebrew) position it reinforces the anti-monarchical comment scattered through the books of Samuel and Kings. The continuing failure of modern draughtsmen to turn these notes into architectural plans has puzzled many readers. Our enquiries lead us to offer this explanation: that even the earliest detectable sources were not contemporary architectural notes or observations, but rather an ancient (though post-exilic) scholar's textual deductions.

2.3.6 I offer one sample cross-check of our hypothesis that the Chronicler preserves an earlier version of Solomon's building operations than the Book of Kings – and that, within the witnesses to the text of Kings, the shorter Greek text is often more original than the longer Hebrew. This is a cedar-wood check – which ought to be neutral! Cedar is mentioned fourteen times in the Hebrew text of 1 Kgs 6–7 (6: 9, 10, 15, 16, 18, 18, 20, 36 and 7: 2, 2, 3, 7, 11, 12). In six cases (in 6: 16–20 and 7: 3, 7) LXX has a shorter text, and does not include mention of cedar. And 2 Chr 3: 1–5: 1 is able to say all that it has to say without any mention of cedar-wood at all. Of course the report in 1 Kgs 7: 1–12 (MT) on the construction of the palace quarters has no counterpart at all in Chronicles. However, that still leaves us to cope with the facts that Chronicles' short report of the construction of the sanctuary itself makes no mention of cedar; that the Greek version of Kings has translated a fuller report that specifies this wood four times; and that our familiar Hebrew text of Kings preserves a slightly fuller report which within its minor additions has mentioned cedar four further times. When we remember that 2 Chr 9: 27 not only shares 1 Kgs 10: 27's closing remark that Solomon 'made silver and gold as common in Jerusalem as stone, and he made cedar as plentiful as the sycamore of the Shephelah', but duplicates the paragraph in which it appears in an anticipatory tribute to the king's success (1: 14–17), and when we remember that Solomon includes cedar among his requests of Hiram in 2 Chr 2: 7 as in the related 1 Kgs 5: 13, 22, 24, we cannot believe that the Chronicler would have extirpated on principle all mention of cedar from his account of the building of the temple. It is equally incredible that the Chronicler, even if seeking to shorten his source in Kings, would have just happened to excise all of the many mentions of cedar in 1 Kgs 6. But we can understand how expansionist scribes in the Kings tradition made more and more use of this material – eight times in the shorter Greek text, and six more in the longer Hebrew. And we may ask ourselves whether, in adding more and more detail about imported wooden decoration, the scribes were

simply making deductions from these general framing remarks
(1Kgs 10: 27 // 2Chr 9: 27) about how plentiful in Solomon's
Jerusalem were such rich materials, or whether they had
alternative access to such information. And of course this critical
question reinforces our discussion of Kings' sources for its
construction of the royal apartments.

2.3.7 Why Kings and Chronicles should offer different, and also
greater and lesser, detail about the Lord's house and some of its
related artefacts is hard to explain. However, even in those
biblical sources which are manifestly from and about the Persian
period we find it impossible to harmonise all the information we
possess about the Jerusalem Temple of those times. In these
more recent times we may fairly deduce that what appear at first
sight to be factual reports, no less than prophetic scoldings and
urgings, are really claims and counter-claims about plans that
have not (yet) been realised – or whose realisation has been less
than satisfactory. The more we come to realise that Kings no less
than Chronicles may be a post-monarchic, post-exilic, creative
text of the Persian period, the more we shall have to cope with the
possibility that Kings like Chronicles is attributing to the early
monarchic period the origins of what is or at least should be the
situation in its own time. Differing dimensions for the Solomonic
temple and its vestibule may have resulted from scribal lapses in
copying the records of a Solomonic reality; but they need not be
explained that way. They may equally reflect either a Persian
reality contemporary to the time of writing or an ideal to be
striven for in that period. It begs the answer to a number of
questions if we take sizes from a biblical text and see where they
might fit in the contours of the rock under the largely Herodian
platform of the *al-Haram al-Sharif.*

2.4 Solomon's Administration

The Book of Kings in Hebrew, the Greek version of that book,
and Chronicles resemble and differ from each other on this topic
in similar fashion to their inter-relationships over the building
reports. 1Kgs 5: 15–30; 9: 10–28 // 2Chr 2; 8: 1–18 provide in all
three versions the immediate frame for the reports of the building

of the temple, the king's prayer, and the following (second) vision. The first panel reports the bargain struck between Solomon and Hiram of Tyre in terms of Tyrian timber and personnel in exchange for food (5: 15–26 // 2: 2–15); and then how Solomon levied and managed labour from Israel for his projects (5: 27–30 // 2: 1,16–17). The second panel returns to further dealings between Solomon and Hiram: first over cities in the north (9: 11– 14 // 8: 2–4) and then over sea trade in the south (9: 26–28 // 8: 17– 18). So far the more or less common tradition. There are differences over these shared matters between the three main 'editions' of the Solomon story; and sometimes these are not insignificant, even when slight in bulk; we shall see shortly that some may form part of larger patterns.

Between these latter dealings with Hiram to north and south, the Hebrew text of Kings and the Book of Chronicles offer notices about other of Solomon's building projects (9: 15b, 17b–19 // 8: 5–6), a fuller statement about his organisation of Israel's labour (9: 15a, 20–23 // 8: 7–10), a note about the housing of his royal Egyptian wife (9: [16–17a] 24 // 8: 11), and a report of arrangements about sacrifice (9: 25 // 8: 12–16). These topics are handled in the same relative order but with rather greater difference over detail. However, in the Greek Book of Kings the corresponding materials are to be found after 10: 22 (labour), after 5: 14 and 9: 9 (daughter of Pharoah and Gezer), and within the large and miscellaneous supplement after 2:46 (sacrifice).

All our other information about Solomonic administration comes only from the Book of Kings. That book follows its plus about the famous judicial decision with further information not found in Chronicles: a list of Solomon's high officers (4: 2–6) and of the twelve regional officials who each had responsibility for providing for the royal household (4: 7–19; 5: 7–8), with summaries of his household's daily needs (5: 2–3, 6) and of the extent of his territories (5: 1, 4–5), and a brief account of Solomon's international reputation for wisdom (5: 9–14). The information at the beginning of chapter 5 (5: 15ff. in English versions) is again very differently arranged in Hebrew and Greek: the latter opens with 5: 7– 8(MT), continues with 5: 2–4, 9–14. But its verses corresponding to 5: 1, 5–6 and indeed 4: 20 are again part of its large plus at the end of chapter 2.

The position of the Hiram materials is quite stable in all three versions of the story: the first two elements surround the central building operations in Jerusalem and the third, about trading operations in the Red Sea, offers a natural transition to the visit of the Queen of Sheba. The opening account of Solomon's arrangement of forced labour in Israel is also non-controversial, at least as to its position in the story. However, the later paragraph about forced labour appears not so much to offer new information as a careful restatement of the earlier paragraph. This cautious afterthought points out that Solomon had conscripted not free-born Israelites, as the unbriefed reader of the earlier account might have supposed, but enclaves of foreign remnants. And it is typical of such an addition to the shared text of the Solomon story that it is placed differently in one of the successor versions (in this case Greek Kings) from the other two (Hebrew Kings and Chronicles). Its content and the variability of its position each point to its secondary status – just as we found with the report of palace-building. Here again the shared text provides a good basis for establishing the shape and extent of the original text. But here the actual content of the paragraph confirms the impression we had gained already from its different position in Greek Kings that the material in question had been added later to the developing story-line. In turn this confirmation supports our use of variable positioning as one criterion for detecting added material.[1]

2.5 Literary Issues

An exchange of articles was launched in the *Journal for the Study of the Old Testament* in 1988 by Kim Parker on how to detect the structure, and so how to control an appropriate holistic reading of 1Kgs 1–11; but it quickly got terribly bogged down. He promised an approach very different from the one being followed in this book, one with resolutely synchronic concerns: 'the present approach will assume that the repetitions and contradictions are

---

[1] I have in mind here variations in positioning larger paragraphs, not short clauses or single sentences such as we discussed in *2.1* above. There it seemed acceptable to conclude that the editors of either or both biblical books had moved the topic of the king's going out or coming in as part of their recasting of the source story.

deliberate and part of a sophisticated narrative strategy' (1988: 20). Essentially, using structural comparisons and contrasts, he was restating Noth's proposal that 1 Kgs 1–8 was favourable to the king, but 1 Kgs 9–11 hostile to him.

2.5.1 The first response came from Brettler, who objected on general literary principles to units of such unequal length being claimed as a balancing structure (1991: 88); proposed that the unit hostile to Solomon was not all of chapters 9–11, but simply 1 Kgs 9:26 – 11:10 (90–94); and reintroduced a modicum of diachronic interest to the discussion of structure and meaning (esp. 95–97). He claimed that only 11: 1–10 was composed by the Deuteronomist; the rest of the hostile portion, which was not similarly saturated with Deuteronomist terminology, was drawn from source-material; the Chronicler, working out of 'his intense pro-Solomon biases', deleted only 1 Kgs 11, 'missed the structure implied by 3: 1–2 // 9: 24–25, and misread 9: 26–10: 29 as aggrandizing Solomon.

2.5.2 The next to take up Parker's challenge was Frisch (1991a), who had completed in 1986 a Bar-Ilan dissertation on 'The Narrative of Solomon's Reign in the Book of Kings'. He offered a number of helpful observations on details of Parker's proposals; argued that 1 Kgs 12 was an integral part of the record of Solomon in 1 Kgs 1–12; and proposed a fresh structural pattern with 6: 1–9: 9 at its heart.

2.5.3 Not surprisingly, Parker's reply(1991) concentrated on the inappropriateness of terming 1 Kgs 12 part of Solomon's story – information about a king was sometimes offered in Kings before the formal report of the opening of his reign, but never after his death notice (11: 41–43 in Solomon's case).

2.5.4 Frisch responded (1991b) with a claim that chapter 12, while of course not part of the historical record of Solomon, was an integral element of the literary-theological complex 1 Kgs 1–12. He repeated his insistence that Parker undervalued a number of internal parallelisms such as 6: 11–13 in relation to 9: 1–9 and 3: 1–3 in relation to 11: 1–8.

2.5.5 Parker then published a substantial new article (1992), apparently prepared before these exchanges with Frisch, which are alluded to but not discussed. Following the schema he had proposed in 1988, he noted evidence of Solomon the ideal king within 1Kgs 1–8 (1992: 77–82); then defended his claim that chapters 9–11 portray Solomon taking Israel symbolically back to Egypt (82-7).

2.5.6 We shall direct our attention in a later chapter to the transition from Solomon to Jeroboam in 1Kgs 11–12 (14). McKenzie (1991: 56ff.), after describing the Jeroboam story in Kings as one of the fountainheads of Dtr, moves almost immediately to write of Dtr being 'forced to periodize Solomon's reign'. I note that the LXX 'supplement' in 12: 24ff. makes no allusion to the most explicit mentions in the 'main text' of the divine promise to Jeroboam – 11: 37–38 (MT and LXX) and 14: 7–8 (MT only).

2.5.7 In the light of our discussion in this book so far, I suspect that the stumbling-block in the debate between Parker and Frisch is their unreadiness to acknowledge as Brettler does that the author of Kings, and Chronicles too, did not just have inherited material *at his disposal*, but rather *had to cope with* the shape and tendencies of his source(s). They are also apparently insensitive to the implications of the very different ordering – and even contents – of 1Kgs 1–11(12) in the Greek Bible. It is presumptuous, for example, of Frisch to placard the structural importance of the parallelism of 6: 11–13 and 9: 1–9 when 6: 11–13 is not even part of the Greek text.[1] And although Parker (especially 1992) has several sensitive exegetical details to offer, he is remarkably selective in what he 'sees' within 1Kgs 1–8. His evidence for its portrayal of the wisdom of the ideal ruler conveniently begins with Solomon's vision at Gibeon, moves on to the judgment between the harlots, and continues with a happy Israel 'as many as the sand by the sea'. But a much more ruthless 'wisdom'

---

[1] That is not to suggest that 6: 11–13 is not an important indicator of the way the Masoretic version of 1 Kings should be read. Yet I prefer to use 'structural' in a strong sense: to refer to load-bearing elements of the main building, rather than secondary features – however prominent these may be at first sight.

operates in chapter 2; and Parker, who never appeals to the Greek text of Kings, although it would help some of his arguments, has to avert his sight from 1 Kgs 3: 1(MT) which I think can only be critical of the king (*2.3* above), and also commend Solomon for imposing forced labour on Israel while blaming him for imposing him it on aliens in Israel (contrast *2.3* above).

2.5.8 It must be insisted that holistic readings of the portrayal of Solomon in Kings – no less than historical ones – have to deal not with a positive picture that shifts to negative at, or somewhere in the middle of, chapter 9; and not even with a positive picture set in a negative outer frame; but with critical if not hostile indicators through and through – enough of them in Greek Kings, and many more in the Hebrew. Jobling (1991) offers the least problematic 'literary' reading of these chapters known to me; he also finds fault with Parker's reading (in this case, in his unpublished dissertation of 1989) of a downturn in 1 Kgs 9–10: an undoing, point for point, of the favourable report in chapters 1–8. For Jobling, the golden age of Solomonic wisdom is inaugurated as the king communes with Lady Wisdom at night (3: 4–15) and not with the 'strange woman' had had just brought into his capitol (3: 1); and it comes to an end as the king returns to sexual interaction with foreign women (11: 1–8). He is a useful ally in reading the text as it stands; and he suggests that the Deuteronomists had been aware of some earlier form of the tradition of Solomon's reign as a Golden Age (1991: 75, n. 6).

2.6 David in Samuel and Chronicles

The elements of the story of David that are common to Samuel and 1 Chronicles offer a perfectly satisfactory introduction to the whole. They start with the flight of Israel before the Philistines, including the death of Saul and his three sons; and move immediately to all Israel making David king at Hebron. The capture of Jerusalem follows. And David enhances his position by building works in that city, including a house for himself, with help from Hiram; by marriages and concubinage; and by a defeat of the Philistines. He then brings the ark to Jerusalem; and receives the dynastic oracle from Nathan. Several military successes are reported, culminating in the defeat of Ammon. There follow, more in note form, mentions of combat between some of his men and various giants and lists of his warriors. The story ends with his census and the acquisition of the threshing floor by Jerusalem where an altar was built.

2.6.1 The David of these narratives is a public figure – appropriately enough for a king! The additional narrative blocks in 2 Samuel largely concern relations between David and Saul's house (2Sam 1–4, 9); Uriah, Bathsheba, and the birth of Solomon (11–12); and the revolt of Absalom (13–18). In all of these Samuel pluses, the characterisation of a person, both private and public, is much more to the fore, and underscores the absence of such concerns from the shared narrative. Only in the census story (2Sam 24//1 Chr 21) does David exhibit a measure of that open grief which is such a well-known feature of the king's response to the loss of Jonathan, or his firstborn by Bathsheba, or Absalom. Scattered though substantial pluses throughout the David story in 1 Chronicles, which relate to matters levitical and liturgical and especially the bringing the ark into Jerusalem, anticipate the large block of eight chapters at the end of that book offering detailed arrangements for the new house of the Lord in Jerusalem, its contents, and its personnel.

2.6.2 A fine microcosmic example of the issues is provided by the brief reports in the two biblical books of David's capture of Jerusalem (2Sam 5: 6–8 // 1Chr 11: 4–6). The most recent detailed treatment of the textual issues (Floss 1989) proposes that the development of the Samuel version was carried out in several stages. I am not concerned here with the adequacy of his general argument. But I do want to point out that his latest Samuel stratum is not reflected in Chronicles: he is typical of the majority of scholars in prefering to assume a deletion by the Chronicler than suppose that the Chronicler had used a prior, not yet completed version of Samuel.

2.6.3 I also find it interesting that Gelander (1991), without apparently making an issue of it, does select for his presentation of *David and his God* (just those) chapters which are found in both

Samuel and Chronicles (though without the military reports in 2Sam 8, 10 // 1Chr 18–19 and the death of Saul in 1Sam 31 // 1Chr 10). He is sensitive to the interpretative suggestiveness of the different editorial collocations of the same narratives in Samuel and Chronicles. But he is probably wrong to ascribe greater freedom to the Chronicler than to the author of Samuel, who (so he states) was writing at a time when 'the details of David's and Solomon's lives were still widely known' (62). On the other hand, when discussing possible connections between 2Sam 24 and 2Sam 21, he wisely notes that some of the links that have been detected would be stronger if the chapters were actually contiguous; and adds: 'Obviously, I have no way of knowing whether the barbs directed at the House of Saul were propaganda weapons employed at the time of the actual conflict, or were used, with the perspective of hindsight, to justify the policies and victory of the House of David' (67).

2.6.4 I do not intend in this book to say much more about the story of David than I already have done. The main differences between Samuel and 1 Chronicles were sketched at the opening of our Overview. Since most of the narrative which we find in Samuel but not repeated in Chronicles is normally attributed to separate sources on David, the question is essentially this: Were all the David sources first gathered together in Samuel, then some of them weeded out by the Chronicler? Or does the Chronicler, shorn of his own manifest supplements, still retain the shape of a shorter collection which was extensively added to in Samuel also? One of my research students is working on the David traditions, and arriving at convergent results. We have published a sample relating to David and Goliath of our views of how the proto-Masoretic text of Samuel could still be substantially reshaped and supplemented in the late biblical period in order to highlight contrasts between Saul and David (Auld and Ho, 1992). And we are confident that this is no isolated example within Samuel of composition by supplementation in that period. Rather more complex inter-relationships are, however, apparent in the following discussion of the texts relating to the transition from father David to Solomon his son.

2.7 From David to Solomon

2.7.1 Kings and Chronicles never differ more substantially than over their presentation of the transition from David to Solomon. In the text they share, there is very little material between David's acquisition of the sacred site (2Sam 24 // 1Chr 21) and Solomon's vision at Gibeon (1Kgs 3: 4–15 // 2Chr 1: 3–13), followed by his negotiations with Hiram (1Kgs 5: 15–26 // 2Chr 2: 2–15). Kings supplies a highly political account (1Kgs 1–2) of how Solomon secured the throne and how the dying David advised him not only to follow divine instruction, but also how to settle some old scores. Chronicles, in a much larger plus or series of pluses (1Chr 22–29), focuses on the main theme of the shared text on Solomon: the construction of the temple. David organises the aliens within Israel as a workforce (22: 2–5, 18); he briefs Solomon about Nathan's oracle and his own practical arrangements for the future building work (22: 6–15), and then formally makes Solomon king over Israel (23: 1). Many details, typical of Chronicles' pluses, are then provided (23:2 – 27:34) of levitical and other organisational arrangements. Finally David calls a national assembly (28–29). He explains to them the Nathan oracle (28: 2–8); briefs Solomon in front of the nation (28: 9–21); asks them to support his son (29: 1); reports his own contributions for the future temple (29: 2–5) - this prompts their freewill offerings (29: 6–9); blesses Yahweh before them (29: 10–19) and has them bless Yahweh in turn (29: 20–21). They then 'ate and drank before Yahweh', and 'made Solomon the son of David king the second time' (29: 22). He in turn sat on the throne in place of his father and received their allegiance (29: 23–25). And 1 Chronicles concludes with a formal death notice for David (29: 26–30).

2.7.2 Very little information is actually shared between Kings and Chronicles about this important transition. Both attribute to David the responsibility for Solomon succeeding to the throne rather than one of his several brothers. Both describe Solomon as actually becoming king before David's death (sitting on his throne instead of him); and both report the aged David as wishing the new king strength and as offering him advice to keep the divine commandments and ordinances. Finally both formally

note David's death, the length of his reign, the succession of
Solomon, and his successful establishment as king. And yet those
few points of convergence of two much longer texts do constitute
– or at least readily permit the reconstruction of – a perfectly
credible transitional narrative. In Kings, an exciting narrative
has been added – crafted like, or as part of, the narrative in much
of 2Sam 9–20 – reporting the tensions and manipulations that
accompanied and might even have voided aged David's
designation of Solomon. In this opening to the Book of Kings,
advice from a David who has intrigued and manipulated his way
through the Book of Samuel is directed towards encouraging
similar statecraft in his son (1 Kgs 2: 5–9).[1] By contrast, in
Chronicles, the strength the old king wishes for Solomon is to
enable him to organise successfully the building of the sanctuary.

2.7.3 It is in many ways appropriate to depict the treatment of
David and Solomon in Samuel and Kings as more political, and
in Chronicles as more religious. As a counter-balance, it is useful
to explore how each presentation of these kings deals with the
significant religious or theological theme of 'rest'. In the Former
Prophets, David is given 'rest' from all his enemies (2Sam 7: 1,
11), just as Yahweh had given to Israel under Joshua (Josh 21: 44;
22: 4; 23: 1). The Joshua passages have no parallel in Chronicles;
however, it is striking that in the Chronicler's version of Nathan's
oracle the topic of rest for David from his enemies is completely
lacking from the opening verse and is differently stated in 1Chr
17: 10 ('I will subdue all your enemies'). On the other hand, the
claim in Solomon's mouth in 1Kgs 5: 18 (no parallel in 2Chr 2, or
indeed elsewhere in 2Chr 1–9) that Yahweh had given Solomon
'rest on every side' is foreseen at the end of Chronicles by David
(1Chr 22: 9), who goes on to explain that Solomon's very name
(*Shelomoh*) points to his being a man of peace (*shalom*), and then
to claim (22: 18) that Yahweh had given the people and David
himself rest from and power over their enemies. If the Former
Prophets extend this theme to the earlier period of Joshua, the
Chronicler extends it in the opposite direction, and attaches it

[1] Koopmans (1991) has recently argued for the poetic unity of all of 1Kgs 2: 1–
     10. That, of course, is not in itself inconsistent with a view of development of the
     text in stages, but it should make one cautious.

also to Asa (2Chr 14: 5, 6; 15: 15) and Jehoshaphat (2Chr 20: 30). At first sight, both Samuel-Kings and Chronicles use the 'rest' theme in connection with both David and Solomon, but always in additions to the shared text. Yahweh gives 'rest' to David in 2Sam 7: 1, 11 (but not in the synoptic parallel 1Chr 17) and in 1Chr 22: 18, and to Solomon in 1Kgs 5: 18 (but not in the synoptic parallel 2Chr 2) and in 1Chr 22: 9.

2.7.4 Before we try to probe further in an attempt to plot exactly where the topic may have been original, we should note that 'rest' is also associated in two pluses in Chronicles with a resting place for Yahweh and his ark: not only in 2Chr 6: 40, quoting Ps 132: 8, at the end of Solomon's prayer, but also in David's restatement of the Nathan material before the national assembly (1Chr 28: 2). Interestingly 1Kgs 8: 56, within the larger Kings plus (8: 54–61) that reports Solomon's benediction of the people after his long prayer, uses the term in the other sense: of Yahweh giving rest to his people. All in all, because I find it more probable that the Chronicler attributed to David preparations towards the construction of the temple of which the common text knew nothing than that Samuel-Kings removed that role from David, I will treat the rest from enemies theme as original to 1Kgs 5: 18 in my reconstruction of the common text on David and Solomon which will be presented as our next chapter.

2.8 Afterthoughts

Several of the issues we have begun to discuss in these pages deserve much fuller exposition; that, however, might best be accomplished in the context of a commentary on the book of Kings. Before presenting our results in our next chapter in the form of a reconstruction of what may have been the source-text used both by the author/editor of Samuel-Kings and by the Chronicler, and – perhaps even more important – before seeking in the chapter after that to apply these ideas to the more intractable problems in the remainder of Kings and Chronicles, a small stocktaking is appropriate here.

2.8.1 We have sampled several representative portions of the

biblical narratives on Solomon (and to a tiny extent David). We
have suggested that the much reduced text actually common to
Samuel-Kings and Chronicles is coherent and self-sufficient.
Here and there we have found evidence convergent with our
fresh approach to the material – and nowhere have we had to
confront a counter-argument.[1] A reading of this shared text on
Solomon, whether holistic or historical, should take note of the
prominence of Hiram who makes the first of his several
appearances almost at the beginning and the last almost at the
end. In fact the first and last mentions of Hiram are framed by the
vision at Gibeon with its divine promise to Solomon of wisdom
and riches and by a closing summary which notes how Solomon
'excelled all the kings of the earth in riches and wisdom'. This
symmetry is lost in Kings and is much less apparent in Chronicles.

2.8.2 Much of the material in the Chronicler's extended transition
from David to Solomon (at least 1 Chr 22; 28–29) could have been
generated from the shared source. The first of the two long
chapters, special to Kings, and which open 1 Kings, provides a
narrative expansion of the statement in the source that the aged
David had designated Solomon as his successor out of all his sons,
exploring the ways and means. The second chapter demonstrates
similar insight into how power is wielded, as it disposes in a very
few strokes both with Solomon's rivals and with his own idealised
reputation as enshrined in that same common source.

2.8.3 The details about Solomon's administration of non-cultic
matters, which bulk much larger in Kings than Chronicles, may
or may not furnish us with authentic information – that is a
separate historical question. But in studying that question it will
be important to pay attention to our finding that these details are
secondary additions to this form of the Solomon story. Many
attempted reconstructions of the growth of the Solomonic
materials in Kings have supposed that the direction of
development was from the matter-of-fact, even archival, to the
more religious or theological. Our results commend a radical

---

[1] My first published sketch of some of these ideas (Auld 1983a) did draw criticism
    from Williamson (1983). I replied to each point of detail (1983b), and am not
    aware of further discussion of these issues.

reversal of this common view: the high theology of Solomon's visions and of his long prayer was already in place, and attached to a much shorter account of the construction of the temple (and especially of its interior), before the lineaments were added of a portrait of Solomon, politician and administrator. The Chronicler did not remove this information in order to create a purified royal ideal: the materials in question were simply not part of his source. Though inventive at many points, the Chronicler was in fact much more conservative in his handling of David's son. It is the Kings presentation of Solomon, with its freedom to criticise, which is the much more innovative.

3

David and Solomon:
The Shared Text

Saul's Death (1Sam 31: 1–13; 1Chr 10: 1–12)

Now the Philistines fought against Israel; and the men of Israel fled before the Philistines, and fell slain on Mount Gilboa. And the Philistines overtook Saul and his sons; and the Philistines slew Jonathan and Abinadab and Malchishua, the sons of Saul. The battle pressed hard upon Saul, and the archers found him; and he was badly wounded by the archers. Then Saul said to his armourbearer, 'Draw your sword, and thrust me through with it, lest these uncircumcised come and thrust me through, and make sport of me.' But his armourbearer would not; for he feared greatly. Therefore Saul took his own sword, and fell upon it. And when his armourbearer saw that Saul was dead, he also fell upon his sword, and died with him. Thus Saul died, and his three sons, and his armourbearer, and all his men, on the same day together. And when the men of Israel who were on the other side of the valley and those beyond the Jordan saw that the men of Israel had fled and that Saul and his sons were dead, they forsook their cities and fled; and the Philistines came and dwelt in them.

On the morrow, when the Philistines came to strip the slain, they found Saul and his three sons fallen on Mount Gilboa. And they cut off his head, and stripped off his armor, and sent messengers throughout the land of the Philistines, to carry the good news to their idols and to the people. They put his armour in the temple of Ashtaroth; and they fastened his body to the wall of Bethshan. But when the inhabitants of Jabesh-gilead heard

what the Philistines had done to Saul, all the valiant men arose,
and went all night, and took the body of Saul and the bodies of
his sons from the wall of Bethshan; and they came to Jabesh and
burnt them there. And they took their bones and buried them
under the tamarisk tree in Jabesh, and fasted seven days.

Jerusalem Taken (2Sam 5: 1–3, 6–10; 1Chr 11: 1–9)

Then all the tribes of Israel came to David at Hebron, and said,
'Behold, we are your bone and flesh. In times past, when Saul was
king over us, it was you that led out and brought in Israel; and
Yahweh said to you, "You shall be shepherd of my people Israel,
and you shall be prince over Israel."' So all the elders of Israel
came to the king at Hebron; and King David made a covenant
with them at Hebron before Yahweh, and they anointed David
king over Israel. David was thirty years old when he began to
reign, and he reigned forty years. At Hebron he reigned over
Judah seven years and six months; and at Jerusalem he reigned
over all Israel and Judah thirty-three years.

And the king and his men went to Jerusalem against the
Jebusites, the inhabitants of the land, who said to David, 'You will
not come in here[, but the blind and the lame will ward you off'
– thinking, 'David cannot come in here].' Nevertheless David
took the stronghold of Zion, that is, the city of David. And David
said on that day, 'Whoever would smite the Jebusites, let him get
up the water shaft to attack the lame and the blind, who are hated
by David's soul.' Therefore it is said, 'The blind and the lame shall
not come into the house.' And David dwelt in the stronghold, and
called it the city of David. And David built the city round about
from the Millo inward. And David became greater and greater,
for Yahweh, the God of hosts, was with him.

Hiram's Embassy – David's Wars (2Sam 5: 11–25; 1Chr 14: 1–
17)

And Hiram king of Tyre sent messengers to David, and cedar
trees, also carpenters and masons who built David a house. And
David perceived that Yahweh had established him king over
Israel, and that he had exalted his kingdom for the sake of his

people Israel.

And David took more concubines and wives from Jerusalem, after he came from Hebron; and more sons and daughters were born to David. And these are the names of those who were born to him in Jerusalem: Shammua, Shobab, Nathan, Solomon, Ibhar, Elishua, Nepheg, Japhia, Elishama, Eliada, and Eliphelet. When the Philistines heard that David had been anointed king over Israel, all the Philistines went up in search of David; but David heard of it and went down to the stronghold. Now the Philistines had come and spread out in the valley of Rephaim. And David inquired of Yahweh, 'Shall I go up against the Philistines? Wilt thou give them into my hand?' And Yahweh said to David, 'Go up; for I will certainly give the Philistines into your hand.' And David came to Baal-perazim, and David defeated them there; and he said, 'Yahweh has broken through my enemies before me, like a bursting flood.' Therefore the name of that place is called Baal-perazim. And the Philistines left their idols there, and David and his men carried them away.

And the Philistines came up yet again, and spread out in the valley of Rephaim. And when David inquired of Yahweh, he said, 'You shall not go up; go around to their rear, and come upon them opposite the balsam trees. And when you hear the sound of marching in the tops of the balsam trees, then bestir yourself; for then Yahweh has gone out before you to smite the army of the Philistines.' And David did as Yahweh commanded him, and smote the Philistines from Geba to Gezer.

Ark at Perez-Uzzah (2Sam 6: 1–11; 1Chr 13: [1–4]5–14)

David again gathered all the chosen men of Israel, thirty thousand. And David arose and went with all the people who were with him from Baale-Judah, to bring up from there the ark of God, which is called by the name of Yahweh of hosts who sits enthroned on the cherubim. And they carried the ark of God upon a new cart, and brought it out of the house of Abinadab which was on the hill; and Uzzah and Ahio, the sons of Abinadab, were driving the new cart with the ark of God; and Ahio went before the ark. And David and all the house of Israel were making merry before Yahweh with all their might, with songs and lyres and harps and tambourines and castanets and cymbals.

And when they came to the threshing floor of Nacon, Uzzah put out his hand to the ark of God and took hold of it, for the oxen stumbled. And the anger of Yahweh was kindled against Uzzah; and God smote him there because he put forth his hand to the ark; and he died there beside the ark of God. And David was angry because Yahweh had broken forth upon Uzzah; and that place is called Perez-uzzah, to this day. And David was afraid of Yahweh that day; and he said, 'How can the ark of Yahweh come to me?' So David was not willing to take the ark of Yahweh into the city of David; but David took it aside to the house of Obededom the Gittite. And the ark of Yahweh remained in the house of Obededom the Gittite three months; and Yahweh blessed Obededom and all his household.

Ark brought to Jerusalem (2Sam 6: 12–20a; 1Chr 15: 1–16: 3*, 43)

And it was told King David, 'Yahweh has blessed the household of Obededom and all that belongs to him, because of the ark of God.' So David went and brought up the ark of God from the house of Obededom to the city of David with rejoicing; and when those who bore the ark of Yahweh had gone six paces, he sacrificed an ox and a fatling. And David danced before Yahweh with all his might; and David was girded with a linen ephod. So David and all the house of Israel brought up the ark of Yahweh with shouting, and with the sound of the horn.

As the ark of Yahweh came into the city of David, Michal the daughter of Saul looked out of the window, and saw King David leaping and dancing before Yahweh; and she despised him in her heart. And they brought in the ark of Yahweh, and set it in its place, inside the tent which David had pitched for it; and David offered burnt offerings and peace offerings before Yahweh. And when David had finished offering the burnt offerings and the peace offerings, he blessed the people in the name of Yahweh of hosts, and distributed among all the people, the whole multitude of Israel, both men and women, to each a cake of bread, a portion of meat, and a cake of raisins. Then all the people departed, each to his house. And David returned to bless his household.

Nathan's Oracle (2Sam 7; 1Chr 17)

Now when the king dwelt in his house,[1] the king said to Nathan the prophet, 'See now, I dwell in a house of cedar, but the ark of God dwells in a tent.' And Nathan said to the king, 'Go, do all that is in your heart; for Yahweh is with you.'

But that same night the word of Yahweh came to Nathan, 'Go and tell my servant David, "Thus says Yahweh: Would you build me a house to dwell in? I have not dwelt in a house since the day I brought up the people of Israel from Egypt[2] to this day, but I have been moving about in a tent for my dwelling. In all places where I have moved with all the people of Israel, did I speak a word with any of the judges of Israel, whom I commanded to shepherd my people Israel, saying, 'Why have you not built me a house of cedar?'" Now therefore thus you shall say to my servant David, "Thus says Yahweh of hosts, I took you from the pasture, from following the sheep, that you should be prince over my people Israel; and I have been with you wherever you went, and have cut off all your enemies from before you; and I will make for you a great name, like the name of the great ones of the earth. And I will appoint a place for my people Israel, and will plant them, that they may dwell in their own place, and be disturbed no more; and violent men shall afflict them no more, as formerly, from the time that I appointed judges over my people Israel; and I will subdue all your enemies. Moreover Yahweh declares to you that Yahweh will make you a house. When your days are fulfilled and you lie down with your fathers, I will raise up your offspring after you, who shall come forth from your body, and I will establish his kingdom. He shall build a house for my name, and I will establish the throne of his kingdom for ever. I will be his father, and he shall be my son. When he commits iniquity, I will chasten him with the rod of men, with the stripes of the sons of men; but I will not take my steadfast love from him, as I took it from Saul, whom I put away from before you. And your house and your kingdom shall be made sure for ever before me; your

---

[1] The Samuel plus (2Sam 7: 1b) introduces the theme of rest from the king's enemies all around (see p. 38 above).
[2] 'from Egypt' is not attested in 1Chr 17: 5, but may have been lost from this version of the text.

throne shall be established for ever."' In accordance with all these words, and in accordance with all this vision, Nathan spoke to David.

Then King David went in and sat before Yahweh, and said, 'Who am I, Divine Yahweh, and what is my house, that thou hast brought me thus far? And yet this was a small thing in thy eyes, Divine Yahweh; thou hast spoken also of thy servant's house for a great while to come, and hast shown me future generations, Divine Yahweh! And what more can David say to thee? For thou knowest thy servant, Divine Yahweh! Because of thy promise, and according to thy own heart, thou hast wrought all this greatness, to make thy servant know it. Therefore thou art great, Divine Yahweh; for there is none like thee, and there is no God besides thee, according to all that we have heard with our ears. What other nation on earth is like thy people Israel, whom God went to redeem to be his people, making himself a name, and doing for them great and terrible things, by driving out before his people a nation and its gods? And thou didst establish for thyself thy people Israel to be thy people for ever; and thou, Yahweh, didst become their God. And now, Divine Yahweh, confirm for ever the word which thou hast spoken concerning thy servant and concerning his house, and do as thou hast spoken; and thy name will be magnified for ever, saying, "Yahweh of hosts is God over Israel," and the house of thy servant David will be established before thee. For thou, Yahweh of hosts, the God of Israel, hast made this revelation to thy servant, saying, "I will build you a house'; therefore thy servant has found courage to pray this prayer to thee. And now, Divine Yahweh, thou art God, and thy words are true, and thou hast promised this good thing to thy servant; now therefore may it please thee to bless the house of thy servant, that it may continue for ever before thee; for thou, Divine Yahweh, hast spoken, and with thy blessing shall the house of thy servant be blessed for ever.'

Further Wars of David (2Sam 8; 1Chr 18)

After this David defeated the Philistines and subdued them, and David took Metheg-ammah out of the hand of the Philistines. And he defeated Moab, and measured them with a line, making them lie down on the ground; two lines he measured to be put to death, and one full line to be spared. And the Moabites became servants to David and brought tribute.

David also defeated Hadadezer the son of Rehob, king of Zobah, as he went to restore his power at the river Euphrates. And David took from him a thousand and seven hundred horsemen, and twenty thousand foot soldiers; and David hamstrung all the chariot horses, but left enough for a hundred chariots. And when the Syrians of Damascus came to help Hadadezer king of Zobah, David slew twenty-two thousand men of the Syrians. Then David put garrisons in Aram of Damascus; and the Syrians became servants to David and brought tribute. And Yahweh gave victory to David wherever he went. And David took the shields of gold which were carried by the servants of Hadadezer, and brought them to Jerusalem. And from Betah and from Berothai, cities of Hadadezer, King David took very much bronze.

When Toi king of Hamath heard that David had defeated the whole army of Hadadezer, Toi sent his son Joram to King David, to greet him, and to congratulate him because he had fought against Hadadezer and defeated him; for Hadadezer had often been at war with Toi. And Joram brought with him articles of silver, of gold, and of bronze; these also King David dedicated to Yahweh, together with the silver and gold which he dedicated from all the nations he subdued, from Edom, Moab, the Ammonites, the Philistines, Amalek, and from the spoil of Hadadezer the son of Rehob, king of Zobah.

And David won a name for himself. When he returned, he slew eighteen thousand Edomites in the Valley of Salt. And he put garrisons in Edom; throughout all Edom he put garrisons, and all the Edomites became David's servants. And Yahweh gave victory to David wherever he went.

So David reigned over all Israel; and David administered justice and equity to all his people. And Joab the son of Zeruiah was over the army; and Jehoshaphat the son of Ahilud was recorder; and Zadok the son of Ahitub and Ahimelech the son of Abiathar were priests; and Seraiah was secretary; and Benaiah the son of Jehoiada was over the Cherethites and the Pelethites; and David's sons were priests.

Campaigns against Ammon and Aram (2Sam 10; 1Chr 19)

After this the king of the Ammonites died, and Hanun his son reigned in his stead. And David said, 'I will deal loyally with Hanun the son of Nahash, as his father dealt loyally with me.' So David sent by his servants to console him concerning his father. And David's servants came into the land of the Ammonites. But the princes of the Ammonites said to Hanun their lord, 'Do you think, because David has sent comforters to you, that he is honouring your father? Has not David sent his servants to you to search the city, and to spy it out, and to overthrow it?' So Hanun took David's servants, and shaved off half the beard of each, and cut off their garments in the middle, at their hips, and sent them away. When it was told David, he sent to meet them, for the men were greatly ashamed. And the king said, 'Remain at Jericho until your beards have grown, and then return.'

When the Ammonites saw that they had become odious to David, the Ammonites sent and hired the Syrians of Bethrehob, and the Syrians of Zobah, twenty thousand foot soldiers, and the king of Maacah with a thousand men, and the men of Tob, twelve thousand men. And when David heard of it, he sent Joab and all the host of the mighty men. And the Ammonites came out and drew up in battle array at the entrance of the gate; and the Syrians of Zobah and of Rehob, and the men of Tob and Maacah, were by themselves in the open country.

When Joab saw that the battle was set against him both in front and in the rear, he chose some of the picked men of Israel, and arrayed them against the Syrians; the rest of his men he put in the charge of Abishai his brother, and he arrayed them against the Ammonites. And he said, 'If the Syrians are too strong for me, then you shall help me; but if the Ammonites are too strong for you, then I will come and help you. Be of good courage, and let us play the man for our people, and for the cities of our God; and may Yahweh do what seems good to him.' So Joab and the people who were with him drew near to battle against the Syrians; and they fled before him. And when the Ammonites saw that the Syrians fled, they likewise fled before Abishai, and entered the city. Then Joab returned from fighting against the Ammonites, and came to Jerusalem.

But when the Syrians saw that they had been defeated by Israel, they gathered themselves together. And Hadadezer sent, and brought out the Syrians who were beyond the Euphrates; and they came to Helam, with Shobach the commander of the army of Hadadezer at their head. And when it was told David, he gathered all Israel together, and crossed the Jordan, and came to Helam. And the Syrians arrayed themselves against David, and fought with him. And the Syrians fled before Israel; and David slew of the Syrians the men of seven hundred chariots, and forty thousand horsemen, and wounded Shobach the commander of their army, so that he died there. And when all the kings who were servants of Hadadezer saw that they had been defeated by Israel, they made peace with Israel, and became subject to them. So the Syrians feared to help the Ammonites any more.

Rabbah Captured (2Sam 11: 1; 12: 26, 30–31; 1Chr 20:1–3)

In the spring of the year, the time when kings go forth to battle, David sent Joab, and his servants with him, and all Israel; and they ravaged the Ammonites, and besieged Rabbah. But David remained at Jerusalem. Now Joab fought against Rabbah of the Ammonites, and took the royal city. And he took the crown of their king from his head; the weight of it was a talent of gold, and in it was a precious stone; and it was placed on David's head. And he brought forth the spoil of the city, a very great amount. And he brought forth the people who were in it, and set them to labour with saws and iron picks and iron axes, and made them toil at the brickkilns; and thus he did to all the cities of the Ammonites. Then David and all the people returned to Jerusalem.

Philistine Giants (2Sam 21: 18–22; 1Chr 20:4–8)

After this there was again war with the Philistines at Gob; then Sibbecai the Hushathite slew Saph, who was one of the descendants of the giants. And there was again war with the Philistines at Gob; and Elhanan the son of Jaareoregim, the Bethlehemite, slew Goliath the Gittite, the shaft of whose spear was like a weaver's beam. And there was again war at Gath, where there was a man of great stature, who had six fingers on each hand, and six toes on each foot, twenty-four in number; and he also was descended from the giants. And when he taunted Israel, Jonathan the son of Shimei, David's brother, slew him. These four were descended from the giants in Gath; and they fell by the hand of David and by the hand of his servants.

David's Heroes (2Sam 23: 8–39; 1Chr 11:10–47)

These are the names of the mighty men whom David had: Josheb-basshebeth a Tahchemonite; he was chief of the three; he wielded his spear against eight hundred whom he slew at one time. And next to him among the three mighty men was Eleazar the son of Dodo, son of Ahohi. He was with David when they defied the Philistines who were gathered there for battle, and the men of Israel withdrew. He rose and struck down the Philistines until his hand was weary, and his hand cleaved to the sword; and Yahweh wrought a great victory that day; and the men returned after him only to strip the slain. And next to him was Shammah, the son of Agee the Hararite. The Philistines gathered together at Lehi, where there was a plot of ground full of lentils; and the men fled from the Philistines. But he took his stand in the midst of the plot, and defended it, and slew the Philistines; and Yahweh wrought a great victory.

And three of the thirty chief men went down, and came about harvest time to David at the cave of Adullam, when a band of Philistines was encamped in the valley of Rephaim. David was then in the stronghold; and the garrison of the Philistines was then at Bethlehem. And David said longingly, 'O that some one would give me water to drink from the well of Bethlehem which is by the gate!' Then the three mighty men broke through the camp of the Philistines, and drew water out of the well of Bethlehem which was by the gate, and took and brought it to David. But he would not drink of it; he poured it out to Yahweh, and said, 'Far be it from me, Yahweh, that I should do this. Shall I drink the blood of the men who went at the risk of their lives?' Therefore he would not drink it. These things did the three mighty men.

Now Abishai, the brother of Joab, the son of Zeruiah, was chief of the thirty. And he wielded his spear against three hundred men and slew them, and won a name beside the three. He was the most renowned of the thirty, and became their commander; but he did not attain to the three. And Benaiah the son of Jehoiada was a valiant man of Kabzeel, a doer of great deeds; he smote two ariels of Moab. He also went down and slew a lion in a pit on a day when snow had fallen. And he slew an Egyptian, a handsome man. The Egyptian had a spear in his hand; but Benaiah went down to him with a staff, and snatched the spear out of the Egyptian's hand, and slew him with his own spear. These things did Benaiah the son of Jehoiada, and won a name beside the three mighty men. He was renowned among the thirty, but he did not attain to the three. And David set him over his bodyguard.

Asahel the brother of Joab was one of the thirty; Elhanan the son of Dodo of Bethlehem, Shammah of Harod, Elika of Harod, Helez the Paltite, Ira the son of Ikkesh of Tekoa, Abiezer, of Anathoth, Mebunnai the Hushathite, Zalmon the Ahohite, Maharai of Netophah, Heleb the son of Baanah of Netophah, Ittai the son of Ribai of Gibeah of the Benjaminites, Benaiah of Pirathon, Hiddai of the brooks of Gaash, Abialbon the Arbathite, Azmaveth of Bahurim, Eliahba of Shaalbon, the sons of Jashen, Jonathan, Shammah the Hararite, Ahiam the son of Sharar the Hararite, Eliphelet the son of Ahasbai of Maacah, Eliam the son of Ahithophel of Gilo, Hezro of Carmel, Paarai the Arbite, Igal the son of Nathan of Zobah, Bani the Gadite, Zelek the Ammonite, Naharai of Beeroth, the armourbearer of Joab the son of Zeruiah, Ira the Ithrite, Gareb the Ithrite, Uriah the Hittite: thirty-seven in all.

Census and Threshing-floor (2Sam 24: 1–25; 1Chr 21: 1–27)

Again the anger of Yahweh was kindled against Israel, and he incited David against them, saying, 'Go, number Israel [and Judah][1].' So the king said to Joab and the commanders of the army, who were with him, 'Go through all the tribes of Israel, from Dan to Beersheba, and number the people, that I may know the number of the people.' But Joab said to the king, 'May Yahweh your God add to the people a hundred times as many as

---

[1] Here, as elsewhere in this chapter, the brackets enclose Sam pluses. This first is reminiscent of the Kings plus in 1Kgs 4: 20, mentioned on p. 30 above, and discussed below on p. 172.

they are, while the eyes of my lord the king still see it; but why does my lord the king delight in this thing?' But the king's word prevailed against Joab and the commanders of the army. So Joab and the commanders of the army went out from the presence of the king to number the people of Israel. [They crossed the Jordan, and began from Aroer, and from the city that is in the middle of the valley, toward Gad and on to Jazer. Then they came to Gilead, and to Kadesh in the land of the Hittites; and they came to Dan, and from Dan they went around to Sidon, and came to the fortress of Tyre and to all the cities of the Hivites and Canaanites; and they went out to the Negeb of Judah at Beersheba.] So when they had gone through all the land, they came to Jerusalem at the end of nine months and twenty days. And Joab gave the sum of the numbering of the people to the king: in Israel there were eight hundred thousand valiant men who drew the sword, and the men of Judah were five hundred thousand.

But David's heart smote him after he had numbered the people. And David said to Yahweh, 'I have sinned greatly in what I have done. But now, Yahweh, I pray thee, take away the iniquity of thy servant; for I have done very foolishly.' And when David arose in the morning, the word of Yahweh came to the prophet Gad, David's seer, saying, 'Go and say to David, "Thus says Yahweh, Three things I offer you; choose one of them, that I may do it to you."' So Gad came to David and told him, and said to him, 'Shall three years of famine come to you in your land? Or will you flee three months before your foes while they pursue you? Or shall there be three days' pestilence in your land? Now consider, and decide what answer I shall return to him who sent me.' Then David said to Gad, 'I am in great distress; let us fall into the hand of Yahweh, for his mercy is great; but let me not fall into the hand of man.'

So Yahweh sent a pestilence upon Israel from the morning until the appointed time; and there died of the people from Dan to Beersheba seventy thousand men. And when the angel stretched forth his hand toward Jerusalem to destroy it, Yahweh repented of the evil, and said to the angel who was working destruction among the people, 'It is enough; now stay your hand.' And the angel of Yahweh was by the threshing floor of Araunah the Jebusite. Then David spoke to Yahweh when he saw the angel who was smiting the people, and said, 'Lo, I have sinned, and I have done wickedly; but these sheep, what have they done? Let thy hand, I pray thee, be against me and against my father's house.'

And Gad came that day to David, and said to him, 'Go up, rear an altar to Yahweh on the threshing floor of Araunah the Jebusite.' So David went up at Gad's word, as Yahweh commanded. And when Araunah looked down, he saw the king and his servants coming on toward him; and Araunah went forth, and did obeisance to the king with his face to the ground. And Araunah said, 'Why has my lord the king come to his servant?' David said, 'To buy the threshing floor of you, in order to build an altar to Yahweh, that the plague may be averted from the people.' Then Araunah said to David, 'Let my lord the king take and offer up what seems good to him; here are the oxen for the burnt offering, and the threshing sledges and the yokes of the oxen for the wood. All this, O king, Araunah gives to the king.' And Araunah said to the king, 'Yahweh your God accept you.' But the king said to Araunah, 'No, but I will buy it of you for a price; I will not offer burnt offerings to Yahweh my God which cost me nothing.' So David bought the threshing floor and the oxen for fifty shekels of silver. And David built there an altar to Yahweh, and offered burnt offerings and peace offerings. So Yahweh heeded supplications for the land, and the plague was averted from Israel.

From David to Solomon (1 Chr 23: 1; 28: 5* [cf. 1 Kgs 1: 1a]; 1 Kgs 2: 1–3* [cf. 1 Chr 28: 7–8*]; 1 Kgs 2: 10–12 [cf. 1 Chr 29: 26–28; 2 Chr 1: 1])

When David was old and full of days, he made Solomon his son king over Israel out of all his sons. When his time to die drew near, he charged Solomon, saying, 'I am about to go the way of all the earth. Be strong, and keep all the commandments and ordinances of Yahweh in order that you may succeed in all that you do. Then David slept with his fathers, and was buried in the city of David. And the time that David reigned over Israel was forty years; he reigned seven years in Hebron, and thirty-three years in

Jerusalem. So Solomon sat upon the throne of David his father; and his kingdom was firmly established.

Solomon at Gibeon (1Kgs 3: 4–15; 4: 1; 2Chr 1: 6b–13)

And he went to Gibeon to sacrifice there, for that was the great high place; Solomon used to offer a thousand burnt offerings upon that altar. And God appeared to Solomon by night; and he said, 'Ask what I shall give you.' And Solomon said, 'Thou hast shown great loyalty to David my father, and hast made me king in his place, over a people numerous as the dust of the earth, and I am but a little lad; I do not know how to go out or come in. Give me therefore wisdom; for who may govern this thy people?' And God said to Solomon, 'Because this was in your heart, and you have not asked for riches [or the life of your enemies], and have not even requested long life, but have asked for yourself wisdom to rule this people, wisdom is granted you, and riches and honour will I give you, such as kings did not have before you nor will have such after you. And Solomon came to Jerusalem, and became king over Israel.

Solomon and Hiram (1Kgs 5: 15–25; cf. 2Chr 2: 1–11,14–15)

Now Hiram king of Tyre sent his servants to Solomon, when he heard that they had anointed him king in place of his father; for Hiram always loved David.[1] And Solomon sent word to Hiram, 'You know that David my father could not build a house for the name of Yahweh his God because of the warfare with which his enemies surrounded him, until Yahweh put them under the soles of his feet. But now Yahweh my God has given me rest[2] on every side; there is neither adversary nor misfortune. And so I purpose to build a house for the name of Yahweh my God, as

---

[1] It is Kings which is being followed in this section. However, this opening sentence should perhaps be removed: it is itself a Kings plus, and the anointing of Solomon to which it refers is described in 1Kgs 1 (also a plus), but is not alluded to in Chronicles. The references to David in the divergent texts of Kings and Chronicles here are noted below on pp. 132-35.

[2] For the theme of 'rest' in connection with David and Solomon see pp. 38-39 above.

Yahweh said to David my father, "Your son, whom I will set upon your throne in your place, shall build the house for my name." Now therefore command that cedars of Lebanon be cut for me; and my servants will join your servants, and I will pay you for your servants such wages as you set; for you know that there is no one among us who knows how to cut timber like the Sidonians.'

When Hiram heard the words of Solomon, he rejoiced greatly, and said, 'Blessed be Yahweh this day, who has given to David a wise son to be over this great people.' And Hiram sent to Solomon, saying, 'I have heard the message which you have sent to me; I am ready to do all you desire in the matter of cedar and cypress timber. My servants shall bring it down to the sea from Lebanon; and I will make it into rafts to go by sea to the place you direct, and I will have them broken up there, and you shall receive it; and you shall meet my wishes by providing food for my household.' So Hiram supplied Solomon with all the timber of cedar and cypress that he desired, while Solomon gave Hiram twenty thousand cors of wheat as food for his household, and twenty thousand cors of beaten oil. Solomon gave this to Hiram year by year. And Yahweh gave Solomon wisdom, as he promised him; and there was peace between Hiram and Solomon; and the two of them made a treaty.

Solomon's Forced Labour from Israel (1 Kgs 5: 27, 29–30; 2 Chr 2: 1,17)

King Solomon raised a levy of forced labour out of all Israel; and the levy numbered thirty thousand men. Solomon also had seventy thousand burden-bearers and eighty thousand hewers of stone in the hill country, besides Solomon's three thousand three hundred chief officers who were over the work, who had charge of the people.

Temple: The Main Structure (1 Kgs 6: 1–22*; 2 Chr 3: 1–9*)

In the fourth year of Solomon's reign, in the second month, .. The house which King Solomon built for Yahweh was sixty cubits long. The vestibule in front of the nave was twenty cubits, opposite the width of the house, and ten cubits [deep]. And he overlaid the inside with pure gold. And he overlaid the house with gold.

Temple: The Most Holy Place (1 Kgs 6: 23–28*; 2 Chr 3: 10–13*)

In the inner sanctuary he made two cherubim [of olivewood]. Five cubits was the wing of the one, and five cubits the wing of the second. And the cherubim spread out their wings. [And he constructed a covering.]

Temple: Jachin and Boaz (1 Kgs 7: 15–22*; 2 Chr 3: 15–17*)

And he made the two pillars. [Eighteen] cubits was the height. [.. capitals] upon the tops .. five cubits. .. chain work .. on the head of the pillars. And he made a hundred pomegranates. He set up the pillars at the vestibule of the temple; the right one he called Jachin; and the left one he called Boaz.

Temple: The Rest of the Work (1 Kgs 7: 23–51; 2 Chr 4: 2–5: 1)

Then he made the molten sea; it was round, ten cubits from brim to brim, and five cubits high, and a line of thirty cubits measured its circumference. Under its brim were gourds, for thirty cubits, compassing the sea round about; the gourds were in two rows, cast with it when it was cast. It stood upon twelve oxen, three facing north, three facing west, three facing south, and three facing east; the sea was set upon them, and all their hinder parts were inward. Its thickness was a handbreadth; and its brim was made like the brim of a cup, like the flower of a lily; it held two thousand baths.

And he made ten lavers; and he set five on the right and five on the left. And the sea he set on the right flank to the east facing the south.

Hiram made the pots, the shovels, and the basins. And Hiram finished the work that he did for King Solomon [on?] the house of Yahweh; the two pillars, the two bowls of the capitals that were on the tops of the pillars, and the two networks to cover the two bowls of the capitals that were on the tops of the pillars; and the four hundred pomegranates for the two networks, two rows of pomegranates for each network, to cover the two bowls of the capitals that were upon the pillars; the ten stands, and the ten lavers upon the stands; and the one sea, and the twelve oxen underneath the sea.

Now the pots, the shovels, and the basins, all these vessels in the house of Yahweh, which Hiram made for King Solomon, were of burnished bronze. In the plain of the Jordan the king cast them, in the clay ground between Succoth and Zarethan. And Solomon left all the vessels unweighed, because there were so many of them; the weight of the bronze was not found out.

So Solomon made all the vessels that were in the house of Yahweh: the golden altar, the golden table for the bread of the Presence, the lampstands of pure gold, five on the south side and five on the north, before the inner sanctuary; the flowers, the lamps, and the tongs, of gold; the cups, snuffers, basins, dishes for incense, and firepans, of pure gold; and the sockets of gold, for the doors of the innermost part of the house, the most holy place, and for the doors of the nave of the temple.

Thus all the work that King Solomon did on the house of Yahweh was finished. And Solomon brought in the things which David his father had dedicated, the silver, the gold, and the vessels, and stored them in the treasuries of the house of Yahweh.

Ark Brought to the Temple (1 Kgs 8: 1–11; 2Chr 5: 2–11a, 14b)

Then Solomon assembled the elders of Israel [and all the heads of the tribes, the leaders of the fathers' houses of the people of Israel, to Jerusalem,] to bring up the ark of the covenant of Yahweh out of the city of David, which is Zion. [And all the men of Israel assembled to King Solomon at the feast] in the month Ethanim, [which is the seventh month]. And [all the elders of Israel came, and] the priests/levites took up the ark. [And they brought up the ark], the tent of meeting, and [all] the holy vessels that were in the tent [the priests (and) the Levites brought them up]. And King Solomon and all [the congregation of] Israel, [who had assembled before him,] were before the ark, sacrificing [so many] sheep and oxen without number [that they could not be counted or numbered]. Then the priests brought the ark [of the covenant of Yahweh] to its place, in the inner sanctuary of the house, in the most holy place, underneath the wings of the cherubim. For the cherubim spread out their wings over the place of the ark, so that the cherubim made a covering above the ark and its poles. And the poles were so long that the ends of the poles were seen from the holy place before the inner sanctuary; but they could not be seen from outside [and they are there to this day].[1] There was nothing in the ark except the two tables of stone which Moses put there at Horeb, where Yahweh made a covenant with the people of Israel, when they came out of Egypt. And when the priests came out of the holy place, a cloud filled the house of Yahweh, so that the priests could not stand to minister because of the cloud; for the glory of Yahweh filled the house of Yahweh.

Solomon's Prayer of Dedication (1 Kgs 8: 12–50a; 2Chr 6: 1–39)

Then Solomon said,
      'Yahweh has set the sun in the heavens,
      but has said that he would dwell in thick darkness.
      I have built thee an exalted house,
      a place for thee to dwell in for ever.'
Then the king faced about, and blessed all the assembly of Israel, while all the assembly of Israel stood. And he said, 'Blessed be Yahweh, the God of Israel, who with his hand has fulfilled what he promised with his mouth to David my father, saying, "Since the day that I brought my people out of Egypt, I chose no city from all the sceptres of Israel to build a house for my name to be there; and I chose no man to be ruler over my people Israel; but I have chosen Jerusalem for my name to be there, and I have chosen David to be over my people Israel." Now it was in the heart of David my father to build a house for the name of Yahweh, the God of Israel. But Yahweh said to David my father, "Whereas it was in your heart to build a house for my name, you did well that it was in your heart; nevertheless you shall not build the house, but your son who shall be born to you shall build the house for my

---

[1] The several expressions in brackets since the beginning of this paragraph are not represented in Kings LXX. It is attractive to see this shorter text as also more original than Kings MT, which is close to Chronicles both MT and LXX, though Chronicles LXX also 'lacks' the opening words of v. 5). The issues involved will be separately discussed. See also pp. 145-46 below.

name." Now Yahweh has fulfilled his promise which he made; for I have risen in the place of David my father, and sit on the throne of Israel, as Yahweh promised, and I have built the house for the name of Yahweh, the God of Israel. And there I have placed the ark, in which is the covenant of Yahweh which he made with the people of Israel.'

Then Solomon stood before the altar of Yahweh in the presence of all the assembly of Israel, and spread forth his hands toward heaven; and said, 'Yahweh, God of Israel, there is no God like thee, in heaven or on earth, keeping covenant and showing steadfast love to thy servants who walk before thee with all their heart; who hast kept with thy servant David my father what thou didst declare to him; yea, thou didst speak with thy mouth, and with thy hand hast fulfilled it this day. Now therefore, Yahweh, God of Israel, keep with thy servant David my father what thou hast promised him, saying, "There shall never fail you a man before me to sit upon the throne of Israel, if only your sons take heed to their way, to walk before me as you have walked before me." Now therefore, O God of Israel, let thy word be confirmed, which thou hast spoken to thy servant David.'

'But will God indeed dwell on the earth? Behold, heaven and the highest heaven cannot contain thee; how much less this house which I have built! Yet have regard to the prayer of thy servant and to his supplication, Yahweh my God, hearkening to the cry and to the prayer which thy servant prays before thee; that thy eyes may be open night and day toward this house, the place of which thou hast said, "My name shall be there", that thou mayest hearken to the prayer which thy servant offers toward this place. And hearken thou to the supplication of thy servant and of thy people Israel, when they pray toward this place; yea, hear thou in heaven thy dwelling place; and when thou hearest, forgive.'

'If a man sins against his neighbour and is made to take an oath, and comes and swears his oath before thine altar in this house, then hear thou in heaven, and act, and judge thy servants, condemning the guilty by bringing his conduct upon his own head, and vindicating the righteous by rewarding him according to his righteousness.'

'When thy people Israel are defeated before the enemy because they have sinned against thee, if they turn again to thee, and acknowledge thy name, and pray and make supplication to thee in this house; then hear thou in heaven, and forgive the sin of thy people Israel, and bring them again to the land which thou gavest to their fathers.'

'When heaven is shut up and there is no rain because they have sinned against thee, if they pray toward this place, and acknowledge thy name, and turn from their sin, when thou dost afflict them, then hear thou in heaven, and forgive the sin of thy servants, thy people Israel, when thou dost teach them the good way in which they should walk; and grant rain upon thy land, which thou hast given to thy people as an inheritance.'

'If there is famine in the land, if there is pestilence or blight or mildew or locust or caterpillar; if their enemy besieges them in any of their cities; whatever plague, whatever sickness there is; whatever prayer, whatever supplication is made by any man or by all thy people Israel, each knowing the affliction of his own heart and stretching out his hands toward this house; then hear thou in heaven thy dwelling place, and forgive, and render to each whose heart thou knowest, according to all his ways (for thou, thou only, knowest the hearts of all the children of men); that they may fear thee all the days that they live in the land which thou gavest to our fathers.'

'Likewise when a foreigner, who is not of thy people Israel, comes from a far country for the sake of thy great name, and thy mighty hand, and thy outstretched arm – when he comes and prays toward this house, hear thou in heaven thy dwelling place, and do according to all for which the foreigner calls to thee; in order that all the peoples of the earth may know thy name and fear thee, as do thy people Israel, and that they may know that this house which I have built is called by thy name.'

'If thy people go out to battle against their enemy, by whatever way thou shalt send them, and they pray to Yahweh toward the city which thou hast chosen and the house which I have built for thy name, then hear thou in heaven their prayer and their supplication, and maintain their cause.'

'If they sin against thee – for there is no man who does not sin – and thou art angry with them, and dost give them to an enemy, so that they are carried away captive to a land far off or near; yet if they lay it to heart in the land to which they have been carried captive, and repent, and make supplication to thee in the land of their captors, saying, "We have sinned, and have acted perversely and wickedly"; if they repent with all their mind and with all their heart in the land of their enemies, who carried them captive, and pray toward their land, which thou gavest to their fathers, the city which thou hast chosen, and the house which I have built for thy name; then hear thou in heaven thy dwelling place their prayer and their supplication, and maintain their cause and forgive thy people who have sinned against thee. Let thy eyes be open to the supplication of thy servant.'

Solomon's Dedicatory Sacrifice (1 Kgs 8: 54a*, 62–66; 2Chr 7: 1a*, 4–5, 7–8, 10)

Then as Solomon finished praying, the king and all the people offering sacrifice before Yahweh, he offered sacrifice of twenty-two thousand oxen and a hundred and twenty thousand sheep. So the king and all the people dedicated the house of Yahweh. Solomon consecrated the middle of the court that was before the house of Yahweh; for there he offered the burnt offering [and the cereal offering] and the fat pieces of the peace offerings, because the bronze altar that was before Yahweh was too small to receive the burnt offering and the cereal offering and the fat pieces of the peace offerings. So Solomon held the feast at that time, and all Israel with him, a great assembly, from the entrance of Hamath to the Brook of Egypt, before Yahweh our God, seven days.[1] On the eighth day he sent the people away to their homes joyful and glad of heart for all the goodness that Yahweh had shown to David his servant and to Israel his people.

Solomon's Vision in Jerusalem (1 Kgs 9: 1–9; 2Chr 7: 11–12, 16–22)

And Solomon finished building the house of Yahweh and the king's house and everything that came to Solomon's heart to do.

---

[1] Both Kings and Chronicles, but in somewhat different order, report an additional seven-day period. Dismissal on the eighth day could simply be conventional, but I take it as a pointer that the second week was a later addition to each.

And Yahweh appeared to Solomon at night, and said to him, 'I have heard your prayer; I have consecrated this house which you have built, and put my name there for ever; my eyes and my heart will be there for all time. And as for you, if you will walk before me, as David your father walked, doing according to all that I have commanded you, and keeping my statutes and my ordinances, then I will establish your royal throne, as I promised David your father, saying, "There shall not fail you a man ruling in[1] Israel." But if you yourselves turn aside from following me, and abandon[2] my commandments and my statutes which I have set before you, but go and serve other gods and worship them, then I will pluck them up from the land which I have given them; and the house which I have consecrated for my name I will cast out of my sight; and I will make it[3] a proverb and a byword among all peoples. And this house which was exalted will become a heap of ruins; everyone passing by it will be astonished; and they will say, "Why has Yahweh done thus to this land and to this house?" Then they will say, "Because they abandoned Yahweh their God who brought them out of the land of Egypt, and laid hold on other gods, and worshiped them and served them; therefore he has brought all this evil upon them."'

Cities Disputed between Solomon and Hiram (1 Kgs 9: 10–14[15–25]26–28*; 2 Chr 8: 1–2[3–16]17–18*)

At the end of twenty years, in which Solomon had built [the two houses,] the house of Yahweh and the king's house, and Hiram king of Tyre had supplied Solomon with cedar and cypress timber and gold, as much as he desired, King Solomon gave to Hiram twenty cities in the land of Galilee. But when Hiram came from Tyre to see the cities which Solomon had given him, they did not please him. Therefore he said, 'What kind of cities are these which you have given me, my brother?' So they are called the land of Cabul to this day. Hiram had sent to the king one hundred and twenty talents of gold.

[1] So C 18 [*mwšl byśr'l*]; K5 ends with 'from the throne of Israel' [*m'l ks' yśr'l*].

[2] Following Chronicles here – Kings has 'do not keep'. This issue is discussed on p. 93 below.

[3] K7 promises that Israel rather than the temple will be the object of the proverb.

And this[1] is the account[2] of the forced labour which King
Solomon levied to build the house of Yahweh and his own house
and the Millo and the wall of Jerusalem and Hazor and Megiddo
and Gezer (Pharaoh king of Egypt had gone up and captured
Gezer and burnt it with fire, and had slain the Canaanites who
dwelt in the city, and had given it as dowry to his daughter,
Solomon's wife; so Solomon rebuilt Gezer) and Lower Beth-
horon and Baalath and Tamar in the wilderness, in the land of
Judah, and all the store-cities that Solomon had, and the cities for
his chariots, and the cities for his horsemen, and whatever
Solomon desired to build in Jerusalem, in Lebanon, and in all the
land of his dominion. All the people who were left of the
Amorites, the Hittites, the Perizzites, the Hivites, and the Jebusites,
who were not of the people of Israel – their descendants who were
left after them in the land, whom the people of Israel did not
finish – these Solomon made a forced levy, and so they are to this
day. But of the people of Israel Solomon made no slaves; they
were the soldiers, [they were his officials],[3] his commanders, his
captains, his chariot commanders and his horsemen. These were
the chief officers who were over Solomon's work:[4] five hundred
and fifty who had charge of the people. But[5] Pharaoh's daughter
went up from the city of David to her own house which Solomon
had built for her; then he built the Millo. Then Solomon offered
up burnt offerings to Yahweh upon Yahweh's altar which he had
built before the nave.[6]

[1] As discussed on p. 30 above, this paragraph, though attested in each of the three
ancient witnesses under consideration, may be a later addition to the common
text, since it appears here in Kings MT and Chronicles but after 10: 22 in Kings
LXX.
[2] See discussions in Williamson (1982) and Willi (1972). McKenzie (1985)
appears to ignore these.
[3] C9 does not include this word, literally 'and his servants'.
[4] C10, perhaps rightly, reads 'who were King Solomon's [*'šr lmlk šlmh*] rather than
'who were over Solomon's work' [*'šr 'l-hml'kh lšlmh*] as in K23.
[5] This 'but' of K24 (MT) I find strange; C11's 'And the daughter of Pharaoh did
Solomon bring up . . . ' reads more easily.
[6] I have followed the shorter Chronicles text here. Williamson (1982) and
McKenzie (1985) both find this shorter text tendentious. The following C13–
16 certainly do offer a fuller account of Solomon's regular sacrificial practice;
but I wonder whether K25 has not already taken a first step down that
expansive route by turning what was a simple report into a record of the
habitual.

King Solomon built a fleet of ships at Ezion-geber, which is near Eloth on the shore of the Red Sea, in the land of Edom. And Hiram sent with the fleet his servants, seamen who were familiar with the sea, together with the servants of Solomon; and they went to Ophir, and brought from there gold, to the amount of four hundred and twenty talents; and they brought it to King Solomon.

The Queen of Sheba (1Kgs 10: 1–13; 2Chr 9: 1–12)

The queen of Sheba heard of the fame of Solomon. She came to Jerusalem to test him with hard questions with a very great retinue, with camels bearing spices, and much gold, and precious stones; and when she came to Solomon, she told him all that was on her mind. And Solomon answered all her questions; there was nothing hidden from the king which he could not explain to her. And when the queen of Sheba had seen all the wisdom of Solomon, the house that he had built, the food of his table, his officials as they sat, and his servants as they stood in attendance, their clothing, his cupbearers, and his burnt offerings which he offered at the house of Yahweh, there was no more spirit in her. And she said to the king, 'The report was true which I heard in my own land of your affairs and of your wisdom, but I did not believe the reports until I came and my own eyes had seen it; and, behold, the half was not told me; your wisdom and prosperity surpass the report which I heard. Happy are your wives! Happy are these your servants, who continually stand before you and hear your wisdom! Blessed be Yahweh your God, who has delighted in you and set you on the throne of Israel! Because Yahweh loved Israel for ever, he has made you king, that you may execute justice and righteousness.' Then she gave the king a hundred and twenty talents of gold, and a very great quantity of spices, and precious stones; never again came such spices as these which the queen of Sheba gave to King Solomon. Moreover the fleet of Hiram, which brought gold from Ophir, brought almug wood and precious stones. And the king made of the almug wood supports for the house of Yahweh, and for the king's house, lyres also and harps for the singers; no such almug wood has come or been seen, to this day. And King Solomon gave to the queen of

Sheba all that she desired, whatever she asked besides what was given her by the bounty of King Solomon. So she turned and went back to her own land, with her servants.

Solomon's Trade (1Kgs 10: 14–28a; 2Chr 9: 13–25, 27–28)

Now the weight of gold that came to Solomon in one year was six hundred and sixty-six talents of gold, besides that which came from the traders and from the traffic of the merchants, and from all the kings of Arabia and from the governors of the land. King Solomon made two hundred large shields of beaten gold; six hundred shekels of gold went into each shield. And he made three hundred shields of beaten gold; three minas of gold went into each shield; and the king put them in the House of the Forest of Lebanon. The king also made a great ivory throne, and overlaid it with the finest gold. The throne had six steps, and at the back of the throne was a calf's head, and on each side of the seat were arm rests and two lions standing beside the arm rests, while twelve lions stood there, one on each end of a step on the six steps. The like of it was never made in any kingdom. All King Solomon's drinking vessels were of gold, and all the vessels of the House of the Forest of Lebanon were of pure gold; none were of silver, it was not considered as anything in the days of Solomon. For the king had a fleet of ships of Tarshish at sea with the fleet of Hiram. Once every three years the fleet of ships of Tarshish used to come bringing gold, silver, ivory, apes, and peacocks.

Thus King Solomon excelled all the kings of the earth in riches and in wisdom. And the whole earth sought the presence of Solomon to hear his wisdom, which God had put into his mind. Every one of them brought his present, articles of silver and gold, garments, myrrh, spices, horses, and mules, so much year by year. And [Solomon gathered together chariots and horsemen;][1] he had fourteen hundred chariots and twelve thousand horsemen, whom he stationed in the chariot cities and with the king in Jerusalem. And the king made silver as common in Jerusalem as stone, and he made cedar as plentiful as the sycamore of the

---

[1] Surely a pejorative addition in K26, in line with the Deuteronomic warning (Dt 17: 16).

Shephelah. And Solomon's import of horses was from Egypt and from all the earth.

Solomon Dies – Rehoboam Succeeds (1 Kgs 11: 41–43; 2Chr 9: 29–31)

Now the rest of the acts of Solomon, and all that he did, and his wisdom, are they not written in the book of the acts of Solomon? And the time that Solomon reigned in Jerusalem over all Israel was forty years. And Solomon slept with his fathers, and was buried in the city of David his father; and Rehoboam his son reigned in his stead.

4

Judah's Other Kings

4.0 Introduction

The kings from Rehoboam to the fall of Jerusalem receive much more summary mention in Kings and Chronicles than the great founders of the royal line – and even more so in the shorter account they share. However, as we turn to Solomon's successors from Rehoboam onwards we meet very similar broad questions. The common story has nothing beyond the formulaic to report about Abijam/Abijah; and even Rehoboam, Hezekiah, and Josiah about whom most detail is provided are despatched in around thirty verses each. The Chronicles pluses, while all typical of his interests, are more varied in character. The Kings pluses have achieved a more patterned narrative, well described – but not so well explained – in Hoffmann (1980). Most of the differences on both sides can be attributed to simple supplementation of a shared source, as in the David and Solomon narratives; and so in the majority of cases it is easy to recover the text of that source. However, here and there we meet more substantial rewriting, and we will require to elaborate criteria to decide whether one or the other or both texts have recast the older story available to them. The most acute questions relate to shared material in longer accounts such as those of Hezekiah and Josiah, and to the several brief reports of the kings following Josiah in the years of collapse.

All accounts of the books of Kings reckon that they have at least three principal sources: records of the kings of Judah and of the kings of Israel, both drawing ultimately on royal archives, and a stock of prophetic narratives mostly connected with Elijah and

Elisha and with the northern kingdom. As with the David and Solomon stories, we have to ask here too: Did the Chronicler unpick a package put together by the editors of Kings, selecting from Kings only its account of the monarchy in Judah? Or does Chronicles, shorn of its own special material, preserve relatively unaltered that very record of the kings of Judah which served also as the major source of the book of Kings? There is some evidence of awareness of Israel and Elijah traditions 'at the margins' of Chronicles; but these could be cross–references from one book to another rather than evidence of a source used in composition. But is there compelling evidence within the main body of the Chronicler's narrative that he almost–successfully–but–not–quite– so eliminated from his record all the material which the authors of Kings had carefully added to and intermingled with their prime source – the record of Judah's kings?

4.1 Overview

The *overview* now offered of the biblical records for the kings of Judah from Rehoboam onwards is laid out, like those already offered for David and Solomon, with the text more or less common to Kings and Chronicles at the centre, clearly separated from the pluses within each book on either side. The textual relationships are rather more complex than those relating to the first two kings. These summary tables can document only larger discrepancies between the biblical books. The pluses recorded are of at least a half–verse in length. The synoptic discussion of Manasseh (4.2) which follows the tables will show just how many small differences of wording there are between blocks of text which are very similar in extent and content.

King's name (approx verses)	Kgs + 's	Kgs close to Chr		Chr + 's
Rehoboam (31)	12: 20	12: 1–19	10: 1–19	
		12: 21–24	11: 1–4	
				11: 5–23
	12: 25–33 13: 1–34			

	14: 1-20			
	14: 22b-24	14: 21-22a	(12: 13-14a)	12: 1
		14: 25	12: 2*	
				12: 3-9a
		14: 26-28	12: 9b-11	
		(14: 21-22a)	12: 13-14a	12: 12,14b
		14: 29-31	12: 15-16	
Abijam/h		15: 1-2	13: 1-2a	
(4)	15: 3-6			
		15: 7b	13: 2b	
				13: 3-21
		15: 7a, 8	13: 22-23a	
	15: 9-10			
				13: 23b
Asa		15: 11a	14: 1	
(13)	15: 11b			
	15: 12			14: 2-15: 15
		15: 13-22	15: 16-16: 6	16: 7-10
		15: 23	16: 11-12a	
		15: 24a	16: 13a, 14a	
Jehoshaphat		15: 24b	17: 1a	
				17: 1b-19
(Elijah)	15: 25-16: 34			
Jehoshaphat	17-21			
(41)	22: 1	22: 2-35a	18: 1-34	
				19
	22: 35b-41			20: 1-30
		22: 42-44a	20: 31-33a	20: 33b
	22: 44b-45			
		22: 46	20: 34	
	22: 47-48			
		22: 49-50	20: 35-37	
		22: 51	21: 1	
(Ahaziah of Israel)	22: 52-54			
				21: 2-4
	2K1: 1-8: 16			
Jehoram (6)		8: 17-22	21: 5-10a	
	8: 23-24a			21: 10b-20
		8: 24b	22: 1a	
Ahaziah (6)	8: 25			22: 1b
		8: 26-29	22: 2-6	
	9: 1-10: 36			22: 7-9
		(9: 21,27b)	(22: 7b,9*)	
Athaliah		11: 1-3	22: 10-12	
		11: 4a	23: 1a	
				23: 1b-3a

King				
		11: 4b	23: 3b	
		11: 5–20	23: 4–21	
Joash		12: 1–3	24: 1–2	
(15?)	12: 4			24: 3
		12: 5*–9*	24: 4*–7*	
		12: 10*–17*	24: 8*–14*	
				24: 15–22
		12: 18*–22*	24: 23*–26*	
				24: 27
(Jehoahaz)	13: 1–14: 1			
Amaziah		14: 2–3a	25: 1–2	
(16)	14: 3b–4			
		14: 5–6	25: 3–4	
				25: 5–10
		14: 7	25: 11	
				25: 12–16
		14: 8–11a	25: 17–20a	
				25: 20b
		14: 11b–14	25: 21–24*	
	14: 15–16			
		14: 17–20	25: 25–28	
Azar/Uzziah		14: 21–22	26: 1–2	
(7)	14: 23–29			
	15: 1			
		15: 2–3	26: 3–4	
	15: 4			26: 5–20
		15: 5–7	26: 21–23	
(Jeroboam II)	15: 8–31			
	15: 32			
Jotham		15: 33–34	27: 1–2a	
(4)	15: 35a			27: 2b
		15: 35b	27: 3a	
				27: 4–6
		15: 36	27: 7	
	15: 37			27: 8
		15: 38	27: 9	
	16: 1			
Ahaz		16: 2–3a	28: 1–2a	
(5)				28: 2b–3a
		16: 3b–4	28: 3b–4	
	16: 5–18			28: 5–25
		16: 19–20	28: 26–27	
	17: 1–18: 1			
Hezekiah		18: 2–3	29: 1–2	
(18)	18: 4–13a	18: 4*	31: 1*	29: 3–32: 1a
		18: 13b	32: 1b	

	18: 14–16			32: 2–8
		18: 17	32: 9	
		18: 19, 20b	32: 10	
		18: (27)32b	32: 11	
		18: 22b	32: 12	
		(18: 29, 33, 35	32: 13–15	
		(19: 11–12		
				32: 16
		19: 14	32: 17	
		18: 28	32: 18	
				32: 19
		19: 2–4.14f.	32: 20	
		19: 35–37	32: 21	
				32: 22–23
	20: 1*–11*	20: 1a,2b,9a*	32: 24	
				32: 25–30
		20: 12–13	32: 31	
	20: 14–19			
		20: 20–21	32: 32–33	
Manasseh		21: 1–10a	33: 1–10a	
(12)	21: 10b–16			33: 10b–17
		21: 17a	33: 18a	
				33: 18b
		21: 17b	33: 19*	
		21: 18*	33: 20	
Amon		21: 19–21	33: 21–22	
(4)	21: 22			
				33: 23
		21: 23–24	33: 24–25	
	21: 25–26			
Josiah		22: 1–2	34: 1–2	
(35?)	(23: 4–14			34: 3–5
	23: 15–18			
	23: 19–20a)	(23: 20b)	34: 7b	34: 6–7a
		22: 3–7	34: 8–12a	
				34: 12b–14
		22: 8–23: 3	34: 15–32a	
	23: 4–20			34: 32b–33
		23: 21a	35: 1a	
	23: 21b			
				35: 1b–17
		23: 22–23	35: 18–19	
	23: 24–27			
				35: 20a
		28: 28	(35: 26–27)	
		23: 29a	35: 20b	

						35: 21–22
		23: 29b*		35: 23a*		
		23: 30a		35: 24a		
						35: 24b–25
		(28: 28)		35: 26–27		
Jehoahaz		23: 30b		36: 1		
(2)		23: 31a		36: 2		
	23: 31b–33a					
Jehoiakim		23: 33b–34a		36: 3–4		
(4)	23: 34b–35					
		23: 36a		36: 5a		
	23: 36b					
		23: 37*		36: 5b		
		24: 1a		36: 6a		
		24: 5a		36: 8a		
Jehoiachin		24: 8a		36: 9a		
(3)	24: 8b					
		24: 9a		36: 9b		
	24: 9b					
		24: 10a, 12b, 13a	36: 10a			
		24: 17		36: 10b		
Zedekiah		24: 18a		36: 11		
(3)	24: 18b					
		24: 19a		36: 12a		
	24: 19b–20a					36: 12b
		24: 20b		36: 13a		
		(25: 10)		(36: 19)		

4.2 Manasseh: First Royal Example

Bad king Manasseh offers a good first sample of text for a more
detailed synoptic examination of the reports in Kings and
Chronicles of a single reign, and this for several reasons. The
reports in Kings and Chronicles are of similar, middling length
(18 verses in Kgs and 20 in Chr). They begin (1–10a) almost
identically, and end (21:17–18//33:18–20) in similar fashion. But
in between, the ways they take are very different though not
wholly unconnected. These Manasseh reports have also been
studied in able recent articles by Ben Zvi (1992) and Smelik
(1992b) who demonstrate wide knowledge of the secondary
literature.

	Kgs + 's	Reconstructed source	Chr + 's	
21: 1		Manasseh was twelve years old when he began to reign, and he reigned fifty-five years in Jerusalem.		33: 1
21: 2	His mother's name was Hephzibah.	And he did what was evil in the sight of Yahweh, according to the abominable practices of the nations whom Yahweh drove out before the people of Israel.		33: 2
21: 3	. . . destroyed;	For he rebuilt the high places which Hezekiah his father had broken down; and he erected altars for Baal, and made an Asherah, and worshiped all the host of heaven, and served	for the Baals, Asherahs,	33: 3
21: 4	. . . as Ahab king of Israel had done.	them. And he built altars in the house of Yahweh, of which Yahweh had said, "In Jerusalem		33: 4
	will I put my name."	shall my name be for ever."		
21: 5		And he built altars for all the host of heaven in the two courts of Yahweh's house.		33: 5
21: 6		And he burned his son as an offering,	. . . his sons as an offering in the valley of the sons of Hinnom,	33: 6
		and practised soothsaying and augury, and dealt with mediums and with wizards. He did much evil in Yahweh's sight provoking him to anger.	. . . and sorcery,	

21: 7		And the graven image of Asherah that he had made he set in the house of which	of the idol . . . . . . of God . . .	33: 7
	. . . Yahweh . . .	God said to David and to Solomon his son, "In this house, and in Jerusalem, which I have chosen out of all the tribes of Israel, I will put my name for ever;		
21: 8		and I will not continue to make Israel's feet wander out of the land which I gave to their fathers, if only they	turn Israel's feet off appointed to your fathers,	33: 8
	according to and . . . that my servant Moses commanded them."	will be careful to do all that I have commanded them by all the *torah*	. . . and the statutes and the ordinances by hand of Moses."	
21: 9	But they did not listen, and . . .	Manasseh seduced them to do more evil than the nations had done whom Yahweh destroyed before the people of Israel.	. . . Judah and the inhabitants of Jerusalem	33: 9
21: 10	. . . by hand of his servants the prophets, saying:	And Yahweh spoke	. . . to Manasseh and to his people, but they gave no heed.	33: 10
21: 11	Because Manasseh king of Judah has practised these abominations, he has done more evil than all that the Amorites did who were before him, and he made Judah sin too by his idols.		Therefore Yahweh brought upon them the commanders of the army of the king of Assyria, who took Manasseh with hooks and bound him with fetters of bronze and	33:11
21: 12	Therefore thus has		brought him to	

	Yahweh God of Israel spoken, Behold, I am bringing upon Jerusalem and Judah such evil that the ears of all of hear of it will tingle. And I will stretch over Jerusalem the line of Samaria and the measure of the house of Ahab; and I will wipe Jerusalem as one wipes a dish, wiping and turning it on its face.	Babylon. And when he was in distress he entreated the favour of Yahweh his God and humbled himself greatly before the God of his fathers.	33: 12
21: 14	And I will cast off the remnant of my possession, and give them into the hand of their enemies, and they shall become a prey and a spoil to all their enemies, because	He prayed to him and God and received his entreaty and heard his supplication and brought him again to Jerusalem into his kingdom. Then Manasseh knew that Yahweh was God.	33: 13
21: 15	they have done evil in my eyes and have been provoking me from the day their fathers came out of Egypt until this day.	Afterwards he built an outer wall for the city of David west of Gihon in the valley, and for the entrance into the Fish Gate, and carried it round Ophel, and raised it to a very great height; he also put commanders of the army in all the fortified cities in Judah.	33: 14
21: 16	Innocent blood also has been shed by Manasseh in very great quantity, till he has filled Jerusalem from one side to the other, apart from his sin which he has made Judah sin, doing evil in Yahweh's eyes.	And he took away the foreign gods and the idol from Yahweh's house and all the altars that he had	33: 15

		built on the mountain of Yahweh's house and in Jerusalem, and he threw them outside the city.	
		He also restored the alter of Yahweh and offered upon it sacrifices of peace offering and thanksgiving; and he commanded Judah to serve Yahweh the God of Israel.	33: 16
		Nevertheless the people still sacrificed at the high places, but to Yahweh their God.	33: 17
21: 17		Now the rest of the acts of Manasseh, and	33: 18
		. . . , his prayer to God, and the words of the seers who spoke to him in the name of Yahweh the God of Israel, behold they are in the Chronicles of the Kings of Israel. And his prayer, and all how God received his entreaty, and all	33:19
		his sin,	
. . . , which he sinned		and his faithless-ness the sites on which he built high places and	

Kings Without Privilege

			set up the Asherim and the images before he humbled	
	book of the	are they not written in the Chronicles of the Kings of Judah?	himself, behold they are seers?	
21: 18		And Manasseh slept with his fathers, and		33:20
	the garden	was buried in		
	of in the garden of Uzza	his house		
		and Amon his son reigned in his stead.		

4.2.1 The differences in vv. 1–10a are mostly modest in scale:

4.2.1.1 Kings as usual reports Manasseh's mother's name (1), but only the name itself – Hephzibah. Up to this point, with only the rarest exception, the shared text offers not only the Queen Mother's name but also either her father's name or where she was from. It is with Manasseh that Kings and Chronicles diverge in this matter. Chronicles no longer cites the Queen Mother's name from Hezekiah and after; while Kings becomes fuller from Amon onwards (21: 19), offering both the father's name and where the queen was from (Halpern and Vanderhooft 1991: 197–199). Kings also makes a cross-reference to Ahab king of Israel (3). It may also have made the minor adjustments to wording we find in v. 3, '*bd* for *nts;*[1] in v. 7, Yahweh for God; and the assimilation in v. 4 to 'I will put my name' of v. 7 in the common text.[2]

4.2.1.2 Chronicles makes Baal and Asherah (3) and son (6) plural;

---

[1] Chronicles never used '*bd*, but shares *nts* with Kings in one clear instance (2Kgs 11: 18//2Chr 23: 17), where both texts attest the *qal* theme of the verb. It is likely that both books also found *nts* in their source for Josiah's reform: Kings uses the *qal* four times (2Kgs 23: 7, 8, 12, 15), and Chronicles the *piel* twice (2Chr 34: 4, 7).

[2] There is variation in both directions between these phrases in the ancient witnesses to the Nathan oracle (2Sam 7 // 1Chr 17) and Solomon's prayer (1Kgs 8 // 2Chr 6).

adds 'in the valley of the sons of Hinnom' and 'and sorcery' (6) and 'of God' (7); replaces Asherah by 'the idol' (*hsml*) in v. 7;[1] and 'gave' by 'appointed' [8].[2]

4.2.1.3 In a couple of instances, I am less confident over reconstructing the original wording: in v. 8, Kings uses *lhnyd* and Chronicles *lhsyr* – the Kings expression is unique, while Chronicles' *hsyr* is often shared with Kings, but not with *rgl* as object;[3] and at the end of that verse Kings has 'and[4] by all the *torah* which my servant Moses commanded them',[5] while Chronicles offers 'by all the *torah* and the statutes and ordinances by hand of Moses'.[6]

4.2.2 Thereafter the accounts of Manasseh proceed in radically different directions:

4.2.2.1 K 10–15 reports a bleak divine threat 'by hand of his servants the prophets'[7] to the effect that the remnant of his heritage will be cast off. Then 16 adds as an afterthought to the

---

[1] *hsml* is found only here (2Chr 33: 7, 15) and in Ezekiel 8: 3, 5 and Deuteronomy 4: 16. It is clear here that this rare word is a euphemism for Asherah. The two verses in Ezekiel 8 use the combination *sml hqn'h* ('the idol of (i.e. that provokes) jealousy'). Deuteronomy 4: 16 speaks just of 'any image in male or female form': again it may be Asherah among others who is in mind – or is being put out of mind!

[2] *h'myd* ('appoint') is a technical term of Chronicles (and P?), and is not used so much elsewhere.

[3] Finding the right word for the deity denying Israel further use of the land they believed he had given them seems to have been difficult – or at least there were several candidates to choose from: the closest correlate to vv. 7–8 at the beginning of the royal story is in Solomon's second vision, where 1Kgs 9: 7 uses 'cut off' while 2Chr 7: 20 offers 'uproot'.

[4] Fishbane (1985: 546) suggests that the Chronicler has deleted the 'and' to remove a potential disjunction in Kings between *torah* and other divine commands of which David and Solomon had been made aware. This possiblity must be borne in mind; but we must also take account of other small reformulations of these texts. But note now Trebolle's proposal (in press) of a *torah*-revision of 1Kgs 1: 1–2: 11 and of 1Kgs 22–2Kgs 25. It appears that parallel passages in Chronicles were also revised, but not always in identical fashion.

[5] Cf. Jos 1: 7, 13; 8: 31, 33, 35; 11: 12; 22: 2, 5; 2Kgs 18: 12.

[6] The closest parallel in Chronicles is 2Chr 19: 10 – and otherwise: Dt 5: 28; 6: 1, 20; 12: 1.

[7] This phrase is fully reviewed in its wider, biblical context in Auld (1983: 5–9; 1984: 70, 74, 76, 81).

many religious complaints in the shared opening a protest that Manasseh had shed much innocent blood – an accusation repeated in 24: 4, the only other mention of innocent blood in Kings or Chronicles.[1] Kings emphasises that Manasseh is without excuse or hope.

4.2.2.2 In C 10–17, Manasseh is made an anticipatory type of what Judah's response should be to the final exile: these verses report the lack of attention by Manasseh and his people to the divine word; then his exile to Babylon, repentence, restoration to his throne, and reform.

4.2.2.3 In a sense there is no common content between these reports. One is wholly bleak, the other open to hope. The doomed Manasseh of the Book of Kings is quite as representative of the nation and especially of the kings of Judah in that book as Chronicles' penitent and restored Manasseh is of the other book. And yet in these two very different accounts, and in smaller divergences towards the conclusion of the shared report, there are some similar expressions; and study of these may betray whether and how far one report may have influenced the other, or whether both have supplanted a shorter shared source:

K 12 talks of 'Jerusalem and Judah', a formulation we find only in Jer 40: 1; 52: 3; and in Ezra 2: 1. The not-dissimilar Chronicles plus 'Judah and the inhabitants of Jerusalem' in v. 9 is found also in 2Chr 20: 15, 18, 20; 32: 33 and has close parallels in 2Chr 32: 25, 26; 34: 30; 35: 18; and Jer 4: 4; 11: 12; 17: 25; 19: 3.

To the shared 'and Yahweh spoke' (10a), Kings adds 'by hand of his servants the prophets', reminiscent of Chronicles' 'by hand of Moses' (end of 8) - each can be parallelled in its own book, but not in the other.

Kings reports the national refusal to listen to Yahweh earlier (beginning of 9), Chronicles later (end of 10, using *wl' hqšybw*). The verb Chronicles uses, though common enough in the

---

[1] The other biblical references are Dt 19: 10, 13; 21: 8, 9; 24: 5; 27: 25; 1 S 19: 5 (with the verb 'sin' – cf: *4.2.4* below); Is 59: 7; Jer 7: 6; 22: 3, 17; 26: 15; Jl 4: 19; Jon 1: 14; Ps 94: 21; 106: 38.

prophets, often in parallel to 'hear',[1] is never used in Kings. In fact it is very rare in the narrative books, being found only once in the Former Prophets (1 Sam 15: 22), and once more in 2 Chronicles (20:15).

4.2.3 It is at the point of transition between the largely shared openings and the mostly distinct continuations that we find the key clues which have to be pondered as we attempt to reconstruct the 'original' shared text.

4.2.3.1 Both texts report (vv. 2–7a) much the same catalogue of Manasseh's errors; and then remark (vv. 7b–8) that there had been an ancient divine promise to David and Solomon conditional on attention to the Mosaic *torah*. This shared reminiscence corresponds perfectly with the account of the promise (also shared) in the Nathan oracle and recapitulated in Solomon's vision at Gibeon and referred to in Solomon's Temple prayer – and with the conditions stated in the almost identical reports of Solomon's subsequent vision in Jerusalem. Before it goes on to term the 'Israel' seduced by Manasseh as worse than the people of the land before Israel, Kings inserts into this agreed report the note that 'they did not hear' (9a); and proceeds to announce 'by agency of the prophets' sentence of extinction on Manasseh and his people. Chronicles reports a divine appeal addressed specifically to Manasseh and his people (10a). It is their rejection of that direct approach (10b) which leads to exile ('Therefore . . .', v. 11). On the widespread assumption that the Chronicler's source was the book of Kings, it is not unnatural to suppose with many commentators that Chronicles 10 is a pithy summary of what Kings 10–14 tells at much greater length. Yet, when we read it carefully on its own, we find that 2 Chronicles 33: 10 ('The Lord spoke to Manasseh and his people, but they gave no heed.') is sufficiently ambiguous to have given rise to both interpretative stories. And yet we have to reckon with the fact that such a divine speaking, especially in Chronicles, is unparalleled: a

---

[3] 'But they did not listen' or 'hear' (*wl' šm'w*, 2Kgs 21: 9) is found also in 2Kgs 17: 14, 40 (cf. 18: 12); and 'they did not listen' is used absolutely also in Jer 13: 11, though 'you did not listen' is more common in Jeremiah (7: 13; 25: 3, 4; 26: 5). This use of 'listen' is never found in Chronicles.

contemporary 'word of the Lord' is always mediated elsewhere through a named intermediary. Perhaps this divine word is a back-reference to Yahweh's ancient speaking to David and Solomon – and through them to all their successors – concerning Moses' teaching.

4.2.3.2 I put 'original' in quotation marks at the opening of this paragraph because of the evidence that points to verses 4 and 6 being secondary inserts. They are marked out linguistically from their context by using *qatal* (or perfect) forms of the verb, rather than the surrounding *wa-yiqtol* (or consecutive imperfect) forms regular in narrative. The common opinion is probably correct that these *qatal* forms represent late biblical Hebrew and are intrusive here. Most of them are preceded by the connective 'and'; and Joosten (1992) has usefully discussed the iterative force of many *we-qatal* forms. However, the key clue will be the summary *hrbh*, without connective *we*– at the beginning of v. 6b – it, like all the *qatal* forms of the verb that precede it in vv. 4, 6 will be late forms narrating simple action in the past.

4.2.4 In their conclusions, the two Manasseh reports converge again somewhat. A very important shared item of vocabulary is the term 'sin' (*ḥṭ't*) to summarise his behaviour. Although in 2 Kgs 21: 17 the noun is used with the cognate verb ('the sin which he had sinned') while in 2 Chr 33: 19 it heads a series of similar terms ('his sin and his *m'l*[1] and the places which he built'), it seems very likely that together they attest at least the single noun 'sin' in the shared tradition. In each given text this original solitary noun will have been accentuated: in Kings by adding the cognate verb,[2] and in Chronicles by the reinforcing synonym.[3] Not only so, this is the first significant recurrence of the term within the shared text since both noun and verb figured prominently in Solomon's

---

[1] The term *m'l* is important in P, Ezekiel and Chronicles to express deceitful, faithless behaviour, expecially in the religious sphere.

[2] And also by repeating the theme in its recapitulatory plus (2Kgs 24: 3–4 – mentioned already in *4.2.2.1* above).

[3] We met analogous phenomena in our discussion of Solomon's vision at Gibeon, where we found that both 'wisdom' and 'wealth' had been variously reinforced in both Kings and Chronicles (see *2.1.1.*, 3, 4 above).

prayer.[1] Even in Kings pluses, we find only two further mentions of 'sin' in a Judaean or Davidic context: in 1 Kgs 14: 33b and 15: 3. In Solomon's long exploration of intercession (1 Kgs 8: 31–36, 46–50a // 2Chr 6: 22–27, 36–39), restoration after repentance is seen as possible after sin. And if that record of Judah's kings which we are claiming was the source common to Kings and Chronicles did once exist, then a reader of that text would naturally have sought the implications of Manasseh's catalogue of mistakes being called 'sin' in terms of Solomon's prayer and the possibility of restoration.

4.2.4.1 This is exactly what we see happening in the development of the Chronicler's special form of the Manasseh story; and therefore the Chronicler's plus on Manasseh can be cited as another piece of evidence for the once separate existence of that shared source lying behind Kings and Chronicles. And lest we should still hanker after the view that a radical Chronicler has purged his source (a version of the Book of Kings) of mentions of 'sin' he found there, we should note that he adds the word to his account of Ahaz in 2Chr 28: 13. Some corroboration of this approach is to be found in the mention of Manasseh's 'prayer' (*tplh*) in 2Chr 33: 18, 19 – another term which has not been used in Chronicles since its appearance six times in the reports shared with Kings of Solomon's temple prayer and second vision.[2] In his discussion of the source citations in these two verses, Schniedewind (1991) suggests that the Chronicler was appealing to a source other than Kings for his 'homiletical' recasting of that book's 'history'. Again it is more likely that the Solomon narratives themselves are the source used by the Chronicler for his reworking of the shorter shared story of Manasseh.

4.2.4.2 In the book of Kings, by contrast, this prolonged non-mention of 'sin' in the common text is disguised by some twenty mentions of 'sin' in the stock condemnation of the northern kings

---

[1] In fact the only other shared use of this term is in 2Kgs 14: 6 // 2Chr 25: 4 in an early citation of Deuteronomic law (see *4.7.1* below).

[2] The only Kings pluses, apart from 1 K 8: 54 within the Solomon material, are in 2Kgs 19: 4; 20: 5 (// Is 37: 4; 38: 5). If Kings provides the matrix for the development of the Hezekiah story, then Solomon's prayer may again have been the source; if Isaiah, then the inspiration may have come from the Psalms.

for persisting in the sin(s) of Jeroboam. That sin referred quite specifically to his manufacture of the golden calves for his new shrines. This is underscored by the use of the same noun three times in reference to the golden calf in the time of Moses in each of Exodus 32 and Deuteronomy 9 – and only there in each book.

4.2.4.3 It is natural as we read the present book of Kings to understand why a cross reference was offered in 21: 3 to Ahab king of Israel although even that cross reference could have been derived not from the (added) Israelite material but from the common tradition in 2Kgs 8: 18// 2Chr 21: 6. But we now have to be conscious that with such a link in our minds we may miss whatever precise reference was originally intended by Manasseh's 'sin'.[1] Again this discussion makes it all the more significant that the related Kings plus 2Kgs 24: 3–4 already noted (on p. 80 and p. 82, n. 2) insists that in Manasseh's case Yahweh 'was not willing to forgive' (triggering in turn the warning found also in Deuteronomy 29: 19 – see below). Given the interest of this discussion, it is surprising to find that Burney, Jones, and Hobbs have passed over the issue of Manasseh's 'sin' in silence, apart from Hobbs' confusion (299) over the versional evidence for the singular and plural of the noun.

4.2.5 The idea of Yahweh being provoked or caused irritation (*k's* – 2Kgs 21: 6, 15) is much commoner in Kings than Chronicles.

4.2.5.1 Only two instances in Kings have parallels in Chronicles – 2Kgs 21: 6//2Chr 33: 6; 22:17//34: 25. The only additional use of this theme in Chronicles ends his story of Ahaz's dealings with the king of Asssyria (2Chr 28: 16–25), which is told in terms very different from 2Kgs 16: 10–18 – 2Chr 28: 25 explains Ahaz's provocation of Yahweh in terms of burning incense to other gods at 'high places', nicely linking themes found within the shared text in 34: 25 itself (burning incense to other gods), and in the

---

[1] The Solomonic prayer may also provide a frame of reference for understanding the handling of David's 'sin' in 2Sam 12, and other such references in Samuel. Chronicles has very few such 'sin' pluses. 2Chr 7: 14, part of a larger plus within the second Solomonic vision report and itself typical of the importance in Chronicles of personal repentence, repeats the thought of 2Chr 6: 26f.

immediate context of 33:6 ('high places' rebuilt in 33:3).[1]

4.2.5.2 The fifteen cases in Kings without parallel in Chronicles appear in 1Kgs 14 : 9, 15; 15: 30; 16: 2, 7, 13, 26, 33; 21: 22; 22: 54; 2Kgs 17: 11, 17; 21: 15; 23: 19, 26. Of these, the final three develop the theme already sketched in 21: 6; 22: 17 – the only two passages which we noted as being shared with Chronicles. All of the earlier twelve references in Kings relate to northern Israel. As with the 'sin' theme just discussed *(4.2.4)* and some other stereotyped language and themes in Kings, we face this question: Has the often clichéd language used to scold the north been derived and generalised from the pre-existing narrative about the south? Or is Manasseh the southern scoundrel dressed in northern colours? Kings certainly wants us to view Manasseh in this way. The issue is nicely focussed as we evaluate the Kings 'plus' in 21: 3. This links Manasseh's altar-building for Baal and Asherah with the practices of Ahab, king of Israel – has Chronicles omitted this note along with the whole story of the north, or Kings added it along with that whole story? Smelik (1992:142f, 153) suggests that Hezekiah and Ahab in 21: 3 are both comparative flashbacks, the one positive and the other negative. The Chronicler's text, lacking Ahab, will have used Hezekiah in Smelik's 'fathers and sons' theme.

4.2.5.3 Outside Kings the verb *hk'ys* is most commonly attested in the Bible in Jeremiah, nine times in passages translated in LXX, and two more in MT pluses within contexts where the term was already in use. Weippert's discussion of these passages (1973: 222–7) is concerned to deny that they stem from the same 'Deuteronomistic' authors as the Books of Kings. However, it is of interest to us here that she sees 1Kgs 16: 7 and 2Kgs 22: 17 as pre-Deuteronomist sources of the later expansion of the theme in Kings, and as belonging to the same milieu whose language had also been developed within Jeremiah.

4.2.6 Manasseh's 'provocation' of Yahweh (v. 6) is summarised under several headings in 2Kgs 21: 3–7 and, as we have seen, almost identically in 2Chr 33: 3–7. Yet, though the terms used

---

[1] Nelson (1986) interprets the Kings account of Ahaz more neutrally than most commentators.

appear familiar stereotypes, there are remarkably few echoes in
the non-synoptic portions of Kings and Chronicles, and only two
within the whole *shared* tradition:

'[re]built the *bamoth*' – 1Kgs 14: 23; 2Kgs 17: 9; 2Chr 33: 19[1]
'erected altars for Baal' – 1Kgs 16: 32;
'made an Asherah' – 1Kgs 15: 13//2Chr 15: 16 (one of the
    repeated phrases); 1Kgs 16: 33; 2Kgs 17: 16;
'worshipped all the host of heaven' – 2Kgs 17:16; 23: 4, 5[2]
'built altars in the house of Yahweh' – unique
'burned his son as an offering'[3] – 2Kgs 16: 3//2Chr 28: 3; 2Kgs
    17:17, 31; 23: 10 (the other repeated phrase)
'practised soothsaying and augury' – 2Kgs 17: 17 (augury
    only)[4]
'dealt with mediums and wizards' – 2 K 23: 24[5]

4.3 First Word Study: 'High Places'

The evaluation in Kings of the individual rulers of Judah (and
Israel) appears to use remarkably stereotyped language. There
is, on closer inspection, a degree of variation. On the assumption
of some deliberateness in composition, this has been exploited in
many studies of Kings in the hope that such variety of usage may
be correlated with layers of composition in the text. The evaluation
of the same monarchs in Chronicles is very often expressed
differently from Kings. On the familiar hypothesis, these
differences – or most of them at least – will have been the
Chronicler's creation. 'High places' (*bmwt*) are an important
element of the tradition common to Kings and Chronicles, and
offer a good test of our proposal that Kings and Chronicles, even
when they diverge and follow their own way, are using and
developing the language of their common source.

---

[1]   While *'k hbmwt l' srw* is used in 1Kgs 22: 44//2Chr 20: 33, *rq hbmwt ..* is a plus
      in 2Kgs 12: 4; 14: 4; 15: 4, 35.
[2]   But compare also 1Kgs 22: 19//2Chr 18:18.
[3]   There is a discussion of the translation of this phrase in Cogan and Tadmor
      (1988: 266).
[4]   Cf. also Lv 19: 6; Dt 18:10.
[5]   Cf. also Lv 19: 31; Dt 18: 11.

4.3.1 In that common source, Gibeon at which Solomon sacrifices and has a divine vision is a *bamah* (1Kgs 3: 4//2Chr 1: 3); Jeroboam's new sanctuaries are 'high places' (1Kgs 12: 31, 32//2 Chr 11: 15); Asa and Jehoshaphat, who both 'did right,' did not remove unspecified 'high places' (1Kgs 15: 14//2Chr 15: 17; 1Kgs 22: 44//2Chr 20:33); Ahaz 'sacrificed and burned incense on the high places' (2Kgs 16: 4//2Chr 28: 4); Hezekiah removed the high places (2Kgs 18: 4//2Chr 31: 1; 2Kgs 18: 22//2Chr 32: 12); Manasseh rebuilt those which his father Hezekiah had destroyed (2Kgs 21: 3//2Chr 33: 3); and their final removal was part of Josiah's reformation – though a smaller part according to Chronicles (34:3 only) than to Kings (23: 5, 8, 8, 9,13, 15, 15, 15, 19, 20)! Only from Ahaz onwards were the *bamoth* a serious issue.

4.3.2 Bamah is clearly then one of the key terms (the key term?) of the Kings account of Josiah. And to this fact corresponds the large number of Kings pluses using the term. The shared account of Solomon is bracketted by expansions within Kings expressing more critical attention to 'high places' during his reign (1Kgs 3: 2, 3; 11: 7). Jeroboam's high places and what Josiah would do to them is the topic of 1Kgs 13 (vv. 2, 32, 33, 33) – picked up explicitly in 2Kgs 23: 15, where Jeroboam's altar at Bethel is twice called a *bamah* before we are told that Josiah burned it to dust.[1] If the one reference in Chronicles is any true indicator, the (only?) 'high places' removed in the source account of Josiah's reform were (Manasseh's?) in the south. Rehoboam's reign over Judah is blamed for similar misdemeanours in the south (1Kgs 14: 23 – part of the larger plus in vv. 22b – 24). A qualification in the spirit of 1Kgs 15: 14 and 22: 44 of the common text is added to the reports on Jehoash (2Kgs 12: 4), Amaziah (14:4), Azariah (15:4), and Jotham (15:35). Then 2Kgs 17 complains about northern Israel's behaviour at the 'high places' (vv. 9, 11), and notes

---

[1] The insistence that this altar, already regarded as illegitimate, is also associated with a *bamah*, with all the pejorative associations of that term in the developing book of Kings, is reminiscent of Joshua 22 and, in particular, the LXX evidence there that an original 'high place' has been turned into the 'altar' we now meet in the Hebrew text. It is interesting to speculate whether that story about the legitimacy of a shrine in the Jordan valley was really a parable about sanctuaries in the hill-country rather closer to Jerusalem.

continuing worship there by the incomers settled in the north by the Assyrians (vv. 29, 32, 32). And finally, to return to where this paragraph began, most of the ten instances in 2Kgs 23: 4–20 (against one in 2Chr 34: 3–7) must be deemed Kings pluses.[1]

4.3.3 There are rather fewer *bmwt* pluses in Chronicles. The Gibeon *bamah* theme, associated in the common text only with Solomon, is anticipated twice in 1 Chronicles (16: 39; 21: 29). Asa is credited with removal of 'high places' in 2Chr 14: 2, 4; and the early Jehoshaphat likewise (2Chr 17: 6), when walking in 'the earlier ways of his father' (v. 4). Interestingly, the common source had made the contrary observation that 'high places' had not been removed during their reigns (see more fully *4.4* immediately below). Jehoram 'made high places in the hill country of Judah' (21: 11), copying the kings of Israel rather than Asa and Jehoshaphat (vv. 12, 13). And Ahaz, already blamed in the common text (28: 4), is further accused in 28:25 of making high places 'in every city of Judah'. Again, what is said of Manasseh in the common text (33:3) is supplemented and adjusted by the Chronicler (vv. 17, 19).

4.3.4 This has proved to be a crucial illustration of our case. We have found some reason to believe that all the Kings and Chronicles pluses are in fact also secondary. In future, those who would probe the meaning of the term *bamah* should consider the instances in the text common to Kings and Chronicles as the earliest in these narrative books. A number of further examples will help us to monitor just how appropriate is the assumption of editorial deliberateness and consistency. Some of the language of false worship used in Kings is never found in Chronicles. Has it been edited out, or was it not part of the source?

4.4 Asa and Amon: Second and Third Royal Examples

Asa and Amon provide a cautionary double example, after these

---

[1] I state that simply on the grounds of the overwhelming disparity between ten occurrences in Kings against only one in Chronicles. Reconstructing the 'original' which both texts rewrote is much harder than simply noting that the editor of Kings was liberal in using *bamah*.

demonstrations of how a shared report on Manasseh and shared opposition to worship at 'high places' were differently expanded in Kings and Chronicles, of Chronicles (in these next two cases, at least) rewriting the shared inheritance.

4.4.1 As the overview (4.1 above) has shown, the reports of Kings and Chronicles on Asa begin and end almost identically. However, Chronicles offers a very extended alternative to 1 Kgs 15: 12. That verse reads simply: '(Asa) put away the *qedeshim* out of the land, and removed all the *gelulim* that his fathers had made.' The replacement text is twenty-eight verses long, and concerns many issues not dealt with in 1 Kgs 15: 12. However, for all its length, it remains silent about both *qedeshim* and *gelulim*. The existence of *qdšym* in the land is reported by Kings in criticism of Rehoboam in 1 Kgs 14: 24; Asa is credited with their removal (15:12), but he was not entirely successful for the task had to be completed by his son Jehoshaphat (22:47). Though their reintroduction is never noted, Josiah is credited with breaking down within Yahweh's house the houses of the *qdšym*, 'where women wove hangings for the Asherah' (2 Kgs 23: 7). Three of these four reports are part of larger pluses in Kings (1 Kgs 14: 22b–24; 22: 47–48; 2 Kgs 23: 4–20*). And we may suppose that we are dealing there with an expansion within Kings of tendentious rhetoric. However, the situation in 1 Kgs 15: 12 and whatever may be related to it in Chronicles requires closer examination.

4.4.2 Kings portrays Asa as removing the *qdšym* from the land, and taking away the *gllym* which his fathers had made. Neither of these terms is repeated by the Chronicler, although he treats Asa in fact at much greater length than does Kings. In their opening formulae, Kings and Chronicles exhibit relatively minor differences in wording. They share the words: 'Asa did what was right in the eyes of Yahweh'; but while 2 Chr 14: 1 adds 'good and' before 'right' and 'his God' after 'Yahweh' 1 Kgs 15: 11 adds 'like David his father' at the end of the sentence. However, when each text turns to specifics in the following verse, the details they offer are very different. The Chronicler's much fuller account opens with a double mention (2 Chr 14: 2, 4) of his removal of the 'high places', taking away foreign or incense altars (vv. 2, 4), hacking down Asherim, and shattering pillars (v. 2 only). Yet it closes (15: 17) by sharing with 1 Kgs 15: 14 the remark that 'the high places were not taken away'.[1] And yet it is likely that Chronicles knew part if not all of 1 Kgs 15: 12 – in the reformation he reports as inspired by Oded the prophet, he notes (2Chr 15: 8) that Asa removed the 'abominations' from all the land of Judah ... (which looks very like an expansive recasting of 1 Kgs 15: 12a). It is significant that both texts use *h'byr* for 'remove': this is unique in Kings, which otherwise reserves the word for a fire rite involving a king's son, and also in Chronicles which does not use the verb elsewhere of religious reformation. It is not impossible that in an earlier text only Asa removed *qdšym*; and that Kings has shared out the credit to benefit the reputations of Jehoshaphat and Josiah, and used their prior existence to add blame to Rehoboam. Whatever *qdšym* signified (and the Lucianic *stelas* may have understood *mṣbwt*), the Chronicler replaced it with a clichéd pejorative. The Chronicler's use in 15:8 of the rare *h'byr* (which Kings uses in 15: 12) alerts us to the likelihood that he was betraying, or acknowledging, his source. His use of the much commoner *wysr* in much the same sense at the beginning of 14: 2 (cf. also 1 Kgs 15: 12b) will complete the demonstration that the Chronicler's whole plus is in fact based on 1 Kgs 15: 12.

4.4.3 We have just suggested that whatever *gllym* meant – and the dictionaries offer different accounts of that word – the Chronicler may have understood it and expounded it in terms familiar from Deuteronomy 7. However, *gllym* like *qdšym* is a term he never uses. The term is very common in Ezekiel (some 40 times) but infrequent elsewhere: once each in Leviticus, Deuteronomy, and Jeremiah; and then in 1 Kgs 15:12; 21:26; 2Kgs 17:12; 21:11, 21; 23: 24. The second and third of these occurrences in Kings are part of the story of the north which Chronicles does not tell; and 2Kgs 21:11 and 23:24 are part of larger Kings pluses within its accounts of Manasseh and Josiah. The remaining instance of *gllym*, in 2Kgs 21: 21b, is within a context much more closely parallelled in Chronicles (2Chr 33: 22b) than we found in the case of Asa. But

---

[1] Chronicles adds here 'from Israel' – this is possibly simply to secure consistency, and in any case it reminds us of the complex issue of the meaning of 'Israel' in the Books of Chronicles.

here too there are interesting differences. K20 and C22a begin their evaluation of Amon son of Manasseh in identical terms: 'And he did what was evil in the eyes of Yahweh, just as Manasseh his father had done.' K21a continues with the similarly shaped clause 'and he walked in all the way that his father had walked', which Chronicles does not reflect. Kings continues with a third similarly constructed clause 'and he served the *gllym* which his father had served', adding 'and did homage to them'. C22b offers a possibly related but quite differently structured sentence: 'And to all the idols which Manasseh his father had made Amon sacrificed, and he served them.' Kings and Chronicles share only the idea of continuity in illicit worship from father to son, and the use of the verb 'serve', though at different points in the sentence. The following verse in each book is quite different from the other: K22 reports 'He abandoned [Yahweh] the god of his fathers, and did not walk in Yahweh's way'; while C23 notes that he did not humble himself as Manasseh had done, and concludes with the words 'Yes, that Amon multiplied guilt'.

4.4.4 If *gllym* are found occasionally in Kings but never in Chronicles, the opposite is almost true of *psylym* in 2Chr 33: 22 (LXX translates both nouns by 'idols'). Though it is used only once in 2Kgs 17: 41 – in a chapter without parallel in Chronicles, the latter book uses it again in 2Chr 33:19; 34: 3, 4, 7. In all of these four verses *psylym* immediately follows Asherim, and in 34: 3, 4 is followed by 'molten statues'. These passages may be considered more formulaic, and less deliberately drafted than 2 Chr 33: 22. As we seek to detect the original text on Amon, we are left with a choice between a finely turned piece of rhetoric in Kings using the term *gllym*, which Ezekiel knows well but which appears mainly in pluses and late additions elsewhere, and a more distinctive use of *psylym* than we find elsewhere in Chronicles. If we give Kings the benefit of the doubt again, its source will probably have used *gllym* only twice – this second time, quietly but effectively: Amon was implicitly blamed for not achieving that break with his wicked father's past which the earlier Asa had made.

4.5 Other Word Studies

The preceding paragraphs have suggested that the terms *qdšym* and *gllym*, though suppressed by the Chronicler, did appear in his source-text for Asa and Amon; and that the author of Kings, learning from this same source, has expanded his usage of these words.[1] In the case of these two terms at least, the shared text no longer preserves the common original. The substitution of 'the idol' for 'Asherah' (2Chr 33:7) which we noted when reviewing Manasseh was an occasional example of the Chronicler suppressing an unwelcome term. Here such suppression has been more resolutely practised. However, these cases of resolute rewriting may be exceptions that help to prove a more general rule. It is creeping standardisation of the terminology of a common original which is the main trend in both Kings and Chronicles. And fortunately it did not happen in the same way in both Kings and Chronicles – that is why we can still uncover some of the traces! Several further examples can be suggested.

4.5.1 'The word of Yahweh' (*dbr yhwh*) offers a striking example: it appears very seldom in the common text – only in 1Kgs 12: 24 //2Chr 11: 2; and 22: 5,19//18: 4, 18; but oftener in Chronicles (x 7 in 2 Chronicles) and much more frequently in Kings (x 45).

4.5.2 'Forsake' ('*zb*) and 'keep/observe' (*šmr*) exhibit similar patterns. 'Forsake' is used in common in 1Kgs 9: 9//2Chr 7: 22; 12: 8, 13//10: 8, 13; 2Kgs 22: 17//2Chr 34: 25; and, in addition to these four common instances, nineteen times more in Kings and seventeen times in Chronicles. And 'keep' is found nine times in common: in 1Kgs 8: 23, 24, 25, 25//2Chr 6: 14, 15, 16, 16; 9: 4 //7: 17; 14: 27//12: 10;[2] 2Kgs 11: 7//2Chr 23: 6; 21: 8//33: 8; 23: 3 //34: 31; and twenty-four times more in Kings and three times more in Chronicles. Half of the Kings *šmr* pluses are in the Solomon chapters (1Kgs 2: 3, 3, 4; 3: 6, 14; 6: 12 [MT only]; 8: 58,

---

[1] In his recent discussion of *The Reforming Kings*, Lowery (1991: 89–91) has suggested that the report in the Kings plus 1Kgs 22: 47 that Jehoshaphat dealt with the *qadesh* problem may have been 'triggered by his characterization as one who "walked in all the way of Asa his father" (1Kgs 22.43)'.

[2] Here *šmr* is used not of obedience but literally of 'guard-duty'.

61; 11: 10, 11, 34, 38); and that readily demonstrates how much that book has heightened the issue of both royal and popular disobedience at the beginning of the story. And this makes it the more likely that 'forsake' in 2Chr 7: 19 has been changed by an editor of Kings into 'do not keep' in 1Kgs 9: 6.

4.5.3 David as comparator ('like David his father') was noted above as a Kings plus in 1Kgs 15: 11. The phrase appears four times more in Kings: in 1Kgs 11: 6, 33; 2Kgs 14: 3; 16: 2. The first two of these are in a chapter not reflected in Chronicles. Only the last is repeated in that book, in fact in the introduction to King Ahaz (2Chr 28: 1). And in the case of the remaining instance, Chronicles' parallel offers simply 'but not with a whole heart' (2 Chr 25: 2) for Kings 'but not like David his father' – and in fact the Kings text does not stop there but continues 'like everything Joash his father did'. (Joash's entirely satisfactory behaviour is being compared to David's, rather than to Amaziah's less than perfect.)

4.5.4 That expression is reminiscent of what is said of Asa in 2Chr 15:17 – 'yet the heart of Asa was whole all his days', to which 1Kgs 15: 14 adds the words '(whole) with Yahweh'. A 'whole heart' is found again in 1Chr 12: 39; 28: 9; 29: 9, 19; 2Chr 16: 9; 19: 9, in addition to 2Chr 25: 2 already mentioned. And 'a heart whole with Yahweh' appears also in 1Kgs 8:61; 11:4; 15:3. Each instance, whether in Kings with Yahweh or in Chronicles without, is part of a substantial plus peculiar to that book. Again we appear to be dealing with multiple copying from the original Asa text. And the fact that the one further occurrence of 'with a whole heart' in Kings (2Kgs 20: 3 = Isa 38: 3) lacks 'with Yahweh' might suggest that the shorter form of the Asa text preserved in Chronicles is more original.[1]

4.5.5 The situation as regards mentions of Moses in Kings and 2 Chronicles is rather similar. He appears ten times in 1 and 2

---

[1] However, if that passage was in fact drafted within the Book of Isaiah rather than Kings (see *4.8* below), the evidential value of this comparison is lessened. Various David themes throughout Kings and 2 Chronicles are one of the topics of chapter 6 below.

Kings, though in only eight passages; and twelve times in 2 Chronicles, in ten passages. Only three of these passages are common to Kings and Chronicles. The details are provided in 6.1 (pp. 128–33) below.

4.6 'Rolling Corpus' or Composition on a Grand Scale?

It is time to offer a *preliminary stocktaking*. We have seen that there are several benefits in stripping away the pluses supplied by the authors of Kings and Chronicles. Among these – beyond laying bare the source material that both made use of – is that we begin to detect how that document was composed as well. The sources it had used had let many kings of Judah appear in an even more distinctive light. It was Asa who removed the *qdšym* and *gllym*, and only he whose heart was 'whole with Yahweh all his days'; it was his mother who made an Asherah; it was Ahaz who passed his son through the fire, and who was compared, negatively, with 'David his father'. The shared text did have one clear example of accumulating language of praise and blame – but for a quite specific purpose in the case of Manasseh. However, larger reflective commentary like 1 Kings 14 and 2 Kings 17 was produced first by editors of Kings. Another feature contributed by the later editors is the large-scale use of one keyword in a single narrative: in the case of 'high places' in the reform of Josiah (x 10 in 2Kgs 23: 4–20, only x 1 in 2Chr 34 – v. 3), we are dealing with an author of Kings; in the case of the verb 'trust' in the narrative of Hezekiah (x 9 in 2Kgs 18–19, only x 1 in 2Chr 32: 10), the expansive drafting may have been carried out within the book of Isaiah. And another is thematization by means of a cognate noun, for example the noun trust (*bṭḥwn*) in 2Kgs 18: 19 – a verse which also contains the verb *bṭḥ*, or provocation/vexation/irritation (*k's*) in 1Kgs 15: 30; 21: 22; and 2Kgs 23: 26 (itself a feature that correlates Manasseh with Jeroboam and Ahab of Israel, or is it the other way round? – cf. our discussion of this word in *4.2.5* above). The impression given as all these observations are gathered is that we are not dealing in these books so much with authorship or comprehensive edition as with piecemeal adjustments and contributions and spelling-out of implications. For such a process we are best to borrow McKane's happy coinages from his Jeremiah studies, and speak of each of Kings and Chronicles as a 'rolling corpus' (1986: l), or of our posited shared text as 'reservoir' (1986: lvi) from which the materials further deployed in Kings and Chronicles had been drawn.

4.7 Josiah: Fourth Royal Example

We began by reviewing bad king Manasseh in Kings and Chronicles. Before we close this chapter, we must offer a brief account of good kings Josiah and Hezekiah in the light of our discussion so far. Accounts of Josiah are offered in fifty verses in 2 Kings 22–23 and sixty verses in 2 Chronicles 34–35. Our overview above (*4.1*) has noted that some 30 verses are shared by the two reports. The largest Kings plus is the expansive report of Josiah's cultic reforms in south and north (23: 4–20) which Chronicles tells of earlier and much more briefly in 2Chr 34: 3–7. And the largest Chronicles plus offers a much fuller account of Josiah's passover (35: 1–19), which Kings reports in only three verses (23: 21–23). We have already documented (pp.87–88 above) the exaggerated prominence of 'high places' in Kings' report of the cultic reforms; and at the centre of the Kings version (23: 15–18) we have a cross-reference to the extended Kings plus about the man of God from Judah and the prophet of Bethel in 1 Kings 13: 1–34. Our reconstruction in Chapter 5 will assume that the the original reform report was more of the length of the shorter Chronicles version than of the long text in 2Kgs 23: 4–20, and also that the short passover report in 2Kgs 23: 21–23, or something very like it, was the source of the lengthy account in 2Chr 35.[1] Taking these considerations together, it would seem sensible to suppose that the Josiah report as it had appeared in the common source was some 35 verses long.[2] Most space in it is devoted to the finding of the book, the king's response, and the

---

[1] It appears that either Kings summary reference to 'the book of this covenant' (23: 21b) or at least some of the detail reported very fully in 2Chr 35 is required to give substance to the comparison both books share with passovers of ancient times.

[2] It would have been a text of similar length to the prophetic story about Micaiah in the reign of Jehoshaphat (1 Kgs 22 // 2Chr 18). The Chronicler's much longer account of Jehoshaphat is the focus of Strübind's recent monograph *Tradition als Interpretation* (1991).

consultation of Huldah the prophetess. And the remaining major issue for those who seek to retrace a path back to the common source concerns the relationship between Josiah's cultic reforms and the oracle of Huldah. Chronicles puts the reforms first, Kings puts them second.[1] The complaint in Huldah's oracle against 'this place . . . and its inhabitants' is that 'they have forsaken me and have burned incense to other gods, that they might provoke me to anger with all the work of their hands'. We reviewed the usage of the opening keyword *'zb* in *4.6.2* above. Huldah's oracle was anticipated at the end of Solomon's second (Jerusalem) vision. There too the service of 'other gods' is the correlate of forsaking Yahweh.

4.7.1 Huldah speaks more specifically of 'burning incense' to other gods. The verb *qtr* in the piel appears only once more in the common text – in 2Kgs 16: 4//2Chr 28: 4, where it is complained of Ahaz that 'he sacrificed and burned incense on the high places'. Chronicles concludes its report of Ahaz by restating that charge in terms even more similar to Huldah's oracle: 'In every city of Judah he made high places to burn incense to other gods, provoking to anger Yahweh' (28: 25). And a Chronicles plus on Amaziah claims that he burned incense to the gods of the defeated Edomites from Seir which he set up as his own gods (25:14).

4.7.1.1 Kings uses the piel of this verb much more often: in five identical pluses related to the 'high places' we have already noted in *4.3.2* above (1Kgs 22: 44; 2Kgs 12: 4; 14: 4; 15: 4, 35); in the review of Israel's fall in 2Kgs 17:11; in the complaint about Nehushtan which Hezekiah removed (18:4); and in its fuller report of Josiah's reforms (23: 5, 5, 8). The first of these instances is in fact more problematic than my simple statement has suggested. Only the four *bamoth* notes in 2 Kings are pluses – 2Chr 20: 33a reproduces the note in 1Kgs 22: 44a that 'the high

---

[1] Eslinger offers a useful account of the different patternings of the Josiah story in Kings and Chronicles. He notes that Chronicles' portrait of the king 'seems to be in better agreement with Huldah's oracle than with that of Kings' (1986: 55). And in fact in dismissing earlier (1986: 38) the notion that either version 'go(es) back to one source or to the events themselves', he was principally concerned to deny that Kings was any less patterned than Chronicles.

places, however, were not taken away'. Yet 20: 33b offers not 'and the people were still sacrificing', but 'the people had not yet set their hearts upon the God of their fathers'. The key question here is which, if either, second half-verse is original.

4.7.1.2 We should note that both Kings and Chronicles also use the hiphil theme of the same verb, Kings eight times and 2 Chronicles eleven times. The conventional distinction is quite clear (cf. KB 1022–23), and is almost consistently maintained throughout the Bible, with the piel used of cultic behaviour relating to gods other than Yahweh, and the hiphil reserved for worship of Yahweh, whether the details of that worship are approved of or not. Interestingly, Kings and Chronicles never quite overlap in their use of the hiphil . They come closest over Ahaz – 2Kgs 16: 13, 15 uses this theme of the verb in its version of his cultic imports from Damascus; and 2Chr 28: 3 uses it in its plus about the Hinnom valley. It would seem that both Kings and Chronicles have generalised extensively on the basis of the Ahaz story (he already appeared in our list of typical sinners in *4.6* above – cf. also *4.5.3* and *4.7.1*).

4.7.1.3 If this point is valid, then Provan's discussion of the *bmwt* theme requires rather more nuanced restatement. He denies (1988: 69) any difference in meaning between the two themes of *qṭr*; and claims that, when Kings admits that monarchs whose conduct is broadly judged good had in fact tolerated cultic practices at the 'high places', these practices (described by *qṭr* piel) were in honour of Yahweh, though at outlying shrines. 'Meaning' may be too slippery a term for our purposes here. Provan may well be correct that no difference in actual practice is intended. However, we should focus first on textual history, and seek to orientate ourselves by the only two uses of *qṭr* piel in our shared text. It is clear that Ahaz's sacrificing and burning incense on the high places is part of his Israel-like wrong-doing; and Huldah makes the point crystal-clear by noting that Judah's burning of incense was to other gods, and so tantamount to abandonment and provocation of Yahweh. And, if 1Kgs 22: 44b is either a supplement to the original v.44a or an alteration of the wording still found in 2Chr 20: 33b, there is no counter-evidence to Köhler-Baumgartner on the piel theme. (But 1Kgs 11: 8 is an incontrovertible case of the hiphil used about worship of other named gods by wives of Solomon.) In the Kings pluses we have already discussed (4.3.2), the editor had not been able to change his [shared] text's judgment that early king after early king of Judah had done right in Yahweh's eyes; but he was able to neutralise this favourable judgment by implying that these kings could not control their people's apostasy from Yahweh. In this as in so many other matters, the text of Kings cannot be read both holistically and historically at the same time.

4.7.2 We have already noted (*4.2.6*) that the only other shared use of the verb 'provoke' is in the Manasseh story. The means of provocation specified by Huldah, 'with all the work of their hands' is very rare in Kings and Chronicles. The phrase is used rather differently in just one place in each book – in the reports of Hezekiah and the Assyrian invaders, in 2Kgs 19: 18 and 2Chr 32:19. And that provides a good introduction to our next topic.

4.8 Hezekiah: Fifth Royal Example

It is daunting, and perhaps presumptuous too, to attempt only a short contribution to the criticism of narratives which have repeatedly been the subject of substantial, and even quite massive monographs in recent years (Childs 1967; Clements 1980; Gonçalves 1986; Chamaza 1988; Hardmeier 1990; Seitz 1991 – to which we should add the important article by Smelik (1992a). And yet it might just be the case that the very small place accorded 2Chr 29–32 in any discussion of the Hezekiah materials in Kings or Isaiah results from the repeated overlooking of a vital clue. There is clearly some linkage between the accounts of Hezekiah in Kings and Chronicles. But their reports of this earlier prominent reformer diverge much more markedly than those concerning the later Josiah. A very sketchy attempt to plot the shared content has been offered in our Overview. And that sketch could only point to common content in less than 20 shared verses out of 95 in 2 Kings 18–20 and 117 in 2 Chronicles 29–32. And even in these twenty or so verses the common content is much less similarly expressed than most of what we have reviewed to this point in our study. If our main point in this whole book is valid, then the source material on Hezekiah must have been much more substantially recast, whether in Kings or in Chronicles or in both. Haag (1951) did argue that Chronicles used a source much shorter than Kings, from Isaiah or his circle. Childs paid some attention to his article (1967: 17, 75, 108), but found it largely unconvincing. Neither 2 Chronicles 32 nor Haag finds any mention in Clements (1980). The latest large-scale commentary adopts the usual two-strand approach to 2 Kings: B1 containing 18: 17–19: 9a, 36 and B2 19: 9b–35 (Cogan and Tadmor 1988).

4.8.1 The discussion of the Hezekiah narratives in 2 Kings and Isaiah has been substantially advanced in the most recent studies of Seitz (1991) and Smelik (1992a, cf. also 1986). In default of a full review, let me simply note my sympathy with Smelik (1986), Seitz (1991) and Smelik (1992a) over the two vital points on which they are agreed: the broad unity of the Isaiah/Kings report on Hezekiah and the deliverance of Jerusalem; and the relative priority of Isaiah 36–39 over 2 Kings 18–20, though Seitz in fact would except Isaiah 39 from that general conclusion.[1]

4.8.1.1 By the first of these points, both scholars are rejecting the widespread view that the undoubted repetitions in the present account(s) in Is 36–37 or 2Kgs 18–19 are best explained as the result of an editorial combination of two not dissimilar and largely parallel source documents. Smelik and Seitz are claiming that these repetitions function to provide emphasis within a text that should be read holistically: it is a document which stresses certain important issues by repeating them and only gradually unpacking their implications. Here I am wholly sympathetic. So much for the points of agreement. Seitz is the more open to agree that these materials in Isaiah had passed through several drafts; and yet he assigns only some twenty years to the process which he believes was completed soon after the death of Sennacherib in 681. Smelik insists that the materials were drafted whole, just as they should be read – but assigns them firmly to a post-exilic date. I prefer to select elements from each of these two scholars' approaches. I tend to agree with Smelik both about the date of the

---

[1] The issues have been usefully rehearsed again, with close attention to text-critical issues, in Konkel 1993.

Hezekiah chapters and about the cumulative effect of those repetitions which persuaded many earlier readers that the text had been composed from separate sources. However, on the basis of my argument so far, I would also suppose with Seitz that several of them result from expansive redrafting of a once shorter text, even if the original shape of that text is no longer readily recoverable from its various reshapings in Isaiah, Kings, and Chronicles.

4.8.1.2 As to the relative priority of 2Kgs 18–20 and Is 36–39, the issues are much more complex, and the arguments advanced are of different weight. Seitz (1991: 51–66) makes a strong case for 2 Kgs 18:14–16 being secondary to the remainder of 2 K 18: 13–20: 19, so reversing the received opinion which deems 18: 14–16 to be the basic annalistic 'source A', while the remainder is divided between sources 'B1' and 'B2'. Seitz's argument is of course conducive to the wider case that Isaiah, which lacks these verses, was the source of the narrative in Kings. But it is equally consistent with the view that Isaiah was copied from a version of Kings to which 2Kgs 18: 14–16 had not yet been added. Neither Seitz nor Smelik cites the evidence discussed by Hurvitz (1957), that the LXX of Is 36–39 was by a different translator from the remainder of the book. Smelik is right to note (1986: 88, n. 31) that Is 7: 1, while a reference to the Book of Kings, was not a part of it. Its formulation may well have drawn on 2Kgs 16: 1. But equally 2Kgs 16: 5, which has no parallel in 2Chr 28, and which is loosely attached to the previous four verses by 'z ('then'), may be drawn from Is 7:1 rather than – as is often urged – the other way round. And Uriah the Priest of Is 8: 2 appears four times in 2Kgs 16 (vv. 10, 11, 15, 16), but not at all in 2Chr 28. It seems crucial to me in this discussion that it must have been an author of Isaiah and not of Kings who elaborated the parallelism of Isaiah's encounters with Ahaz and then Hezekiah: the location 'at the end of the channel' (7: 3//36: 2); the king's distress at the invasion news (7: 2//37: 1); the 'fear not' oracle (7: 4–9//37: 6–7); the offer of a sign to the king (7: 10–16//37: 30–32); the concluding future threat (7: 17–25//39: 6–7) – not to speak of the resumption in 37: 32 of the 'zeal of the Lord of Hosts' from Is 9:6 (cf. Ackroyd 1982).

4.8.2 The Shared Text on Hezekiah opened in standard fashion with 2Kgs 18: 1–3 (cf. 2Chr 29: 1–2). The report in Kings of his reformation is very much shorter (18: 4–8) than that in Chronicles (29–31), and yet there are some grounds for suspicion that even this short version has been recast and expanded, and was not itself the source of the much longer narrative in Chronicles.

4.8.2.1 Of the cultic items destroyed according to 18:4, three are shared with the list in 2Chr 31: 1; yet only of the standing stones (*hmṣbt*) is the same verb 'shatter' (*šbr*) used. Hezekiah's removal of the 'high places' is not only put in (advanced to?) first position, but is emphasised in Kings by the opening *hw'*: 'he it was who removed the high places.'[1]

4.8.2.2 Verse 5 has caused many commentators problems with its unqualified preference for Hezekiah over all kings of Judah both before and after him – in language most reminiscent of Solomon's vision at Gibeon.[2] It is the negative implications for Josiah that are the most obvious. But if comparison with Solomon is hinted at in 18:5, then the next verse is quick to stress a contrast.

4.8.2.3 The rare use of *dbq* (18: 6) is striking, and apparently part of a small pattern – it is never used in a religious sense in Chronicles. It is used in Kings to criticise Solomon (1Kgs 11: 2) who 'clung to (foreign wives) in love', and Jehoram of Israel (2Kgs 3: 3) who 'clung to the sin of Jeroboam . . .'. After these two negative instances Hezekiah is very much the 'good guy'. (In particular 2Kgs 3: 3 and 18: 6 appear deliberately contrasted.) 'Clinging' to Yahweh is commended in apparently later strata of Deuteronomy (10: 20; 11: 22; 13: 5, 18; 28: 60; 30: 20) and Joshua (22: 5; 23: 8, 12) – and to his 'testimonies' in Psalm 119: 31. Relationships between Kings and other Deuteronomistic books will be further probed in chapter 8 below – there is no link here with Jeremianic usage.

---

[1] There is evidence (Cogan and Tadmor 1988) that this use of the independent pronoun need not be emphatic; yet we should note that the use of *hw'* in 2Kgs 18: 22 is reflected, or at least refracted, in 2Chr 32: 12 – but not the instance in 18: 4. So we have to consider whether Kings or Chronicles or both modified the source in the shared text.

[2] Seitz returns repeatedly to this verse and its implications – for example, pp. 144, 187.

4.8.3 Much critical attention has been paid to the composition of the long report in 2 Kings 18: 13–20: 19, about the deliverance of Jerusalem from military threat and its king from serious illness, and its close relationship to that in Isaiah 36–39. But little attention in all of this has been paid recently to the alternative report in 2Chr 32, though Smelik (1992a) does suggest that Chronicles and Ecclesiasticus appear to know this material as Isaianic. Most scholars suppose that the Chronicler produced 2 Chr 32 by a radical shortening and recasting of the material it found in Kings, whether the ultimate origins of that story were in Kings or Isaiah. Gonçalves helpfully offers a renewed survey (1986: 508–24) of the links between 2Chr 32 and 2Kgs 18: 13–19: 37 and the earlier arguments of Haag (1951) and Le Moyne (1957). While he (rightly) excludes the logical possibility that Kings is derived from Chronicles, he may be too quick to conclude that Chronicles must know the present text of Kings rather than an earlier source on the ground that Chronicles shows knowledge of both main 'sources' of the present text of Kings. There are some typical Chronicles features in 2Chr 32. But we have also noted at several points above how key elements of the whole royal narrative common to Kings and Chronicles appear – or have been retained – in 2Chr 32. If that chapter has summarised a much longer source, then the summary has been made with keen attention to the story of the monarchy as a whole. Yet we have also noted (p.94 above) that 2Kgs 18//Is 36 is something of a repetitive midrash on 'trust'. And other features of 2Kgs 18–20 are no less repetitive – most noticeably the theme of the inadequacy of the gods of other countries to combat the king of Assyria. Many scholars reckon with a complex growth for these chapters. The issue we should be addressing, after our observations on other parts of Kings and Chronicles, is whether 2Chr 32 can be correlated with likely earlier and shorter versions of the Kings story, or whether we have to rest with the general conclusion that the Chronicler must have been aware of the fuller Kings or Isaiah texts we know. The parallels between Is 7 and Is 36–39 we reported at the end of *4.8.1.2* above tell against this general consensus. On the one hand, as we already remarked, they suggest the priority of Isaiah over Kings. On the other, they are almost entirely lacking from 2Chr 32. Clements argues in a more recent discussion that Isaiah's first two prophecies concerning Sennacherib, in Is 37: 22–29, 30–32, are supplements to the more original critique in vv. 33–35 (1991). But, of course, what interests me is that none of these prophecies is reported by the Chronicler! Further consideration of this issue should await our treatment below (*6.3.7* and *6.4*) of indications of the lateness of both the Isaiah/Kings and the Chronicles versions.

4.9 Concluding Comments

4.9.1 Our review of a selection of the evidence about the interrelationships between the reports on the kings of Judah from Rehoboam to the collapse of Jerusalem has rendered rather more plausible our contention that we are dealing in Kings and Chronicles with diverging expansions of a shorter common story. In many cases what started as occasional remarks or descriptions have become common clichés. In a very few cases, terms from the common story have so scandalised the Chronicler that he has suppressed them.

4.9.2 The short accounts of the final few reigns have not been separately studied. The issues involved are quite complex, and the texts – and especially the texts of the common material they share – provide too little material to allow reliable conclusions. An impression of these issues may be gained from our sketch rendering of the shared text at the end of chapter 5. The chart in *6.3* below also provides some samples of the distinctiveness of this material. It is not just the relationships between the texts of Kings and Chronicles after Josiah, but also the connections between these final reports in both books and the longer story that has gone before, that are difficult to plot. They will repay separate study in the light of the general conclusions of this volume.

5

Rehoboam to the Collapse:
The Shared Text

Rehoboam at Shechem (1 Kgs 12: 1–19, 21–24; 2 Chr 10: 1–11: 4[1])

Rehoboam went to Shechem, for all Israel had come to Shechem
to make him king. And when Jeroboam the son of Nebat heard
of it (for he was [still[2]] in Egypt, whither he had fled from King
Solomon), then Jeroboam returned[3] from Egypt. And they sent
and called him; and Jeroboam and all [the assembly of] Israel
came and said to Rehoboam, 'Your father made our yoke heavy.
Now therefore lighten the hard service of your father and his
heavy yoke upon us, and we will serve you.' He said to them,
'Depart for three days, then come again to me.' So the people
went away.

　　Then King Rehoboam took counsel with the old men, who had
stood before Solomon his father while he was yet alive, saying,
'How do you advise me to answer this people?' And they said to
him, 'If you will be a servant/for good[4] to this people today and
serve them, and speak good words to them when you answer

---

[1] The 'main' text of the LXX offers a rendering of 1 Kgs 12, though without v. 17.
　The extended alternative version preserved after 12: 24 of the main text offers
　a shorter version of this same story, which should perhaps have been adopted
　as our 'Shared text' here. For further discussion, see *7.3.5* below.

[2] 'still' is read only in MT of 1 Kgs 12: 2 – LXX reports the main content of the verse
　within 11: 43; and Chr, which offers no antecedent report corresponding to
　1 Kgs 11: (26–) 40, does not require 'still'.

[3] Following Chronicles; 1 Kgs 12: 2 (MT) reads *wyšb* as 'lived in'.

[4] In several terms Kings prefers 'serve' and Chronicles 'please/be good'.

them, then they will be your servants for ever.' But he forsook the counsel which the old men gave him, and took counsel with the young men who had grown up with him and stood before him. And he said to them, 'What do you advise that we answer this people who have said to me, "Lighten the yoke that your father put upon us"?' And the young men who had grown up with him said to him, 'Thus shall you speak to this people who said to you, "Your father made our yoke heavy, but do you lighten it for us"; thus shall you say to them, "My little finger is thicker than my father's loins. And now, whereas my father laid upon you a heavy yoke, I will add to your yoke. My father chastised you with whips, but I [will chastise you] with scorpions."'

So Jeroboam and all the people came to Rehoboam the third day, as the king said, 'Come to me again the third day.' And the king answered them/the people[1] harshly, and forsaking the counsel which the old men had given him, he spoke to them according to the counsel of the young men, saying, 'My father made your yoke heavy, but I will add to your yoke; my father chastised you with whips, but I will chastise you with scorpions.' So the king did not hearken to the people; for it was a turn of affairs brought about by Yahweh that he might fulfil his word, which Yahweh spoke by Ahijah the Shilonite to Jeroboam the son of Nebat.

And when all Israel saw that the king did not hearken to them, the people answered the king,

'What portion have we in David?
We have no inheritance in the son of Jesse.
To your tents, O Israel!
Look now to your own house, David.'

So Israel departed to their tents. [But Rehoboam reigned over the people of Israel who dwelt in the cities of Judah.[2]] Then King Rehoboam sent Adoram, who was taskmaster over the forced labor, and all Israel stoned him to death with stones. And King Rehoboam made haste to mount his chariot, to flee to Jerusalem. So Israel has been in rebellion against the house of David to this

---

[1] Here 'the people' is a Kings plus – it is already used several times in the common text.

[2] This verse is not part of the 'main' LXX version of this chapter.

day.

When Rehoboam came to Jerusalem, he assembled [all the house of] Judah, and [the tribe of] Benjamin, a hundred and eighty thousand chosen warriors, to fight against the house of Israel, to restore the kingdom[1] to Rehoboam the son of Solomon. But the word of God came to Shemaiah the man of God: 'Say to Rehoboam the son of Solomon, king of Judah, and to all the house of Judah and Benjamin, [and to the rest of the people,] "Thus says Yahweh, You shall not go up or fight against your kinsmen the people of Israel. Return every man to his home, for this thing is from me." So they hearkened to the word of Yahweh, and turned from going [against Jeroboam].[2]

Jeroboam's New Cult (1Kgs 12: 25–33 – cf. 2Chr. 11: 5–23[3])

Then Jeroboam built Shechem in the hill country of Ephraim, and dwelt there; and he went out from there and built Penuel. And Jeroboam said in his heart, 'Now the kingdom will turn back to the house of David; if this people go up to offer sacrifices in the house of Yahweh at Jerusalem, then the heart of this people will turn again to their lord, to Rehoboam king of Judah, and they will kill me and return to Rehoboam king of Judah.' So the king took counsel, and made two calves of gold. And he said to the people, 'You have gone up to Jerusalem long enough. Behold your gods, O Israel, who brought you up out of the land of Egypt.' And he set one in Bethel, and the other he put in Dan. And this thing became a sin, for the people went to the one at Bethel and to the other as far as Dan. He also made houses on high places, and appointed priests from among all the people, who were not of the Levites. And Jeroboam appointed a feast on the fifteenth day of the eighth month like the feast that was in Judah, and he offered

---

[1] The shorter LXX not only reads merely 'every man of Judah and Benjamin' (in fact Chronicles is even shorter with 'Judah and Benjamin'), but does not number them, and has them making war on 'Jeroboam at Shechem'.

[2] Chronicles 'against Jeroboam' corresponds to Luc just quoted above.

[3] 2Chr 11: 5–23 is clearly familiar with 1K gs12: 25–33 or something like it – and is probably dependent on it. I suspect, however, that 1Kgs12: 25–33 was not part of the Shared Text, and that the related Chronicles passage represents later knowledge of the developing Books of Kings.

sacrifices upon the altar; so he did in Bethel, sacrificing to the calves that he had made. And he placed in Bethel the priests of the high places that he had made. He went up to the altar which he had made in Bethel on the fifteenth day in the eighth month, in the month which he had devised of his own heart; and he ordained a feast for the people of Israel, and went up to the altar to burn incense.

Rehoboam's Rule (1Kgs 14: 21–22a; 2Chr 12: 13–14a. 1Kgs 14: 25–31; 2Chr 12: 2*, 9b–11, 15–16)

Now Rehoboam [the son of Solomon] reigned in Judah. Rehoboam was forty-one years old when he began to reign, and he reigned seventeen years in Jerusalem, the city which Yahweh had chosen out of all the tribes of Israel, to put his name there.[1] His mother's name was Naamah the Ammonitess. And [he][2] did what was evil in the sight of Yahweh.[3]

In the fifth year of King Rehoboam, Shishak king of Egypt came up against Jerusalem; he took away the treasures of the house of Yahweh and the treasures of the kings house; he took away everything. He also took away [all] the shields of gold which Solomon had made; and King Rehoboam made in their stead shields of bronze, and committed them to the hands of the officers of the guard, who kept the door of the king's house. And as often as the king went into the house of Yahweh, the guard bore them and brought them back to the guardroom.

Now the rest of the acts of Rehoboam, and all that he did, are they not written in the Book of the Chronicles of the Kings of Judah? And there was war between Rehoboam and Jeroboam continually. And Rehoboam slept with his fathers and was buried [with his fathers] in the city of David. [His mother's name was Naamah the Ammonitess.] And Abijam his son reigned in his stead.

---

[1] Luc lacks the notice of Jerusalem's election – but adds that Naamah was daughter of Ana, son of Nahash, king of Ammon.

[2] This text follows the Chronicler; Kings (MT) makes 'Judah' subject of the verb, Kings (LXX) 'Rehoboam'.

[3] Each tradition adds its own tail-piece – Luc: 'and did not walk in the way of David his father'; Kings and Chronicles are less standard.

Abijam/h (1Kgs 15: 1–2, 7–8; 2Chr 13: 1–2, 22–23a)

Now in the eighteenth year of King Jeroboam [the son of Nebat], Abijam began to reign over Judah.[1] He reigned for three years in Jerusalem. His mother's name was Maacah the daughter of Abishalom. And there was war between Abijam and Jeroboam. The rest of the acts of Abijam, and all that he did, are they not written in the Book of the Chronicles of the Kings of Judah? And Abijam slept with his fathers; and they buried him in the city of David. And Asa his son reigned in his stead.

Asa (1Kgs 15: 11–24a; 2Chr 14: 1–2; 15: 16–16: 6; 16: 11–12a, 13a, 14a)

And Asa did what was right in the eyes of Yahweh. He put away the 'qedeshim' out of the land, and removed all the idols that his fathers had made. He also removed Maacah his mother from being queen mother because she had an abominable image made for Asherah; and Asa cut down her image and burned it at the brook Kidron. But the high places were not taken away. Nevertheless the heart of Asa was wholly true [to Yahweh] all his days. And he brought into the house of Yahweh the votive gifts of his father and his own votive gifts, silver, and gold, and vessels.

And there was war between Asa and Baasha king of Israel all their days. Baasha king of Israel went up against Judah, and built Ramah, that he might permit no one to go out or come in to Asa king of Judah. Then Asa took [all the] silver and [the] gold [that were left] from/in the treasures of the house of Yahweh and [the treasures] of the king's house [and gave them into the hands of his servants]; and [King Asa] sent them to Ben-hadad [the son of Tabrimmon, the son of Hezi-on], king of Syria, who dwelt in Damascus, saying, 'Let there be a league between me and you, as between my father and your father: behold, I am sending to you [a present of] silver and gold; go, break your league with Baasha king of Israel, that he may withdraw from me.' And Ben-hadad hearkened to King Asa, and sent the commanders of his armies

---

[1] LXX in Kings calls him Abijah son of Jeroboam; and LXX in Chronicles says that he ruled over Israel!

against the cities of Israel, and conquered Ijon, Dan, Abel-beth-maacah, and all Chinneroth, with all the land of Naphtali[1] . And when Baasha heard of it, he ceased building Ramah, and he dwelt[2] in Tirzah. Then King Asa [made a proclamation to] took all Judah, none was exempt, and they carried away the stones of Ramah and its timber, with which Baasha had been building; and with them built Geba and Mizpah. Now the rest of all the acts of Asa, [all his might, and all that he did, and the cities which he built,] are they not written in the Book of the Chronicles of the Kings of Judah? But in his old age he was diseased in his feet. And Asa slept with his fathers, and was buried with his fathers in the city of David his father; and Jehoshaphat his son reigned in his stead.

Jehoshaphat and the Prophets (1 Kgs 22: 2–35a; 2 Chr 18: 1–34)

. . . year[s] Jehoshaphat came down to Ahab to Samaria. And Ahab king of Israel said to Jehoshaphat king of Judah, 'Will you go with me to Ramoth-gilead?' And he said to him, 'I am as you are, my people as your people [my horses as your horses].'[3] And Jehoshaphat said to the king of Israel, 'Inquire first [for the word[4]] of Yahweh.' Then the king of Israel gathered the prophets together, about four hundred men, and said to them, 'Shall I go to battle against Ramoth-gilead, or shall I forbear?' And they said, 'Go up; for Yahweh will give it into the hand of the king.' But Jehoshaphat said, 'Is there not here another prophet of Yahweh of whom we may inquire?' And the king of Israel said to Jehoshaphat, 'There is yet one man by whom we may inquire of Yahweh, Micaiah the son of Imlah; but I hate him, for he never prophesies good concerning me, but evil.' And Jehoshaphat said, 'Let not the king say so.' Then the king of Israel summoned an officer and said, 'Bring quickly Micaiah the son of Imlah.' Now the king of Israel and Jehoshaphat the king of Judah were sitting

---

[1] C4 concludes: and Abel-mayim and all the *miskenoth* of the cities of Naphtali.

[2] Kings MT reads *wyšb* as 'lived', LXX as '[re]turned', but Chronicles offers *wyšbt* – 'stopped [his work]'.

[3] Not in C3; but it offers here 'in the battle', not having offered 'battle' in Israel's invitation (K4a).

[4] In neither Kings nor Chronicles does LXX does attest *dbr* ('[for] the word').

on their thrones, arrayed in their robes, at the threshing floor at the entrance of the gate of Samaria; and all the prophets were prophesying before them. And Zedekiah the son of Chenaanah made for himself horns of iron, and said, 'Thus says Yahweh, "With these you shall push the Syrians until they are destroyed."' And all the prophets prophesied so, and said, 'Go up to Ramoth-gilead and triumph; Yahweh will give it into the hand of the king.'

And the messenger who went to summon Micaiah said to him, 'Behold, the words of the prophets with one accord are favourable to the king; let your word be like the word of one of them, and speak favorably.' But Micaiah said, 'As Yahweh lives, what Yahweh says to me, that I will speak.' And when he had come to the king, the king said to him, 'Micaiah, shall we go to Ramoth-gilead to battle, or shall we forbear?' And he answered him, 'Go up and triumph; Yahweh will give it into the hand of the king.' But the king said to him, 'How many times shall I adjure you that you speak to me nothing but the truth in the name of Yahweh?' And he said, 'I saw all Israel scattered upon the mountains, as sheep that have no shepherd; and Yahweh said, "These have no master; let each return to his home in peace." And the king of Israel said to Jehoshaphat, 'Did I not tell you that he would not prophesy good concerning me, but evil?' And Micaiah said, 'Therefore hear the word of Yahweh: I saw Yahweh sitting on his throne, and all the host of heaven standing beside him on his right hand and on his left; and Yahweh said, "Who will entice Ahab, that he may go up and fall at Ramoth-gilead?" And one said one thing, and another said another. Then a spirit came forward and stood before Yahweh, saying, "I will entice him." And Yahweh said to him, "By what means?" And he said, "I will go forth, and will be a lying spirit in the mouth of all his prophets." And he said, "You are to entice him, and you shall succeed; go forth and do so." Now therefore behold, Yahweh has put a lying spirit in the mouth of all your prophets; Yahweh has spoken evil concerning you.'

Then Zedekiah the son of Chenaanah came near and struck Micaiah on the cheek, and said, 'How did the Spirit of Yahweh go from me to speak to you?' And Micaiah said, 'Behold, you shall see on that day when you go into an inner chamber to hide yourself.' And the king of Israel said, 'Seize Micaiah, and take him back to Amon the governor of the city and to Joash the king's son;

and say, "Thus says the king, 'Put this fellow in prison, and feed him with scant fare of bread and water, until I come in peace.'"' And Micaiah said, 'If you return in peace, Yahweh has not spoken by me.' And he said, 'Hear, all you peoples!'

So the king of Israel and Jehoshaphat the king of Judah went up to Ramoth-gilead. And the king of Israel said to Jehoshaphat, 'I will disguise myself and go into battle, but you wear your robes.' And the king of Israel disguised himself and went into battle. Now the king of Syria had commanded the [thirty-two] captains of his chariots, 'Fight with neither small nor great, but only with the king of Israel.' And when the captains of the chariots saw Jehoshaphat, they said, 'It is surely the king of Israel.' So they turned to fight against him; and Jehoshaphat cried out. And when the captains of the chariots saw that it was not the king of Israel, they turned back from pursuing him. But a certain man drew his bow at a venture, and struck the king of Israel between the scale armour and the breastplate; therefore he said to the driver of his chariot, 'Turn about, and carry me out of the battle, for I am wounded.' And the battle grew hot that day, and the king was propped up in his chariot facing the Syrians until evening, and he died at the time of sunset.

Jehoshaphat Summarised (1 Kgs 22: 41–44, 46, 49, 51; 2 Chr 20: 31–37)

Jehoshaphat became king of Judah; he was thirty-five years old when he began to reign, and he reigned twenty-five years in Jerusalem. His mother's name was Azubah the daughter of Shilhi. He walked in the way of Asa his father; he did not turn aside from it, doing what was right in the sight of Yahweh. But the high places they did not take away; still the people were sacrificing and making offerings at the high places.[1]

Now the rest of the acts of Jehoshaphat, and his might that he showed, and how he warred, are they not written in the Book of the Chronicles of the Kings of Judah? Jehoshaphat made ships of Tarshish [to go to Ophir for gold]; but they did not go, for the

---

[1] After 'still the people', C33b offers instead 'did not direct their heart to the god of their fathers'.

ships were wrecked at Ezion-geber. And Jehoshaphat slept with his fathers, and was buried in the city of David; and Jehoram his son reigned in his stead.

J[eh]oram (2Kgs 8: 17–22, 24b. 2Chr 21: 5–10a; 22: 1a)

He/Joram was thirty-two years old when he became king, and he reigned eight years in Jerusalem. And he walked in the way of the kings of Israel, as the house of Ahab had done, for the daughter of Ahab was his wife. And he did what was evil in the sight of Yahweh. Yet Yahweh would not destroy Judah, for the sake of David his servant, since he promised to give a lamp[1] to him and to his sons for ever.

   In his days Edom revolted from the rule of Judah, and set up a king of their own. Then Joram passed over to Zair[2] with all his chariots, and rose by night, and he and his chariot commanders smote the Edomites who had surrounded him [;but his army fled home].[3] So Edom revolted from the rule of Judah to this day. Then Libnah revolted at the same time. [And the rest of the acts of Joram and all that he did, are they not written in the chronicles of the kings of Judah. And Joram slept with his fathers][4] and was buried in the city of David. And Ahaziah his son ruled in his stead.

Ahaziah (2Kgs 8: 26–29; 9: 21, 27b; 2Chr 22: 2–6, 7–9*)

Ahaziah was twenty-two years old when he began to reign, and he reigned one year in Jerusalem. His mother's name was Athaliah; she was a granddaughter of Omri. He also walked in the way of the house of Ahab, and did what was evil in the sight of Yahweh, as the house of Ahab had done, for he was son-in-law to the house of Ahab. He went with Joram the son of Ahab to make war against Hazael king of Syria at Ramoth-gilead, where the Syrians wounded

---

[1] Or 'fief'. Rofé (1988) retains the former interpretation 'lamp' and offers a cross-reference to Psalm 132.
[2] Is K21 ṣ'yrh the same place as the normal ś'yr? ś'yrh would offer a middle position textually between Kings MT and C9 'm-śryw (cf. mention of the commanders at the end of the verse).
[3] Not in C10.
[4] This part of the closing formula is only in K23–24a.

Joram. And King Joram returned to be healed in Jezreel of the wounds which the Syrians had given him at Ramah, when he fought against Hazael king of Syria. And Ahaziah the son of Jehoram king of Judah went down to see Joram the son of Ahab in Jezreel, because he was sick.

And he set out with Jehoram to Jehu son of Nimshi. And he found the commanders of Judah, and the sons of Ahaziah's brothers serving Ahaziah, and he slew them. And he sought Ahaziah, and put him to death; and they buried him.[1]

Athaliah (2Kgs 11: 1–20; cf. 2Chr 22: 10–23: 21)

Now when Athaliah the mother of Ahaziah saw that her son was dead, she arose and destroyed all the royal family. But Jehosheba, the daughter of King Joram, took Joash the son of Ahaziah, and stole him away from among the king's sons who were about to be slain – him and his nurse in a bedchamber. Thus he was hidden from Athaliah, so that he was not slain; and he remained with her six years, hid in the house of Yahweh, while Athaliah reigned over the land.

But in the seventh year Jehoiada sent and brought the captains of the hundreds, and had them come to him in the house of Yahweh; and he made a covenant with them [and put them under oath] in the house of Yahweh [, and he showed them the king's son][2]. And he commanded them, 'This is the thing that you shall do: one third of you coming on the sabbath, one third in the king's house, and one third at the gate Sur, and all the poeple will keep Yahweh's regulations. And you shall surround the king, each with his weapons in his hand; and whoever approaches the ranks is to be slain. Be with the king when he goes out and when he comes in.'

The captains did according to all that Jehoiada the priest commanded, and each brought his men who were to go off duty on the sabbath, with those who were to come on duty on the sabbath. to Jehoiada the priest. And Jehoiada the priest delivered to the captains the spears and shields that had been King David's,

---

[1] Only Kings provides here the note that is normal for kings up to Hezekiah, that the king was buried in Jerusalem in the city of David (2Kgs 9: 28).

[2] Not in C3.

which were in the house of Yahweh; and the guards stood, every man with his weapons in his hand, from the south side of the house to the north side of the house, around the altar and the house. Then he brought out the king's son, and put the crown upon him, and gave him the testimony; and they proclaimed him king, and anointed him; [and they clapped their hands] and said, 'Long live the king!'

When Athaliah heard the noise of the guard and of the people, she went into the house of Yahweh to the people; and when she looked, there was the king standing by the pillar, according to the custom, and the captains and the trumpeters beside the king, and all the people of the land rejoicing and blowing trumpets. And Athaliah rent her clothes, and cried, 'Treason! Treason!' Then Jehoiada the priest commanded the captains who were set over the army, 'Bring her out between the ranks; and slay with the sword any one who follows her.' For the priest said, 'Let her not be slain in the house of Yahweh.' So they laid hands on her; and she went through the horses' entrance to the king's house, and there she was slain.

And Jehoiada made a covenant between himself and [all] the people,[1] that they should be Yahweh's people. Then all the people went to the house of Baal, and tore it down; his altars and his images they broke in pieces, and they slew Mattan the priest of Baal before the altars. And the priest posted watchmen over the house of Yahweh. And he took the captains, and all the people of the land; and they brought the king down from the house of Yahweh, marching through the guards'/highest gate to the king's house. And he took his seat on the throne of the kings. So all the people of the land rejoiced; and the city was quiet after Athaliah had been slain with the sword.

Jehoash (2Kgs 12: 1-3, 5-22*; 2Chr 24: 1-2, 4-14*, 23-26*)

Jehoash was seven years old when he began to reign, and he reigned forty years in Jerusalem. His mother's name was Zibiah of Beer-sheba. And Jehoash did what was right in the eyes of

---

[1] The Kings text is clearly expansive. It seems that the initial *bynw* has been interpreted (appropriately) as 'between the king', and also read as *byn y"*, i.e. 'between Y[ahweh]'.

Yahweh all the days of Jehoiada the priest.

Jehoash said to the priests,[1] 'All the money of the holy things which is brought into the house of Yahweh, the money for which each man is assessed – the money from the assessment of persons – and the money which a man's heart prompts him to bring into the house of Yahweh, let the priests take, each from his acquaintance; and let them repair the house wherever any need of repairs is discovered.' But by the twenty-third year of King Jehoash the priests had made no repairs on the house. Therefore King Jehoash summoned Jehoiada the priest and the other priests and said to them, 'Why are you not repairing the house? Now therefore take no more money from your acquaintances, but hand it over for the repair of the house.' So the priests agreed that they should take no more money from the people, and that they should not repair the house.

Then Jehoiada the priest took a chest, and bored a hole in the lid of it, and set it beside the altar on the right side as one entered the house of Yahweh; and the priests who guarded the threshold put in it all the money that was brought into the house of Yahweh. And whenever they saw that there was much money in the chest, the king's secretary and the high priest came up and they counted and tied up in bags the money that was found in the house of Yahweh. Then they would give the money that was weighed out into the hands of the workmen who had the oversight of the house of Yahweh; and they paid it out to the carpenters and the builders who worked upon the house of Yahweh, and to the masons and the stonecutters, as well as to buy timber and quarried stone for making repairs on the house of Yahweh, and for any outlay upon the repairs of the house. But there were not made for the house of Yahweh basins of silver, snuffers, bowls, trumpets, or any vessels of gold, or of silver, from the money that was brought into the house of Yahweh, for that was given to the workmen who were repairing the house of Yahweh with it. And they did not ask an accounting from the men into whose hand they delivered the money to pay out to the workmen, for they dealt honestly. The money from the guilt offerings and the money from the sin offerings was not brought into the house of

---

[1] 2Chr 24: 5–14 is very different on this topic.

Yahweh; it belonged to the priests.

At that time Hazael king of Syria went up and fought against Gath, and took it. But when Hazael set his face to go up against Jerusalem, Jehoash king of Judah took all the votive gifts that Jehoshaphat and Jehoram and Ahaziah, his fathers, the kings of Judah, had dedicated, and his own votive gifts, and all the gold that was found in the treasuries of the house of Yahweh and of the king's house, and sent these to Hazael king of Syria. Then Hazael went away from Jerusalem. Now the rest of the acts of Joash,[1] and all that he did, are they not written in the Book of the Chronicles of the Kings of Judah? His servants arose and made a conspiracy, and slew Joash in the house of Millo, on the way that goes down to Silla. It was Jozacar the son of Shime-ath and Jehozabad the son of Shomer, his servants, who struck him down, so that he died. And they buried him with his fathers in the city of David, and Amaziah his son reigned in his stead.

Amaziah (2Kgs 14: 2–3a, 5–14, 17–20; 2Chr 25: 1–4, 11, 17–20a, 21–24*, 25–28)

He was twenty-five years old when he began to reign, and he reigned twenty-nine years in Jerusalem. His mother's name was Jeho-addin of Jerusalem. And he did what was right in the eyes of Yahweh, yet not like David his father. And as soon as the royal power was firmly in his hand he killed his servants who had slain the king his father. But he did not put to death the children of the murderers; according to what is written in the book of the law of Moses, where Yahweh commanded, 'The fathers shall not be put to death for the children, or the children be put to death for the fathers; but every man shall die for his own sin.'

He killed ten thousand Edomites in the Valley of Salt. Then Amaziah sent messengers to Jehoash the son of Jehoahaz, son of Jehu, king of Israel, saying, 'Come, let us look one another in the face.' And Jehoash king of Israel sent word to Amaziah king of Judah, 'A thistle on Lebanon sent to a cedar on Lebanon, saying, "Give your daughter to my son for a wife" and a wild beast of Lebanon passed by and trampled down the thistle. You have indeed smitten Edom, and your heart has lifted you up. Be

---

[1] Immediately before the final clause of the paragraph in C27.

content with your glory, and stay at home; for why should you provoke trouble so that you fall, you and Judah with you?' But Amaziah would not listen. So Jehoash king of Israel went up, and he and Amaziah king of Judah faced one another in battle at Beth-shemesh, which belongs to Judah. And Judah was defeated by Israel, and every man fled to his home. And Jehoash king of Israel captured Amaziah king of Judah, the son of Jehoash, son of Ahaziah, at Beth-shemesh, and came to Jerusalem, and broke down the wall of Jerusalem for four hundred cubits, from the Ephraim Gate to the Corner Gate. And he seized all the gold and silver, and all the vessels that were found in the house of Yahweh and in the treasuries of the king's house, also hostages, and he returned to Samaria.

Amaziah the son of Joash, king of Judah, lived fifteen years after the death of Jehoash son of Jehoahaz, king of Israel. Now the rest of the deeds of Amaziah, are they not written in the Book of the Chronicles of the Kings of Judah? And they made a conspiracy against him in Jerusalem, and he fled to Lachish. But they sent after him to Lachish, and slew him there. And they brought him upon horses; and he was buried in Jerusalem with his fathers in the city of David.

Azariah (2Kgs14: 21–22; 15: 2–3, 5–7. 2Chr 26: 1–4, 21–23)

And all the people of Judah took Azariah, who was sixteen years old, and made him king instead of his father Amaziah. He built Elath and restored it to Judah, after the king slept with his fathers. He was sixteen years old when he began to reign, and he reigned fifty-two years in Jerusalem. His mother's name was Jecoliah of Jerusalem. And he did what was right in the eyes of Yahweh, according to all that his father Amaziah had done. And Yahweh smote the king, so that he was a leper to the day of his death, and he dwelt in a separate house. And Jotham the king's son was over the household, governing the people of the land. Now the rest of the acts of Azariah, and all that he did, are they not written in the Book of the Chronicles of the Kings of Judah? And Azariah slept with his fathers, and they buried him with his fathers in the city of David, and Jotham his son reigned in his stead.

Jotham (2Kgs 15: 33–34, 35b–36, 38; 2Chr 27: 1–2a, 3a, 7, 9)

He was twenty-five years old when he began to reign, and he reigned sixteen years in Jerusalem. His mother's name was Jerusha the daughter of Zadok. And he did what was right in the eyes of Yahweh, according to all that his father Uzziah had done.[1] He built the upper gate of the house of Yahweh. Now the rest of the acts of Jotham, and all that he did, are they not written in the Book of the Chronicles of the Kings of Judah? Jotham slept with his fathers, and was buried in the city of David; and Ahaz his son reigned in his stead.

Ahaz Introduced (2Kgs 16: 2–4, 5; 2Chr 28: 1–2a, 3b–4, 5–15*)

Ahaz was twenty years old when he began to reign, and he reigned sixteen years in Jerusalem. And he did not do what was right in the eyes of Yahweh, as his father David had done, but he walked in the way of the kings of Israel. He even passed his son through fire like the abominations of the nations whom Yahweh removed from before the people of Israel. And he sacrificed and burned incense on the high places, and on the hills, and under every green tree. Then Rezin king of Syria and Pekah the son of Remaliah, king of Israel, came up to wage war on Jerusalem, and they besieged Ahaz but could not conquer him.[2]

Ahaz and Assyria (2Kgs 16: 7–18*, 19–20; 2Chr 28: 16–25*, 26–27)

So Ahaz sent messengers to Tiglath-pileser king of Assyria, saying, 'I am your servant and your son. Come up, and rescue me from the hand of the king of Syria and from the hand of the king

---

[1] It may be that the common text here continued 'Yet the high places were not removed; the people were still sacrificing and making offerings at the high places.' Certainly here uniquely C2 offers 'Only he did not come to the temple of Yahweh; and the people were still acting destructively.' Yet since Chronicles does also render the critical formula more literally, this could be a secondary addition in Chronicles following a secondary addition in Kings.

[2] 2Chr 28: 5–15, though much longer, does not include the words of 2Kgs 16: 5 (cf. Is 7: 1); yet it is not unlikely that it was framed in awareness of them.

of Israel, who are attacking me.'[1] And the king of Assyria hearkened to him; . . . [2] When King Ahaz went to Damascus to meet Tiglath-pileser king of Assyria, he saw the altar that was at Damascus. Then the king drew near to the altar, and went up on it, and burned his burnt offering and his cereal offering, and poured his drink offering, and threw the blood of his peace offerings upon the altar.[3] And Ahaz collected the implements of the house of Yahweh, and chopped them up, and closed the doors of Yahweh's house.[4] Now the rest of the acts of Ahaz which he did, are they not written in the Book of the Chronicles of the Kings of Judah? And

---

[1] There is no counterpart in Chronicles to what follows in Kings (v. 8): 'Ahaz also took the silver and gold that was found in the house of Yahweh and in the treasures of the king's house, and sent a present to the king of Assyria.' Has Chronicles suppressed it, or is it one of Kings' pejorative additions?

[2] The remainder of 2Kgs 16: 9 reads: 'the king of Assyria marched up against Damascus, and took it, carrying its people captive to Kir, and he killed Rezin.' The alternative text in Chronicles is probably tendentious; and yet this text in Kings is probably also not original: it uses *hglh* ('exiled'/'took captive') which is never found in the shared text, and it is strongly reminiscent of Amos 1: 5 – indeed the adaptation from Amos may have happened in stages, for LXX is (still) without 'Kir'.

[3] Here too I follow the shorter Chronicles text. K14–18 is much fuller: 'And the bronze altar which was before Yahweh he removed from the front of the house, from the place between his altar and the house of Yahweh, and put it on the north side of his altar. And King Ahaz commanded Uriah the priest, saying, "Upon the great altar burn the morning burnt offering, and the evening cereal offering, and the king's burnt offering, and his cereal offering, with the burnt offering of all the people of the land, and their cereal offering, and their drink offering; and throw upon it all the blood of the burnt offering, and all the blood of the sacrifice; but the bronze altar shall be for me to inquire by." Uriah the priest did all this, as King Ahaz commanded. And King Ahaz cut off the frames of the stands, and removed the laver from them, and he took down the sea from off the bronze oxen that were under it, and put it upon a pediment of stone. And the covered way for the sabbath which had been built inside the palace, and the outer entrance for the king he removed from the house of Yahweh, because of the king of Assyria.'

[4] Weinfeld (1972: 182) has noted that 2Kgs 16: 10–16 'is pervaded with ritual expressions encountered only in P, e.g. the combination of "burnt offering, cereal offering, and drink offering" (*'wlh, mnḥh, nsk*), "throwing blood upon the altar" (*zrq dm 'l hmzbḥ*), "the north side of the altar" (*yrk hmzbḥ ṣpwnh*), "the morning burnt offering" (*'lt hbqr*), "model" (*dmwt*), "pattern" (*tbnyt*), and the like. . . . The same is true of a similar annalistic pasage in 2Kgs 12: 5–17 which also pertains to Temple affairs (the repair of the temple) and also contains many Priestly terms, such as "the money for which each man is assessed" (*ksp npšwt 'rkw*), "guilt offering" (*'wn*), "sin offering" (*ḥṭ't*).'

Ahaz slept with his fathers, and was buried with his fathers in the city of David; and Hezekiah his son reigned in his stead.

Hezekiah Introduced (2Kgs 18: 2–3, 4*, (5–8,)13b; 2Chr 29: 1–2; 31: 1*; 32: 1b)

Hezekiah was twenty-five years old when he began to reign, and he reigned twenty-nine years in Jerusalem. His mother's name was Abi[jah] the daughter of Zechariah. And he did what was right in the eyes of Yahweh, according to all that David his father had done. He [it was who] removed [the high places and] the pillars, and cut down the Asherah. And he broke in pieces the bronze serpent that Moses had made, for until those days the people of Israel had burned incense to it; it was called Nehushtan.[1] [He trusted in Yahweh the God of Israel; so that there was none like him among all the kings of Judah after him, nor among those who were before him. For he held fast to Yahweh; he did not depart from following him, but kept the commandments which Yahweh commanded Moses. And Yahweh was with him; wherever he went forth, he prospered. He rebelled against the king of Assyria, and would not serve him. He smote the Philistines as far as Gaza and its territory, from watchtower to fortified city.]

Jerusalem Delivered (2Chr 32: 9–12, 14*, 20–21*, 24*; cf. 2Kgs 18: 17–22, 35; 19: 2–4*, 14–15*, 35–37; 20: 1a*, 5b*, 8–11*)

Sennacherib, king of Assyria came [up] against the fortified cities of Judah and took[2] them. The king of Assyria sent . . . from Lachish to king Hezekiah at Jerusalem, saying: 'Thus has the king of Assyria said: "On what are you trusting, that you live under seige[3] in Jerusalem? Is not Hezekiah misleading you,

---

[1] I give prominence to breaking the pillars: it is not only the first act in Chronicles' brief list of cultic changes (31: 1), and the only one where Kings and Chronicles share noun and verb; but it is typical of Kings to give prominence in 2Kgs 18: 4 to removal of 'high places'. Chronicles has introduced a distinction between reforms in Jerusalem (2Chr 29–30) and in outlying centres (31: 1). I have placed 2Kgs 18: 5–8 in brackets: they do not appear to be reflected in the text of 2Chr 29–32.

[2] 2Chr 32: 1 is less definite: 'thinking to win them for himself'.

[3] 2Kgs 18: 20 offers instead 'that you have rebelled against me'. The only instance of *mrd* shared between Kings and Chronicles relates to the rebellion against the king of Babylon by Zedekiah (2Kgs 24: 20 // 2Chr 36: 13).

giving you over to die by famine and thirst, telling you: 'Yahweh our God will deliver us from the king of Assyria.'? Has not this same Hezekiah taken away his high places and his altars, saying to Judah and Jerusalem: 'Before this[1] altar you shall prostrate yourselves.' Has any of the gods of the nations ever delivered his land out of the hand of the king of Assyria, that your god should deliver you out of my hand?"' And Hezekiah prayed; and Yahweh sent a messenger and obliterated . . . [2] in the camp of Assyria; and he returned [to his land] and he came to the house of his god, and his sons felled him with the sword. In those days, Hezekiah was mortally sick; and he prayed to Yahweh, and he said: 'Behold, I will heal you.' And he even granted him a sign.

Hezekiah's End (2Kgs 20: 12–15*, 20–21; cf. 2Chr 32: 27–31, 32–33)

[And the king of Babylon sent envoys; . . . And Hezekiah welcomed them, and he showed them all his treasure house, the silver, the gold, the spices, the precious oil, his armoury, all that was found in his storehouses; there was nothing in his house or in all his realm that Hezekiah did not show them.][3] The rest of the deeds of Hezekiah, and all his might, and how he made the pool and the conduit and brought water into the city, are they not written in the Book of the Chronicles of the Kings of Judah? And Hezekiah slept with his fathers; and Manasseh his son reigned in his stead.

Manasseh (2Kgs 21: 1–10a, 17, 18*; 2Chr 33: 1–10a, 18a, 19*, 20)

Manasseh was twelve years old when he began to reign, and he reigned fifty-five years in Jerusalem. [His mother's name was Hephzibah.] And he did what was evil in the sight of Yahweh,

[1] 2Chr 32: 12 (MT) reads 'one' for 'this' – LXX agrees with 2Kgs 18: 22.
[2] 2Chr 32: 21 details 'the mighty warriors and commanders and officers', while 2Kgs 19: 35 quotes only a total: 'one hundred and eighty-five thousand'.
[3] Something like this short report from Kings appears to be reflected in Chronicles; yet it may be a further case of secondary adaptation in Chronicles from later additions to Kings – not evidence for an original element in the Shared Text.

according to the abominable practices of the nations whom
Yahweh drove out before the people of Israel. For he rebuilt the
high places which Hezekiah his father had destroyed; and he
erected altars for Baal, and made an Asherah, and worshiped all
the host of heaven, and served them. And he built altars in the
house of Yahweh, of which Yahweh had said, 'In Jerusalem will
I put my name.' And he built altars for all the host of heaven in
the two courts of the house of Yahweh. And he burned his son as
an offering, and practiced soothsaying and augury, and dealt
with mediums and with wizards. He did much evil in the sight of
Yahweh, provoking him to anger. And the graven image of
Asherah that he had made he set in the house of which Yahweh
said to David and to Solomon his son, 'In this house, and in
Jerusalem, which I have chosen out of all the tribes of Israel, I will
put my name for ever; and I will not cause the feet of Israel to
wander any more out of the land which I gave to their fathers, if
only they will be careful to do according to all that I have
commanded them, and according to all the law that my servant
Moses commanded them.' Manasseh seduced them to do more
evil than the nations had done whom Yahweh destroyed before
the people of Israel. And Yahweh spoke to Manasseh and his
people, but they did not listen.[1] Now the rest of the acts of
Manasseh, and his sin, are they not written in the Book of the
Chronicles of the Kings of Judah? And Manasseh slept with his
fathers, and was buried in his house; and Amon his son reigned
in his stead.

Amon (2Kgs 21: 19–21, 23–24; 2Chr 33: 21–22, 24–25)

Amon was twenty-two years old when he began to reign, and he
reigned two years in Jerusalem. [His mother's name was
Meshullemeth the daughter of Haruz of Jotbah.] And he did
what was evil in the sight of Yahweh, as Manasseh his father had
done. He [walked in all the way in which his father walked, and]
served the idols that his father served, and worshiped them; he

[1] This follows 2Chr 33: 10, rather than 2Kgs 21: 9a, 10 – the issue is discussed
above on p.81. The presentation of the texts in parallel on p. 75 attempts to
present what is strictly the shared text – here we have suggested what may have
been the more original text.

forsook Yahweh, the God of his fathers, and did not walk in the way of Yahweh. And the servants of Amon conspired against him, and killed him in his house. But the people of the land slew all those who had conspired against King Amon, and the people of the land made Josiah his son king in his stead. [Now the rest of the acts of Amon which he did, are they not written in the Book of the Chronicles of the Kings of Judah? And he was buried in his tomb in the garden of Uzza; and Josiah his son reigned in his stead.]

Josiah (2Kgs 22: 1–23: 3; [23:4-20] 23: 21a, 22–23, 28–30a 2Chr 34: 1–2, 8–12a, 15–32a, 3–7*; 35: 1a, 18–19, 20b, 23a*, 24a, 26–27)

Josiah was eight years old when he began to reign, and he reigned thirty-one years in Jerusalem. [His mother's name was Jedidah the daughter of Adaiah of Bozkath.][1] And he did what was right in the eyes of Yahweh, and walked in the way of David his father, and he did not turn aside to the right hand or to the left.

In the eighteenth year of his reign, he sent Shaphan the son of Azaliah, the secretary, to the house of Yahweh, saying, 'Go up to Hilkiah the high priest, that he may reckon the amount of the money which has been brought into the house of Yahweh, which the keepers of the threshold have collected from the people; and let it be given into the hand of the workmen who have the oversight of the house of Yahweh; and let them give it to the workmen who are at the house of Yahweh, repairing the house, that is, to the carpenters, and to the builders, and to the masons, as well as for buying timber and quarried stone to repair the house[. But no accounting shall be asked from them for the money which is delivered into their hand], for they deal honestly.'

And Hilkiah said to Shaphan the secretary, 'I have found the book of the law in the house of Yahweh.' And Hilkiah gave the book to Shaphan. And Shaphan the secretary came to the king, and reported to the king, 'Your servants have emptied out the money that was found in the house, and have delivered it into the hand of the workmen. Then Shaphan the secretary told the king,

[2] Not in C1.

'Hilkiah the priest has given me a book.' And Shaphan read it before the king.

And when the king heard the words of the law, he rent his clothes. And the king commanded Hilkiah, and Ahikam the son of Shaphan, and Achbor the son of Micaiah, and Shaphan the secretary, and Asaiah the king's servant, saying, 'Go, inquire of Yahweh for me, and for the people, and for all Judah, concerning the words of the book that has been found; for great is the wrath of Yahweh that is kindled against us, because our fathers have not obeyed the words of this book, to do according to all that is written concerning us.'

So Hilkiah, and Ahikam, and Achbor, and Shaphan, and Asaiah went to Huldah the prophetess, the wife of Shallum the son of Tikvah, son of Harhas, keeper of the wardrobe (now she dwelt in Jerusalem in the Second Quarter); and they talked with her. And she said to them, 'Thus says Yahweh, the God of Israel: "Tell the man who sent you to me, Thus says Yahweh, Behold, I will bring evil upon this place and upon its inhabitants, all the words of the book which the king of Judah has read. Because they have forsaken me and have burned incense to other gods, that they might provoke me to anger with all the work of their hands, therefore my wrath will be kindled against this place, and it will not be quenched. But as to the king of Judah, who sent you to inquire of Yahweh, thus shall you say to him, Thus says Yahweh, the God of Israel: Regarding the words which you have heard, because your heart was penitent, and you humbled yourself before Yahweh, when you heard how I spoke against this place, and against its inhabitants,[1] and you have rent your clothes and wept before me, I also have heard you, says Yahweh. Therefore, I will gather you to your fathers, and you shall be gathered to your grave in peace, and your eyes shall not see all the evil which I will bring upon this place.' And they brought back word to the king.

Then the king sent, and all the elders of Judah and Jerusalem were gathered to him. And the king went up to the house of Yahweh, and all the men of Judah and the inhabitants of Jerusalem, and the priests and the prophets, all the people, both

[1]   K19 adds here 'that they should become a desolation and a curse'.

small and great; and he read in their hearing all the words of the book of the covenant which had been found in the house of Yahweh. And the king stood by the pillar and made a covenant before Yahweh, to walk after Yahweh and to keep his commandments and his testimonies and his statutes, with all his heart and all his soul, [to perform] the words of this covenant that were written in this book; and all the people joined in the covenant.

And they pulled down before him the altars of the Baals, and the . . . that were above them he chopped to pieces, and the Asherim and the graven and molten images he shattered and ground and scattered over the graves of those who sacrificed to them. And the bones of the priests he burned on their altars. And he pulled down the altars, and the Asherim and the graven images he chopped and ground, and all the . . . he hacked to pieces in all the land of Israel.[1]

And the king commanded all the people, 'Keep the passover to Yahweh your God, as it is written[2] in this book of the covenant.' Surely no such passover was celebrated since the days of the judges who judged Israel, or during all the days of the kings of Israel or of the kings of Judah; but in the eighteenth year of King Josiah this passover was kept [to Yahweh in Jerusalem].[3]

Now the rest of the acts of Josiah, and all that he did, are they not written in the Book of the Chronicles of the Kings of Judah? In his days Pharaoh Neco king of Egypt went up to the king of Assyria to the [river] Euphrates. Josiah went to meet him; and he slew him at Megiddo, when he saw him. And his servants carried him dead in a chariot from Megiddo, and brought him to Jerusalem, and buried him in his [fathers'] tomb.[4] And the people of the land took Jehoahaz the son of Josiah, [and anointed him,]

---

[1] Since Chronicles regularly makes at least small changes to the source reports of cultic modifications, this paragraph will only give an impression of the original wording. But it can hardly be doubted that the long report in 2 Kgs 23: 4–20 has been substantially expanded, and in more than one stage.

[2] This clause is strictly a Kings plus, but may have provided from the original text the basis for the double mention of Moses in the much expanded 2 Chronicles 35 (vv. 6, 12).

[3] These words are not in Chronicles MT – but cf. the longer LXX.

[4] Williamson (1982) has suggested that Chronicles' *Vorlage* here was expanded from what we know as the text of Kings.

5

and made him king in his father's stead.

Jehoahaz (2Kgs 23: 30b–31a, 33b–34a; 2Chr 36: 1–4)[1]

Jehoahaz was twenty-three years old when he began to reign, and he reigned three months in Jerusalem. [His mother's name was Hamutal the daughter of Jeremiah of Libnah. And he did what was evil in the sight of Yahweh,[2] according to all that his fathers had done.] And Pharaoh Neco [put him in bonds at Riblah in the land of Hamath,] removed him that he might not reign in Jerusalem, and laid upon the land a tribute of a hundred talents of silver and a talent of gold. And Pharaoh Neco made Eliakim the son of Josiah king, and changed his name to Jehoiakim. But he took Jehoahaz away; and he came to Egypt.

Jehoiakim (2Kgs 23: 36a, 37*; 24: 1a, 5a. 2Chr 36: 5–6a, 8a)

Jehoiakim was twenty-five years old when he began to reign, and he reigned eleven years in Jerusalem. [His mother's name was Zebidah the daughter of Pedaiah of Rumah.] And he did what was evil in the sight of Yahweh [, according to all that his fathers had done]. [In his days] Nebuchadnezzar king of Babylon came up [and Jehoiakim became his servant three years; then he turned and rebelled against him].[3] Now the rest of the deeds of Jehoiakim, and all that he did, are they not written in the Book of the Chronicles of the Kings of Judah? So [Jehoiakim slept with his fathers, and] Jehoiachin his son reigned in his stead.

Jehoiachin (2Kgs 24: 8a, 9a, 10a, 12b, 13a, 17; 2Chr 36: 9–10)

Jehoiachin was eighteen years old when he became king, and he reigned three months in Jerusalem. [His mother's name was

---

[1] In this attempt at a rendering of a more original text of the final short reports, the material in brackets appears in Kings only.

[2] MT in 2Chr 36: 2 (and 1 Es 1: 33) lacks the evaluative note, but it is offered in the LXX.

[3] C6b–7 reports that Nebuchadnezzar 'bound him in fetters to take him to Babylon. Nebuchadnezzar also carried part of the vessels of the house of Yahweh to Babylon and put them in his palace in Babylon.'

Nehushta the daughter of Elnathan of Jerusalem.] And he did what was evil in the sight of Yahweh. [At that time the servants of] King Nebuchadnezzar [of Babylon] came up and took him into captivity to Babylon; and carried off [all] the treasures of the house of Yahweh [and the treasures of the king's house].[1] And the king of Babylon made Mattaniah, Jehoiachin's uncle, king in his stead, and changed his name to Zedekiah.[2]

Zedekiah (2Kgs 24: 18a, 19a, 20b; 2Chr 36: 11, 12a, 13a)

Zedekiah was twenty-one years old when he became king, and he reigned eleven years in Jerusalem. [His mother's name was Hamutal the daughter of Jeremiah of Libnah.] And he did what was evil in the sight of Yahweh. And he rebelled against the king of Babylon.

---

[1] The fuller Kings text, which goes on in v. 14 to mention the gold decoration of the temple made by Solomon, is discussed in Brettler (1991b). Four of the five earlier Kings passages where he notes mention of transfer of precious metals to foreign treasuries (1Kgs 14: 26; 15: 18; 2Kgs 14: 14; 16: 8) are shared with Chronicles (2Chr 12: 9; 16: 2; 25: 24; 28: 21); but the fifth (in 2Kgs 18: 14-16) in its entirety, like most of this report here, is a Kings plus.

[2] C10 makes no mention of the renaming, and calls Zedekiah Jehoiachin's brother, not uncle.

6

Moses and David in the Story of Judah's Kings from Solomon

6.0 Introduction

Having sampled comparisons between David and Solomon and then the remaining Kings of Judah as they are portrayed in Samuel-Kings on the one side and Chronicles on the other, and having offered a reconstruction of our hypothetical main source for both biblical presentations, it is time now to return to where we started. A fuller review of the uses made of Moses and David throughout Samuel-Kings and Chronicles will set our opening remarks about the two endings of Solomon's great prayer in in a better researched context. It will also help us to move beyond our somewhat arbitrary division of the textual material between David and Solomon on the one side and the rest of the kings on the other.

6.1 Moses in Kings and 2 Chronicles

It was noted above (*4.5.5*) that Moses appears ten times in 1 and 2 Kings, though in only eight passages; and twelve times in 2 Chronicles, in ten passages. Only three of these passages are common to Kings and Chronicles.

6.1.1 The first is within the report of the placing of the Ark in the innermost holy place of the new Solomonic temple: it is noted (1 Kgs 8: 9 // 2 Chr 5: 10) that the Ark contained nothing but the two tables of stone which Moses put there at Horeb (cf. Dt 10: 1–5). The second is part of the report of Amaziah's liquidation of those responsible for the assassination of his father Joash. The almost identical 2Kgs 14: 6 and 2Chr 25: 4 cite his respect for Moses' lawbook (cf. Dt 24: 16) to explain why the new king did not also kill the sons of the assassins. And finally Manasseh's evil actions are related to his scorn of the divine promises that Yahweh would put his name for ever in his house and in Jerusalem and that Israel's feet would remain in their land provided simply that they were careful to act in accordance with his commands as mediated by Moses (2Kgs 21: 8 // 2Chr 33: 8). Some of his crimes can in fact be correlated with Deuteronomy 18: 9–14 (see p. 86 above).

6.1.2 The five passages in Kings with Moses pluses are all within the accounts of Solomon, Hezekiah, and Josiah.

6.1.2.1 At the begining of 1Kings 2 (vv. 1–4), David on his deathbed advises Solomon to observe carefully the divine precepts as written in Moses' *torah*. De Vries (1985: 34) squirms over the presence of apparently late features such as *šmr mšmrt* (2: 3), which is not part of the related and rather fuller reports in 1Chr 22: 12–13 or 28: 7–10, 20. Braun (1986: 222–3) unfortunately pays more attention to the links of 1Chr 22 with Jos 1: 7–8 than to those with 1Kgs 2: 1–4.

6.1.2.2 The next two mentions of Moses are at the end of Solomon's dedicatory prayer: 1Kgs 8: 53, 56. The first has already been discussed; the second is part of a more substantial Kings plus (vv. 54–61) which report a blessing of the people by Solomon in between his prayer and the following sacrifice. This opens: 'Blessed be the Lord who has given rest to his people Israel, according to all that he promised; not one word has failed of all his good promise, which he uttered by Moses his servant.'

6.1.2.3 Kings and Chronicles handle Hezekiah very differently: they begin in tandem (2Kgs 18: 1–3 // 2Chr 29: 1–2) and intersect again with Sennacherib's invasion half way through his reign (2Kgs 18: 13 // 2Chr 32: 1). The only detail in the intervening three-chapter report in Chronicles at all reminiscent of the much briefer report in 2Kgs 18: 4–8 (and especially vv. 5–7a) is the note at its end: 'and he did what was good and right and faithful before the Lord his God. And every work that he undertook in the service of the house of God and in accordance with the law and the commandments, seeking his God, he did with all his heart, and prospered.' The shorter Kings text includes two mentions of Moses that appear to make contrary points: he had manufactured Nehushtan, the bronze serpent, which Hezekiah broke in pieces as part of his cultic reforms; but he was also the medium through whom had been delivered the divine commandments which Hezekiah followed. This second plus could well represent precision added to 2Chr 31: 21 just cited.

6.1.2.4 The next mention of the Mosaic commandments follows immediately, at the end of the summary report (2Kgs 18: 9–12)[1] of Shalmaneser's capture of Samaria and exiling of Israel because of their transgression of the divine covenant.

6.1.2.5 Finally the praise heaped on Josiah culminates in 2Kgs 23: 25: 'Before him there was no king like him, who turned to the Lord with all his heart and with all his soul and with all his might, according to all the law of Moses; not did any like him arise after him.' This is a perfect reappropriation of the promise to Solomon in the Kings plus 1Kgs 3: 12b, except that the wisdom of which it speaks has been replaced here with the words of Dt 6: 5! Note that 6: 5 has been more briefly cited in 1Kgs 2: 3.

6.1.3 Five of the seven passages with Mosaic pluses in 2 Chronicles relate also to Solomon, Hezekiah, and Josiah, but are very different in flavour; the other two are from his report of the period of influence of Jehoiada the priest:

6.1.3.1 The first (1: 3) notes at the beginning of the report of the vision at Gibeon that Moses had made the tent of meeting (*'hl mw'd h'lhym*) which was at that shrine.

6.1.3.2 Moses is next mentioned (8: 13) within a much larger plus (vv. 12–15) which apparently expands the summary mention of Solomon's sacrificial practice in 1Kgs 9: 25. The sacrificial duties

---

[1] Those verses have a relationship with 2Kgs 17: 1–6 – a common core expanded in two directions?

for each sabbath and pilgrim festival had been prescribed by Moses, while the various priestly orders had been defined by his father David, 'the man of God'.

6.1.3.3 A similar two-fold point about David and Moses is made (23:18) within a report of Jehoiada's reform (23: 16–21) that extends the shorter 2Kgs 11: 17–20.

6.1.3.4 Mosaic authority is claimed (24: 6, 9) for a temple tax which the shorter report in 2Kgs 12: 4–16 appears to understand as simply customary. The second verse (24: 9) locates the Mosaic instruction in the desert; the first verse (24: 6) notes that his original prescription had related to 'the tent of testimony' (*l'hl h'dwt*). This expression is unique in Chronicles (Williamson 1982); but two points may be noted: (1) it is familiar in the middle of Numbers (9: 15; 17: 22, 23; 18: 2 – and cf. *mškn h'dwt* in 10: 11); and (2) it closely follows an occurrence of '*dwt* in the common text (2Kgs 11: 12 // 2Chr 23: 11).[1]

6.1.3.5 The account of Hezekiah's passover reports that those involved took their places 'according to their ruling/custom' (*kmšptm*), which is further explained by the appositional phrase 'according to the *torah* of Moses the man of God' (30:16).

6.1.3.6 The report of Josiah's reforms goes beyond 2Kgs 22: 8 in having Hilkiah specify as Mosaic (2Chr 34: 14) the *torah*-book found in the temple.

6.1.3.7 Finally, and in a similar spirit, the detailed account of the reforming passover under Josiah notes twice (35: 6, 12) that its conduct followed instructions mediated by Moses or in his book.[2]

6.1.4 The three mentions of Moses common to Kings and Chronicles can readily be correlated with material in the Book of Deuteronomy. And this is also true (if rather more generally?) of the five further mentions of Moses in the Books of Kings. However, most though not all of the seven pluses mentioning

---

[1] The only mention of this sacred tent common to Sam–Kings and Chr is when it is brought with the ark to the new temple (1Kgs 8: 4 // 2Chr 5: 5). There, both Hebrew texts call it *'hl mw'd*, but both Greek translations offer 'tent of testimony'.

[2] See Shaver (1990) for a discussion of the identity of the Chronicler's law-book.

Moses in 2 Chronicles attribute priestly and sacrificial regulations to him. Even where they cannot quite be squared with the text of the Pentateuch as we know it, they relate more to the book of Numbers than to Deuteronomy (cf. Shaver 1990). In these pluses either one of two things seems to be happening – and sometimes perhaps both together: additions to the text are felt to require the sanction of Mosaic authority; and the separate emphases of the diverging texts of Kings and Chronicles are variously correlated with different strands of what we know as the Pentateuch.

6.2 David in Kings and 2 Chronicles

Within the story of Judah's kings, Moses is of course always and only a figure, a symbol, a name, from the distant past. David has a double function: he is a principal character at the beginning, and only later becomes the symbol of his line. In what follows, I want to explore this symbol through the shared text from Solomon onwards, through the many pluses relating to David in Kings and 2 Chronicles, to the references to David elsewhere in the Bible – I exclude 1–2 Samuel and 1 Chronicles, where he is clearly a full character, and Psalms, where his symbolic status is both so prevalent and so well known.

6.2.1 In the Shared Text, David appears fourteen times in the Solomon story (mostly in his prayer)[1] and ten times thereafter.[2] Most of the references in the prayer relate to the legitimacy of Solomon's succession to David; and that is also the topic of Hiram's congratulatory blessing of Yahweh in 1Kgs 5. Then, while the opening vision at Gibeon underscores Yahweh's loyalty to David, Solomon's later Jerusalem vision makes the continuance of the promise conditional on each king maintaining the integrity of David's behaviour. Of the remaining shared mentions of David, the first three relate to the rebellion of the north against Rehoboam; four compare much later monarchs with David,

[1] In 1Kgs 3: 6; 5: 21; 7: 51; 8: 15, 16, 17, 18, 20, 24, 25, 26, 66; 9: 4, 5 – and the parallels in Chronicles. I have excluded the references to the 'city of David' in 8: 1 and 9: 24.

[2] In 1Kgs 12: 16, 16, 19; and 2Kgs 8: 19; 11: 10; 14: 3; 16: 2; 18: 3; 21: 7; 22: 2 – and the parallels in Chronicles.

Ahaz unfavourably, Hezekiah and Josiah favourably, and Joash cautiously favourably; the Manasseh story refers back to the link of promise and demand in Solomon's second vision; Judah is saved from disaster under Jehoram because of the divine promise to David; and finally 2Kgs 11: 10 (cf. 2Chr 23: 9) reports Jehoiada's action, as he prepared for the revolt against Queen Athaliah, of arming of the guards with spears and shields that had once belonged to a more flesh-and-blood David.

6.2.2 The David pluses in Kings[1] are quite varied in nature:

6.2.2.1 A first group are added into portions of the shared text on Solomon. Three relate to the Gibeon vision – 3: 7 simply adds the name where it was clearly implied by the context; 3:14 adds to this vision a conditional promise that following Yahweh as David had would bring Solomon long life;[2] while 3: 3 qualifies the claim that 'Solomon loved Yahweh, walking in the statutes of David his father' with the admission 'only, he sacrificed and burnt incense at the high places'. Three more (5: 15, 17, 19) appear in the immediate context of 5: 21//2: 11 of the Shared Text, and may indeed represent the source-text of the clearly related 2Chr 2: 2, 6. And 6: 12 is part of 6: 11–14, which is not just a Kings plus, but also an MT plus not represented in the Greek text of Kings.

6.2.2.2 Many more David pluses are clustered in chapter 11, which is of course a Kings plus in its entirety. Verses 15, 21, 24 of that chapter offer historical references to David's wars in Transjordan. The remainder either deal with the promise to David (vv. 12, 13, 32, 34, 36, 38)[3] or use him as a comparator (vv.

---

[1] I start by excluding 1Kgs 1–2 from consideration, along with the Books of Samuel.

[2] This plus is different from the condition expressed in the Shared Text of the second vision, which connects the continuance of the Davidic line to obedience (9: 4–5).

[3] The promise to David functions to mitigate Yahweh's anger against Solomon, and is recalled in several ways:

for the sake of David your father	11: 12
for the sake of David my servant	11: 13, 34 – cf. 2Kgs 8: 19//2 Chr21: 7; 2Kgs 19: 34; 20: 6
for the sake of my servant David	11:32
that David my servant may always have a *nyr*	11:36 – cf. 1Kgs 15: 4; 2Kgs 8: 19// 2Chr 21: 7
as I built for David	11:38

4,6,33,38)[1]. I leave unclassified for the moment 11:39, an MT plus not represented in the LXX and somewhat reminiscent of Jeremiah.

Many of this cluster of references to David in 1Kgs 11 are related to the carrying forward to Solomon of the promise to David; yet the terms in which they are expressed have been drawn from much later portions of the Shared Text (2Kgs 8: 19//2Chr 21: 7; 16: 2//28: 1; 18: 3//29: 2). We shall discuss later (*7.3.5* below) the evidence that 1Kgs 11 was not part of the first draft of the Books of Kings. Their repeated concern with this theme should make me reconsider having excluded 1Kgs 1–2 from this survey. Although David does still function as a full character in those opening chapters, there is also a decided stress on the question of who will next sit on the Davidic throne (see *2.6.2* and *2.7.2* above and Auld 1992: 350–1).

6.2.2.3 Many of the remaining David pluses in Kings have already been mentioned above in cross-references (1Kgs 15: 3, 4, 5, 11; 2Kgs 14: 3; 19: 34; 20: 5, 6). Of the remainder, 1Kgs 12:20,26; 13:2; 14:8; and 2Kgs 17:21 are all in passages that deal with the division of the kingdom.[2]

6.2.3 The additions to 2 Chronicles relating to David are of a very different sort, and exhibit less continuity with the text that book shares with Kings.

6.2.3.1 Solomon is surnamed 'son of David' in 1: 1; 11: 18; 13: 6; 30: 26; 35: 3. And the 'sons of David' are simply the rightful kings according to 13: 8; 23: 3;[3] and 'house of David' has similar force in 10:19 and 21:7, though in the latter text 'house of David' seems not so much a plus as an alteration by the Chronicler of the more

---

[1] David is used in comparisons in the following:

as was the heart of David his father	11: 4 – cf. 1Kgs 8: 17//2Chr 6: 7; 1Kgs 15: 3
as David his father	11: 6(MT only), 33 – cf. 15: 11; 2Kgs 14: 3; 16: 2//2Chr 28: 1
as David my servant did	11:38 – cf. 15: 5; 2Kgs 18: 3//2Chr 29: 2

[2] 1Kgs 14: 8 (MT) is one of the parts of that chapter which has no parallel in the extended LXX 'supplement' following 1Kgs 12: 24. This alternative text is discussed more fully below (*7.3.5*).

[3] Cf. 32: 33, where it comes to discussion of Hezekiah's rightful burial place.

original 'Judah' of 2 Kgs 8: 19.[1] The rights of David and of his sons to the kingship for ever are enshrined according to 13:5 in a covenant of salt.

6.2.3.2 David is the organiser of the orders of priests and levites, and of worship and praise and its instruments, as in 7: 6 and 8: 14 and 23: 18 (twice each); and in 29: 25, 26, 27, 30 and 33: 4, 15. This is exactly the role David always plays in Ezra and Nehemiah – cf. also the musical recollection in Amos 6: 5.

6.2.3.3 The remaining Chronicles pluses are more varied. There are historical notes in 1: 4; 2: 13, 16;[2] 3: 1; 8: 11. Yahweh is styled 'God of David' in 21: 12 and 34: 3[3] – 2Chr 21: 12 in fact offers a negative comparison between Jehoram and both his father Jehoshaphat and the earlier Asa. And a similar comparison is made in 11: 17 – Rehoboam did manage three years of walking 'in the way of David and of Solomon'.

6.3 David and Moses in the Kings of Judah after Solomon

Those readers who prefer text only should ignore the following chart, and move straight to the notes. Chart and notes offer an overview of the roles played by David and Moses in the assessment of Judah's kings: first of all in the text shared by Kings and Chronicles, and then in the Kings and Chronicles pluses.

---

[1] Judah had been destroyed; the Chronicler, however, still had hopes for a continuing house of David.

[2] 2Chr 2: 2, 6 were already mentioned in *6.2.2.1* above.

[3] Elsewhere in the Bible, only in 2 Kgs 20: 5 // Is 38: 5.

King	walked in way of	right /evil	like	David	Moses	K D+	K M+	Ch D+	Ch M+	other
Rehoboam		evil		3x				1x		
Abijam		—				3x				
Asa		right				1x				
Jehoshaphat	Asa	right								
Jehoram	kings of Israel	evil		promise						
Ahaziah	house of Ahab	evil								
Joash		right		weapons				1x	2x	
Amaziah		right, but	[Joash]¹		law	unlike				like J
Azar/Uzziah		right	Amaziah							
Jotham		right	Uzziah							
Ahaz	kings of Israel	not right	not David							
Hezekiah		right	David			3x	3x	4x	1x	
Manasseh		evil	all the nations	word to	law					
Amon		evil	Manasseh							
Josiah	David – no turn	right					1x	2x	2x	
Jehoahaz		—								
Jehoiakim		evil								
Jehoiachin		evil								
Zedekiah		evil								

Notes

6.3.1 Only two kings of Judah do not have summary judgment passed on them in the common text – Abijam who reigned three years, and Jehoahaz who occupied the throne only three months. And apart from them, only Amaziah and Ahaz escape the simple verdict 'right' or 'evil'.

6.3.2 The ten or eleven middle kings on the list have their rightness or wrongness compared with that of another or of others. The exceptions, beyond Solomon's first three successors and the last four, are Joash, with whom a fresh start was made

¹ While 2Kgs 14: 3 qualifies the 'right' verdict on Joash in the words 'yet not like David his father; he did in all things as Joash his father had done', 2Chr 25: 2 says more simply 'yet not with a blameless heart'. It is not easy to deduce what the common text had read; but presumably it was shorter than the present text of Kings, even if one of the elements in Kings is more original than the Chronicler's phrase.

after the usurpation of Athaliah, and possibly Amaziah, unless Kings is to be followed.

6.3.3 The comparators used are David (3x), the king's father (4x), the kings of Israel or house of Ahab (3x), and the nations that preceded Israel (1x). Only in the case of Ahaz are two comparisons offered: he was like the kings of Israel, and unlike David. The one comparator never used in a Judaean context is Jeroboam – and that is a resounding silence (see pp. 153-54 below).

6.3.4 Apart from Joash, with whom a new start is made and who benefits from the wise priestly counsel of Jehoiada, and the 'star' kings, Hezekiah and Josiah, most mention of David is concentrated in the stories of Solomon's immediate successors: of Rehoboam in the shared text, and – largely in Kings pluses – of Abijam and Asa.[1]

6.3.5 David functions in many different ways. However, the Chronicler's David who offers instruction about levitical duties and matters musical, is cited only in the case of kings who do right: Joash, Hezekiah, and Josiah.

6.3.6 Although the shared text only states about Josiah that he was an unswerving walker in David's way, Kings mentions Moses and Chronicles makes mention of Moses and further mention of David in their extensions to this Shared Text.

6.3.7 It leaps out of the chart above that it is in their reports about Hezekiah that both books are most generous in further citations of these potent names (see further 6.4 below).

6.3.8 The use made of Moses' name is rather more nuanced than of David's. In the common text (see also *4.5.5* above), Solomon sets the Ark containing the terms of the Mosaic covenant at the heart of the new Temple; Amaziah, who has been rated not "Alpha" but only "Alpha-" ('right, but'), does act on one stipulation

---

[1] Several issues are drawn together in Kings expanded portrait of Rehoboam. 1Kgs 14: 22b–24, for example, draws him as a precursor of wicked Manasseh.

of the Mosaic *torah*; and the third shared mention of Moses, contained in the common text on Manasseh, aligns with Mosaic *torah* the divine demands laid on David and Solomon. The Chronicler's Moses pluses relate to Solomon, Joash, Hezekiah, and Josiah; and he rates all of these kings positively – and even re-presents the wicked Manasseh of the common text as a penitent. But the Kings Moses pluses, relating to three of these same four (Solomon, Hezekiah, and Josiah), indicate different perspectives. His Hezekiah and Josiah remain undiminished stars; but Solomon in Kings is a much more complex figure.

6.4 Hezekiah again

Both in Kings and in Chronicles, more space is allotted to Hezekiah than to any of Solomon's successors in Judah. Even granted this, however, the chart just discussed above makes plain a greater than average concern with David and Moses in both accounts of this king.

6.4.1 References to David are strewn through 2Chr 29–32. They start with the formulaic introduction (29: 2) shared with Kings. Three of the pluses listed in the chart concern instructions relating to temple music (29: 25, 27, 30); the fourth surnames Solomon 'son of David' (30: 26). In this wider context, it may also be significant that the report of Hezekiah's construction works twice mentions the 'city of David' (32: 5, 30), and that the king is finally buried 'in the tombs of the sons of David' (32: 33). These later phrases including David's name, though unremarkable in themselves, do resonate with the earlier possibly more deliberate references. The Chronicler's one Moses plus concerns Passover rules (30: 16).

6.4.2 As for the David pluses in 2 Kings 18–20, these are 'for my sake and for David's sake' (19: 34; 20: 6) and 'Thus says Yahweh, the God of David your father' (20: 5). The first of these usages was mentioned above (*6.2.2.2*) in connection with the large Kings addition (1Kgs 11) at the end of the Solomon story. 2Kgs 20: 6 is also a Kings plus relative to the Isaiah parallel: Is 38: 5 corresponds to 2Kgs 20: 5, and Is 38: 6 to 2Kgs 20: 7; but this second Kings' mention within the Hezekiah story of 'Yahweh's and David's sake' is not represented in Isaiah. The Moses pluses all occur in 18: 4, 6, 12 – all, that is, before the narrative shared with Isaiah begins.

6.4.3 I suspect that this greater enthusiasm in both books, though differently, for citing Moses and David in respect of Hezekiah – greater than in relation to any other king – is evidence for the relative lateness of their elaborations of the account of this king. The account in the Shared Text, by contrast, deals with Hezekiah more briefly than either Jehoshaphat or Josiah. It would go beyond the purposes of this book to probe in any detail how these remarks bear on the discussion by Seitz and Smelik (see 4.8 above) of relations between Isaiah 36–39 and 2Kgs 18–20. It would of course help if only we could reconstruct with greater confidence the Hezekiah portion of what I have been calling the 'Shared Text'! We should have to plot afresh the relationship between this shorter text and the developing book of Isaiah – and do so while lacking most of the familiar landmarks for orientation.

6.5 David, Moses, and Solomon

Unlike the great majority of the Kings who follow him Solomon is not judged in Chronicles – nor therefore in the text it shares with Kings – by a summary verdict. It seems clear enough from the extended narrative about him that the assessment both in the shared source and by the Chronicler is positive; but that assessment is not stated in so many words. Along with David, Solomon is for them simply part of the ideal beginnings of monarchy (and state and religion?). And it is significant that the shared text does confirm this reading once, much later on, by explicitly linking the names of David and Solomon – interestingly, precisely where that original text is underscoring the seriousness of Manasseh's black record.[1]

6.5.1 Yet the portrait of Solomon in Kings, while it is clearly of the same subject, has been finished by quite a different hand. This Solomon is introduced by variants of the formulae that were

[1] Throntveit (1988) argues that the Chronicler has treated David and Solomon as a pair when comparing Hezekiah to them both, and offers further references.

standard for his successors, and so becomes detached from David and ranked with them. The Solomon of the common text was not the first of many successors of David the founding father: instead Solomon, with David, was one of the founding fathers whom the others were to follow and by whose ways they were to be judged. The introduction in Kings to Solomon's vision at Gibeon (1 Kgs 3: 1–3) breaks new ground by including clauses very reminiscent of the formulae to come. It also includes talk of Solomon's love for Yahweh: and that language is very rare in the Hebrew Bible. Our reading of this introduction must take account of both these factors.

6.5.1.1 The paragraphs on several of Solomon's successors follow the standard first clause of the verdict ('and he did right/wrong in the eyes of Yahweh') with some such statement as 'and walked in the way of . . .'.[1] Solomon, somewhat differently, is said to have '*loved* Yahweh, *walking* in the statutes of David his father' (1 Kgs 3: 3a) – where 'loved' replaces 'did what was right', 'statutes' replaces 'way', and the independent verb 'walked' is reduced to the subordinate 'walking'.

6.5.1.2 'Loved' is suggestively read in the light of one or other of two familiar texts. One is Psalm 97:10 – 'You who love Yahweh must hate evil'. If Solomon did love Yahweh, then saying so should have been understood as subsuming the regular 'did what was right in Yahweh's eyes'. The other is the Shema (Dt 6: 5), and related texts in Deuteronomy – 'you shall love Yahweh your God with your whole heart . . . '. Yet, in whichever of these two directions we might look for guidance in reading 1 Kgs 3:3a, the *rq* at the beginning of 3:3b takes us by surprise. For the love of Yahweh which hates evil, the love for Yahweh which must commit the total effort of the lover, should not be limited by any clause that begins with *rq* - 'only, but, however, yet, except that'. Again the parallel with later kings of Judah is instructive. In the case of several of these we are told that *they* 'did what was right in Yahweh's eyes, except that *the people* was sacrificing and burning incense at the high places'. That could mean that the king's own heart was in the right place, but that he was not fully in control

---

[1] For details, see the chart in *6.3* above.

of his people. Yet in Solomon's case the qualifying *rq* introduces evidence clearly more damning: 'except that *he* sacrificed . . . at the *bamoth*'. Certainly the previous verse does supply the standard statement that 'the people, however, were sacrificing at the high places' and offers the explanation, 'because no house had yet been built for the name of Yahweh'. 1 Kgs 3: 2 is often supposed to have been penned by another hand, and to represent an amelioration of a damning judgment on great king Solomon. However, McConville makes an attractive case that it intends a rebuke for Solomon and not an excuse (1989: 35). And we are all the more open to persuasion that such condemnation was in fact intended in 3:3 when we notice (1) that 'love' makes only two appearances in the books of Kings, (2) that Solomon is the lover both times, (3) that the counterpart to 'Solomon loved Yahweh' in 3:3 is 'Solomon loved many foreign women' in 11:1 – and when we note further (4) that the hatred of evil and the undivided heart, hinted at in this opening statement in 3:3 that the king 'loved Yahweh', have become a heart turned away after other gods in 11:2, 4. Many readers take the opening verses of 1 Kings 3 as straightforward comment, and naturally suppose that Kings portrays a Solomon who went into decline after a glorious start. I suspect on the contrary that there is heavy irony in the report of Solomon's first love! Of course there is variation in the material on Solomon in Kings. And of course there is movement from positive to negative. But that movement is not historical or chronological: from the early Solomon to the late. It is editorial or literary: the turning of a positive source into a negative portrayal. Oh, how Solomon loved Yahweh! Yes, just how!

6.5.2 The negative conclusion of Kings' account of Solomon is clear for all eyes to see: 'So Solomon did what was evil in Yahweh's sight' (1 Kgs 11: 6a). The key exegetical issue is whether that simply states the view of the Book of Kings about Solomon at his end, or whether it also articulates its pervasive judgment on David's son through and through. In this connection, it is important not to misunderstand the observation in v. 4a that Solomon's wives turned away his heart after other gods *when he was old*. That provides no evidence for a periodisation of Solomon's reign which had begun well but ended badly. There is no implication that Solomon's love of many women signified a new response to a mid-life – or even a late-life – crisis. The text states only that the *results* of his actions became manifest in his old age.

6.5.3 In the light of our wider argument in this book, it is sensible to ask where the building blocks of this more extensive tradition about Solomon, and in particular the link between his intermarriage and false worship, might have been found in the shared text. The best candidate is located in the account in 2Kgs 8: 17 // 2Chr 21: 6 about Jehoram, who had married a daughter of Ahab and walked in the ways of Israel's kings. And the following verse in that passage ('Yet Yahweh would not destroy Judah, for the sake of David his servant, since he promised to give a *nyr* to him and to his sons for ever.') gives us some confidence that we are on the right track. For it articulates, even if in somewhat different terms, that divine guarantee to (Judah and) the Davidic line which is re-used to explain the limit set to the punishment of Solomon (1Kgs 11: [11–]13): 'However I will not tear away all the kingdom; but I will give one 'staff' to your son, for the sake of David my servant and for the sake of Jerusalem which I have chosen.'

6.6 David, Moses, and the Kings of Israel after Solomon

David is mentioned only at beginning and end of the Kings pluses that fall within the story of the kings of northern Israel. The shared account of Rehoboam's fateful visit to Shechem ends with the statement (1Kgs 12: 19//2Chr 10: 19) that 'Israel was in rebellion against the house of David until this day'. 1Kgs 12: 20 appends to this the note that the staff/tribe of Judah alone followed the house of David. And a little later, Jeroboam's fears are noted that the kingship might return to the house of David (12: 26). The following narrative about the man of God from Judah opens with his prediction to the altar at Bethel (13: 2) that it would be destroyed by a son called Josiah to be born to the house of David. Ahijah's oracle to Jeroboam notes that Yahweh tore the kingship from the house of David and gave it to him, but that he (Jeroboam) was not obedient 'like my servant David' (14: 8). So much for David at the beginning of Israel's separate story.

Finally the closing review of the failed northern story repeats the first of Ahijah's points, though somewhat differently: 'for he tore Israel off the house of David, and they made Jeroboam king' (2 Kgs 17: 21).

As for Moses – he is never mentioned at all in connection with Israel. It is said once that Jeroboam, although like David in being given kingship torn from another, proved unlike him since he did not keep Yahweh's commandments, or follow him wholeheartedly, or do only what was right in his eyes. But it is nowhere suggested that these commands had been made known through Moses' agency. Loyalty in the north to the divine standards mediated through Moses is simply not an issue: it is not even worth denying.

6.7 Disclosing the Divine Will before Moses: The Evidence of the Shared Text

Prohibiting the service or worship of other gods is a commonplace of the Deuteronomic writings. 'There shall not exist for you other gods over against me' is the negative statement of the issue at the head of the Ten Commandments (Dt 5:7). And 'other gods' are warned against seventeen further times within Deuteronomy alone.[1] The positively stated counterpart of the same principle – the one-ness of Yahweh and the consequent totality of the service required by him – is the very heart of the Shema (Dt 6: 4–9). In our Common Text this issue appears at two points: in Solomon's second vision, where the conditions attached to the royal promise are expressed (1 Kgs 9: 6, 9); and in Huldah's oracle, where the failure to meet these conditions is documented (2 Kgs 22: 17). The first thing I find significant is that these two mentions of 'other gods' bracket the whole story: Solomon belongs with David to the time of ideal beginnings, and by the time of Huldah and Josiah the end has been decreed. The second thing I find significant is the mode of divine utterance: just as Yahweh's key explanations in the time of David and Solomon are given in Nathan's oracle to David and in two visions granted to Solomon, so Yahweh's final judgment on Judah is given in another prophetic

[1] Dt 6: 14; 7: 4; 8: 19; 11: 16, 28; 13: 3, 7, 14; 17: 3; 18: 20; 28: 14, 36, 64; 29: 25; 30: 17; 31: 18, 20.

oracle, this time to Huldah. And I note again (cf. Auld 1983) that only Nathan and Huldah in all of the common text are termed 'the prophet(ess)'. My third remark concerns a silence in these two texts: there is no explicit mention of Moses, even in Huldah's words.

6.7.1 The first two remarks are indicators of the careful structuring of this shared text. 'Other gods' are not repeatedly mentioned, as in Deuteronomy or Jeremiah. However, the one mention is to Solomon in a vision, and the other is to Josiah through a prophetess. And visions and prophetic intermediaries are as rare in the Shared Text as are warnings against other gods. It is clear that our reconstructed 'source' belongs in a period in which avoidance of 'other gods' was already the touchstone of right religion. But my third remark may suggest that Moses was not yet the ubiquitously recognised authority for this right religion.

6.7.2 Such a suggestion already demands a fresh look at the three Common Text mentions of Moses – and recent remarks by Trebolle (in press) within a quite different discussion encourage such a re-examination. Trebolle nicely draws attention to varying word choices in the Hebrew Book of Kings which overlap with the partial (so-called) *kaige* recension of the Greek book. It has long been a puzzle to understand why that obvious re-edition of the Greek text excluded the material corresponding to 1Kgs 2: 12–21: 29. Trebolle points out that *torah*, while relatively prominent in the Hebrew book in 1Kgs 1: 1–2: 11 and in 1Kgs 22–2Kgs 25 (x11), is completely absent from the larger part of 1 Kings. By contrast, other terms such as 'statutes', 'ordinances', and 'commandments', which are common in that larger portion of 1 Kings, are much less prominent elsewhere. The implication is clear: that at least part of the motivation for the revision of Greek Kings was a partial revision carried out on Hebrew Kings in which *torah* had replaced or supplemented other expressions of divine demand. A scrutiny of the three Moses passages in our Shared Text produces some evidence congenial to Trebolle's suggestions.

6.7.2.1 Our discussion of Manasseh in Kings and Chronicles (in

4.2 above) already noted that the Moses reference was differently handled in 2 Kgs 21: 8 and 2 Chr 33: 8. Even there, where we were stressing the phraseology actually shared by Kings and Chronicles, we reconstructed the common text as ' . . . be careful to do all that I have commanded them by all the *torah*', and tentatively assigned Moses to the pluses in both Kings and Chronicles. In the light of Trebolle's remarks, we might conjecture as original only ' . . . do all . . . the statutes and ordinances', excerpted from Chronicles' actual ' . . . do all [I commanded them by all the *torah* and] the statutes and ordinances [by the hand of Moses]'; and suppose that the late *torah* revision did its work more comprehensively in Kings, but followed through less fully in Chronicles.

6.7.2.2 In 2 Kgs 14: 6, grounds are given why Amaziah did not eliminate the offspring of his father's assassins in the following terms: 'as written in the book of the *torah* of Moses where Yahweh commanded saying . . . '. The parallel in 2 Chr 25: 4 differs in two respects: it offers 'for' (*ky* – MT only, LXX and Vulg do not represent this *ky*) before 'as written' (*kktwb*); and the order and construction of the following terms is slightly different – 'for, as written in the *torah* in the book of Moses where Yahweh commanded saying . . . '. Here, if we take seriously the evidence of the received Hebrew text of Chronicles, we might follow up Trebolle's remarks either less or more radically. At the least we might conclude that *torah* had been intruded secondarily, and slightly differently in Kings and Chronicles, into 'as written in the book of Moses'. And yet I wonder if the embarassing 'But their children he did not put to death, *for* . . . ' in 2 Chr 25: 4 was not originally followed immediately by the statement of principle, 'fathers shall not die for children . . . '. In that case, Chronicles' *ky* is a tell-tale leftover from the originally shorter text which survived the addition of the citation formula 'as written . . . '. Logically, the 'for' should have yielded place to the full citation – and it did so in Kings and in versions of Chronicles.

6.7.2.3 We are well short of proof in this move to eliminate Moses not so much from the Shared Text – he is of course in that, although some textual confusion surrounds him there – as from a hypothetical common original behind Kings and Chronicles. The third relevant text is 1 Kgs 8: 9 (cf. 2 Chr 5: 10). Here again

Moses is part of a context marked by considerable textual divergence. Chronicles has a brief text: 'There was nothing in the Ark, except the two tablets which Moses granted at Horeb . . . '. Kings (MT) has the slightly different and fuller ' . . . , except the two *stone* tablets which Moses *laid to rest* there at Horeb . . . '. Kings (LXX) is fuller still: '..., except the two stone tablets, *tablets of the covenant* which Moses *placed* there at Horeb . . . '. It is interesting that this fuller Greek text occurs so soon after the opening of 1 Kgs 8; for in vv. 1–5 the LXX is very much shorter than Kings (MT) or Chronicles, and its evidence suggests that substantial revision has been required to produce the normative Hebrew texts.

6.7.3 How far do these remarks deconstruct my whole case?! I have not yet probed in this book very far behind the actual shared text. Yet the text used by Kings and Chronicles presumably had had a pre-history. And indeed several of the arguments advanced by previous scholars to identify stages in the production of the books of Kings, such as changes in the formulaic presentation of individual kings, may well be indicators of the growth of that shared text. It is at least possible that the authors of that text, though quite familiar with 'statutes and ordinances' of the sort we know in Deuteronomy 12–26, were innocent of any mention of Moses. Were they then 'Deuteronomists'? Can one have 'Deuteronomists' without Moses?

7

Room for a View

Have we now cleared enough of the inherited clutter to enable a clearer view, not only of the emergence of Kings and Chronicles, but also perhaps of Deuteronomy and the so-called Deuteronomistic History – and even the book of Jeremiah?

7.1 Recapitulation

In the previous chapters, we have argued in a variety of ways for a thoroughly fresh understanding of the composition of the Books of Samuel-Kings and Chronicles, and of their interrelatedness too. Most of the consensus view about Chronicles remains unchallenged: that these books were extensively expanded and thoroughly rewritten from a base consisting of material familiar to us from Samuel and Kings. What we have challenged of the consensus view is that the Chronicler also omitted large tracts of material from his source. For we have claimed that Samuel and Kings too have been extensively expanded and thoroughly rewritten from a base of material familiar to us in Chronicles! And of course the neater way of making the same double suggestion is to say that each of the biblical books has been produced by expanding and rewriting a common source. For illustrative purposes only, we have offered in chapters 3 and 5 a rough sketch of the narrative which Samuel-Kings and Chronicles still hold in common, and which moreover we are claiming was not only the source each shared, but also the major source of each. In our treatment of Solomon, we have largely laid bare this Shared Text: a detailed discussion has been

147

offered of the opening vision at Gibeon, where Kings and
Chronicles present substantially different texts; however, some
loose ends have been left in the cases of the correspondence
between Solomon and Hiram and of the interior decoration of
the Temple in Jerusalem. In the narrative of Solomon's successors,
the key texts that still require substantial study are the widely
varying reports on King Hezekiah and on Josiah's four successors.
Our view of Chronicles, in some respects at least, is not very novel.
The Chronicler did radically re-present Judah's story: he intruded
repentance and (at least partial) restoration into the account of
many of Judah's kings, and had several of them talking in the
accents of classical prophets. But we have certainly removed the
need to believe that he also radically shortened his source-
material. And we have challenged the usual assumption that, in
his 'high' view of Solomon, the Chronicler was innovative over
against Kings: he was in fact more conservative in this respect
than Kings. Our major claim is that we have recovered the
principal source of the books of Samuel and Kings. Of course they
had other sources too; but these were spliced into the story of
Judah's kings at much the same stage in its development from
which Chronicles was also developed. Granted our hypothesis,
the skills involved in laying bare this source have been those of the
conservator rather than of the rebuilder – our Shared Text is
strictly the product of conservation rather than reconstruction. A
radical approach to Kings of this sort helps to explain occasional
late Hebrew usages found in Kings but not in the parallel passage
in Chronicles – such as *kyd hmlk* ('thanks to the king') at the end
of the Queen of Sheba story (1 Kgs 10: 13), found elsewhere in the
Hebrew Bible only in Esther, Ezra, and Nehemiah.

7.1.1 Two threads have reappeared throughout our discussion.
Wound together, they appear capable of bearing much of the
weight of our proposals. The first is that the Shared Text exhibits
clear signs of structure and coherence. This is nowhere more
apparent than in the story of Solomon. The source text, which
Chronicles has only lightly supplemented, is a narrative at peace
with itself about an ideal king. Kings has produced from it with
considerable craft a much more nuanced Solomon. It has turned
the older, ideal, almost fairy-tale Solomon – of the visions, of

building god's house on earth, of proverbial wisdom and wealth, of world-wide trade and the fabled queen of Sheba – into a calculating politician who organises an administration and is entrammelled with too many women and their gods. But the skill of the writers of Kings must not blind us to the coherence and structure of that source which they either enhanced or subverted, depending on one's point of view. Aspects of that structure were noted in chapter 2 above. A further example is provided by our remarks at the end of the last chapter (*6.7*) about the significant placing within the Shared Text of narratives about the special disclosure of the divine purpose and of crucial divine demands such as the proscription of 'other gods'. Of course the backbone of the common story may have been provided from a king-list with details of succession and length of reign. But its narrative coherence is a much more important indicator that we are on the right track.

7.1.2 The second thread is that most of the language of the extensive pluses in Kings and Chronicles is already to be found within the Shared Text. Whether fashioned there, or already present in its sources, its expressions were available to be repeated, and more often re-combined and re-used, in the successor texts. This means that we cannot use words and phrases such as we examined in our word-studies (in *4.3–5* above) in any simplistic way as diagnostic of individual literary phases. The same words are often re-used in successive strata of the text. 'Moses', 'other gods', 'high places', 'the word of Yahweh', 'keep', 'forsake' are used differently in Kings from Chronicles. That has often been noted. But we have argued that that fact does not imply that Chronicles has re-applied the language of Kings. Instead, both Kings and Chronicles have reused the terminology of their common source. Not only are the structure of the Shared Text and the patterns of its word-usage clearer – much less jumbled – than those of either Kings or Chronicles, but we can also understand better the lines of rethinking and development, out from that source in two directions, than we could when we tried to argue only from Kings to Chronicles. 'Clearer – much less jumbled', but not 'clear': the case for clarity and straightforwardness of composition should not be overplayed.

Much of the evidence offered, and often recently resurveyed (as in Halpern and Vanderhooft 1991), to prove the existence of diverse strata in the Deuteronomistic History is in fact evidence of the stratification and gradual composition of the text behind both Kings and Chronicles.

7.2 Deuteronomists in Kings?

What was the role of the Deuteronomists in the composition of Kings? The question should perhaps be put more radically: Are there still questions about the writing of the books of Kings whose best answer is 'The Deuteronomists'?

7.2.1 A useful approach to this issue is by means of a further review of the Solomon story. We should distinguish in principle between several strata of materials that have gone to make up the account of Solomon in Kings. And I mention at the outset six layers, or groups of layers, for which objective criteria can be claimed:

(a) materials which are not only in the common text, in the sense that they are shared by the Hebrew and Greek texts of 1 Kings 3–10 and by 2 Chronicles 1–9, but also occupy the same position relative to each other within that common text – in fact most of our Shared Text;

(b) material which is in the common text, but occurs in different positions – such as the nations that remain being put to forced labour (1Kgs 9 [MT]//2Chr 8 – but after 1Kgs 10: 22[LXX]);

(c) Kings pluses documented in both MT and LXX, and appearing in the same order;[1]

(d) Kings pluses documented in MT and LXX, though differently placed;[2]

(e) Kings pluses special to MT (3:1a; 6:11–14; some of the details of temple construction; beginning of 11) and relocations of

---

[1] This list includes 1Kgs 3: 16–28; 4: 1–19; 5: 2–4, 9–14, 15, 17–19; details of the temple interior throughout chapter 6; 1Kgs 8: 54b–61; 9: 12–14; 10: 28b–29a.

[2] This list includes, following the MT order, 1Kgs 3: 1b (LXX 5: 14A); 5: 7–8 (LXX 5: 1); 5: 31–32a (LXX 6: 1A–B); 9: 15 (LXX 10: 22A); and 9: 16–17a (LXX 5: 14B).

common materials (like the palace buildings already discussed, and possibly some of those in category (d) just mentioned);

(f) revisions made both to MT and LXX – such as *torah* in 2: 3 according to Trebolle (in press).

Very likely there will have been more layers within some of the broader groups.

7.2.2 We must first insist that the hand of the Deuteronomists is not to be identified everywhere we find what is termed their 'distinctive terminology'. This so-called Deuteronomistic language was influential, and later scribes could also write it! And so the 'Deuteronomists' had no direct responsibility for strata (e) or (f): neither occasional additions of *torah* (as in 1Kgs 2: 3) if Trebolle is correct; nor Hebrew pluses such as *wythtn slmh* in 1Kgs 3: 1a, however thoroughly Deuteronomic its pedigree in Dt 7, or the exhortation to obedience in 6: 11–13.

7.2.3 More controversially: it seems equally clear to me that their hand is not to be detected in our basic stratum (a), or indeed (b): the extensive material about David, Solomon, and Judah shared by Kings and Chronicles – notwithstanding the fact that we have spent decades calling Solomon's prayer one of the great Deuteronomic speeches that give the whole historical work its structure, and even disagreeing over which parts of it might have been written by earlier or later Deuteronomists.

7.2.3.1 Cross's discussion of 2Sam 7 (1973: 241–261) seeks to document the 'Deuteronomic' affinities of much of the language in that chapter: 'It fairly swarms with expressions found elsewhere in works of the Deuteronomistic school' (252). However, what strikes me most forcibly after scanning his lists of cross-references is not so much the links between Deuteronomy and Nathan's oracle, but just how closely 2Sam 7 shares language with Solomon's prayer, his two visions (the second more than the first), and to a lesser extent the greetings to Solomon, including praise of Yahweh's wisdom, extended by both Hiram and the Queen of Sheba. Such language is, as Cross notes, quite widely known throughout what we call the Deuteronomistic literature

(Deuteronomy-Kings). But where within the wide range of these books and their sources was this talk at home? My strong suspicion is that the language of election out of all Israel's 'staffs' (1Kgs 8: 16) was either coined or at least first pressed into narrative service to depict the divine oracle to David's dynasty and its reaffirmation when Solomon succeeded his father, and was only later reminted to serve re-assessments of the status of Eli's ancestors (1Sam 2: 28), or of the Levites (Nu 17: 20), or even of the nation Israel itself (Dt 7: 6, 7). And if David was the earliest *stated* object of Yahweh's choice, it is not helpful to call election an originally 'Deuteronomic' term, especially if in Deuteronomy the beneficiaries of divine election are not the king, but the nation and the Levites.

7.2.3.2 Wider appropriation, after Jerusalem's fall, of language which had earlier referred to the Davidic dynasty was aided by the essential openness or even ambiguity of some of the statements in the shared text. Solomon's prayer repeatedly mentions Yahweh's 'servant' and/or 'servants'. It is clear that the 'servant' in the singular is the present king. By 'servants' in the plural were originally envisaged, I suspect, the members of the continuing dynasty; but 'thy servants' could quite as readily be taken to refer to the king's wider entourage or even his whole people. And of course, once there was no longer a king in Jerusalem, this very openness of the language allowed the old words to be appropriated to new situations. Many readers have detected similarly within Isaiah 40–55 how several opportunities have been taken to 'democratise' radically or 'nationalise' the old royal Davidic language.

7.2.3.3 In addition to the drafting of new material, there was a tendency to make small adjustments to existing texts in this same spirit. We should recognise as more original the Greek text of 1 Kgs 8: 23 – 'there is no god like you, in heaven above or on earth beneath, keeping covenant and loyalty for your servant who walks before you with all his heart' – while MT in Kings and the parallel in 2Chr 6: 14 offer ' . . . for your servants who walk . . . their heart'.[1]

---

[1] While mentioning this verse, it is worth recording the likelihood that Solomon's prayer is also the literary origin of the rather odd Hebrew phrase *šmr ḥbryt whhsd l-*, here rendered 'keeping covenant and loyalty for'. Like 'choose' or 'elect' (cf. *7.2.3.1* just above), this phrase has been re-applied to the nation in Dt 7: 9.

7.2.3.4 To recapitulate: when we read Solomon's prayer, and the report of his two visions, and Nathan's oracle – purged of a very few pluses from Samuel-Kings or Chronicles – their links are much more richly with the royal psalms than with Deuteronomy. And the few Deuteronomic links that demand attention may be better explained by influence in the opposite direction: from the Solomonic story back to the Mosaic statement of principles. If that is the case, then much of what we have been accustomed to attribute to the Deuteronomistic Historian – or Historians 1 and 2, in the terminology of Cross (1973) and Nelson (1981) or H, P, and N, in the terminology of Smend (1978), Dietrich (1972), and Veijola (1977) – is mis-attributed. It was not a Deuteronomist who scripted the main text of Solomon's prayer – except, possibly, its tailpiece in the Kings version (1Kgs 8: 50b–61).

7.2.4 That leaves only our two middle strata as Deuteronomistic candidates. They were certainly contributed by the hands that created a work recognisable as a form of the books of Kings. And they exemplify two 'Deuteronomic' traits: greater criticism of the king; and a higher profile for Jeroboam.

7.2.4.1 We have noted that the Shared Text, like Chronicles, idealized Solomon. These new elements special to Kings, on the other hand, began to 'realise' him, as we saw above *(7.1.1)* – and then blame the flesh-and-blood king they had created!

7.2.4.2 It is in Kings that the end of Solomon is inter-twined with the beginning of Jeroboam. And typically this feature is further accentuated in MT than in LXX. It is also throughout Kings that Jeroboam is blamed for the whole sad story of the north – *though only in portions talking about the north.* Jeroboam never impinged directly on the old shared story of Judah, once the disruption had taken place; nor does he impinge at all now on the Judah story as still told in both Kings and Chronicles. Judah's bad kings may have been led astray by their own wicked fathers, by Ahab, by the kings of Israel, even by the nations that preceded Israel (for the details of all these, see the chart in *6.3* above) – but Jeroboam is *never* explicitly blamed. You cannot have the book of Kings without Jeroboam; but most of what we read of him has been added in to a well-established text. He is blamed, reign by reign, for the evils of the kings of Israel; and he is the villain of the concluding evaluation of the north in 2Kgs 17. But these are all additions to the Shared Text. Only in the report of his own reign or of Rehoboam's, and of the transition to them from Solomon, do we have to enquire where alterations have been made to the original account in that Shared Text. Part of the purpose of the new end to the Solomon story in Kings (see further 7.3.5 below) is to splice him in.

7.2.5 The authors of these layers within Kings do, therefore, resemble in some ways those we have been calling for decades the 'Deuteronomists'. We shall return below to the question whether they were also responsible for giving the books of Joshua, Judges, or Samuel their shape?

7.3 The Story of Israel's Kings

The two-hundred-year story of the Kingdom of Israel is an essential ingredient of the Books of Kings; and yet it is quite deliberate that we have spent six chapters reviewing several aspects of the growth of Kings with hardly a mention of these vital materials – strange though that may seem in a study pledged to an unprejudiced reading of Kings. Kings may not be Kings without Israel; we have, however, taken trouble to demonstrate not only that the story of Judah can be told in its own terms now – that is proved satisfactorily by Chronicles – but also that it was told at an earlier stage too on its own, and in its own terms, without the accompaniment of Israel's whole story. That is not to say that Israel was never mentioned or that it was portrayed as without influence in Judah's earlier story: Israel did always have a 'bit part' in Judah's drama. The Shared Text does describe the parting of the ways after Solomon; it does record occasional warfare between the monarchies; and its record does lament the baleful influence of Ahab on his immediate in-laws on the throne of Judah, and of kings of Israel in general on Ahaz somewhat later.

7.3.1 The Israel story is told in three main stages:
(a)   There are the beginnings under Jeroboam (1Kgs 12–14) and the six contemporaries of Asa of Judah, which come to their

awful climax with Ahab son of Omri and husband of Jezebel (1Kgs 15–16).

(b) There is the record of the house of Omri, finally swept away by Jehu the furious charioteer (1Kgs 17 – 2Kgs 10).

(c) And there are the final generations before the collapse (2Kgs 13–17), including the five contemporaries of Uzziah of Judah (15: 8–31) who have their place just before the final king Hoshea (17: 1–6).

The central section is the major one: it concerns the 'house of Omri', the name given internationally to what readers of Kings call the 'kingdom of Israel'. This account takes up quite the largest space; it has as its recurring topic the contest between Yahweh and Baal; and its most detailed portraits are of Elijah and Elisha, rather than of the kings whom they confront. In fact, we find prophets much in the foreground throughout the story of the north (see *7.3.4* below)– yet Moses is never as much as named (cf. *6.6* above). And at the end of each section the story pauses for an explanation from the narrator.

7.3.2 Most of the individual kings of Israel are presented in very cursory, and mostly formulaic fashion. As with the story of Judah, there is a model. And, as in the case of the kings of Judah, we are told

    his father's name
    that he reigned over Israel
    the name of his capital city
    the length of his reign
    that he did evil in Yahweh's eyes (a straightforwardly good verdict is never given).

But, beyond the Judahite comparator, we are always informed in addition – though in a variety of forms – that the king in question remained in continuity with 'Jeroboam the son of Nebat, who made Israel to sin'. The opening narrative about Jeroboam himself will be discussed below (*7.3.5*).

7.3.2.1 About the kings from Jeroboam's son Nadab down to Ahab, we are told in one form or another that they 'went in the sins of Jeroboam . . . '. And the fact that Jeroboam's first five (Old

Greek) or six (Hebrew) successors are conveniently grouped in
one textual block (1Kgs 15: 25–16: 28/34) with all of their reigns
overlapping that of the one king Asa in Jerusalem nicely suggests
a contrast between northern impermanence and the stability of
the Judaean cousins. But the contrast encapsulated in these
earlier some forty verses is linguistic as well. As is already familiar
to us from shorter reports on southern kings, much of each
individual report is formal, and also formulaic. But the formulae
about the northern kings, with their repeated talk of continuing
in Jeroboam's sin[s] and of provoking Yahweh, are even more
clichéd than those for the south.

7.3.2.2 The closest we come to specifics is at the end of this series
of sinners: Ahab served Baal by building him a house in Samaria
and erecting an altar for him there, and by making an Asherah
(16: 31–33). And the fact that Ahab is introduced climactically
(30-31) as worse than all his predecessors *including Jeroboam*
makes it likely that his position as last of a series of six is not simply
a result of them all being contemporaries of Asa of Judah, but
involves an element of deliberate presentation. This first comment
on Ahab by the narrator (1Kgs 16: 31–33) is skilfully crafted. It
opens by noting that Jeroboam's sin was too little for Ahab, and
closes with the claim that he provoked Yahweh more than all the
kings of Israel before him. Immediately inside this bracket, we
read in second place that he took Jezebel as his wife – and in
penultimate place that he made the Asherah, symbol of a female
deity.[1] This double frame surrounds five pieces of information
about Ahab's worship of the Baal – and the deity is named in no
less than three of them:

> he served the Baal
> he prostrated before him
> he erected an altar to the Baal
> [this altar was] located in the house of the Baal
> and he built the 'house' in Samaria

– total service, personal and architectural, of a new deity in the
capital city of the kingdom. No wonder he is confronted

---

[1] One wonders how these notes relate to the hostile portrait of Solomon in 1Kgs
11: 1–8.

immediately and persistently by a 'man of God' whose very name
Eli-yahu echoes the nation's confession on Carmel (18: 39), 'It is
Yahweh who is God'. The sketch in 16: 31–33 of Ahab's
'contribution' uses two phrases that also appear once in the
Shared Text: 'erected an altar to the Baal' and 'made the
Asherah' are both reported of Manasseh in 2Kgs 21: 3. As for
related pluses in Kings, 'served the Baal, and prostrated to him'
are repeated in 1Kgs 22: 54, in the assessment of Ahab's son
Ahaziah. And 'made the Asherah' makes one further biblical
appearance, in 2Kgs 17: 16, in addition to its role in the shared
Manasseh report.

7.3.2.3 A second narratorial comment on Ahab is offered in 1Kgs
21: 25–26, in a pause between Elijah's declaration of the divine
sentence of judgment (20–24) and Ahab's response (27). 'Sold
himself for evildoing in Yahweh's eyes' is picked up from v. 20a,
and appears again only in the final account of northern Israel
(2Kgs17: 17). The hitpa'el theme of the verb *mkr* ('sell') makes just
one further biblical appearance: in Dt 28: 68, in the culminating
divine threat within a chapter of curses: namely, that Yahweh will
bring a rebellious Israel back in ships to Egypt where they will 'sell
themselves' to their enemies as slaves, but not find a purchaser.
Whether Dt 28 is an earlier or later text than these in Kings, it
usefully reminds us of the total self-abandonment implicit in 'sell
oneself to evildoing': the neighbouring words 'there was none
[who sold himself] . . . like Ahab' hardly need to be added before
the explanatory 'whom Jezebel his wife incited'. The comment
continues in v. 26 in negative superlatives: 'he committed
abomination' by 'following *gilulim*' (again repeated as 'served the
gllym' in the closing 2Kgs 17: 12), which had been a practice of the
Amorites – and we remember what happened to them when
Yahweh gave Israel their land! This opportunity taken by the
narrator to underscore Elijah's words adds to the dramatic effect
of the passage. And that is further heightened when Ahab – the
wickedest king in the wicked northern kingdom – responds to
Elijah's message by repenting (*nkn'*); and Elijah 'anticipates'
Huldah's response to Josiah and promises a stay of execution till
a later reign. Josiah is the only such penitent in the Shared Text,
and there are many Chronicles pluses that develop this theme.[1]

[1] The verb *nkn'* is used in this religious sense of 'repent' in 2Chr 7: 14; 12: 6, 7,
7, 12; 30: 11; 32: 26; 33: 12, 19 (and in negative in 33: 23; 36: 12).

But Ahab, to our surprise and to all the greater effect, is the only other such penitent in Kings.

7.3.2.4 Of Ahab's son Ahaziah, we are told that 'he walked in the way of his father, and in the way of his mother, and in the way of Jeroboam the son of Nebat, who made Israel to sin' (22: 52). And of his brother Jehoram, we learn that '[he did evil in Yahweh's eyes] though not like his father and mother, for he put away the pillar of Baal which his father had made. Nevertheless he clung to the sin of Jeroboam . . . he did not turn from it'(2Kgs 3: 2–3).

7.3.2.5 Jehu, at the other end of the central section, is quite exceptional: his deeds are presented at length in a famous story, but he is not formally introduced to us readers. It is towards the end of the long report in 2Kgs 9–10 that we read (2Kgs 10: 28–31): 'Thus Jehu wiped out the Baal from Israel. But Jehu did not turn aside from the sins of Jeroboam the son of Nebat, which he made Israel to sin, the golden calves that were in Bethel, and in Dan. And Yahweh said to Jehu, "Because you have done well in carrying out what is right in my eyes, and have done to the house of Ahab according to all that was in my heart, your sons of the fourth generation shall sit on the throne of Israel." But Jehu was not careful to walk in the law of Yahweh the God of Israel with all his heart; he did not turn from the sins of Jeroboam, which he made Israel to sin.'[1]

7.3.2.6 The impression of impermanence (*7.3.2.1* above) is reinforced towards the end of Israel's story: the five kings preceding Hoshea, in whose reign the collapse occurred, appear in a single block within the reign of Azariah/Uzziah of Judah (2Kgs 15: 8–31) that is even briefer than the report of the first kings after Jeroboam (*7.3.2.1* above). In fact, another way of pointing up this contrast between the two kingdoms is to note that Solomon had nineteen successors in each of Judah and Israel; yet those in Israel reigned on average only three years each for every five of their counterparts in Jerusalem. Mostly we

---

[1] Halpern and Vanderhooft (1991: 199–203) nicely describe the pattern according to which the earlier kings of Israel 'walk in the ways of Jeroboam' while the later ones, following the nadir of the enthusiastic Baal-worship of Omri and Ahab, 'do not turn' from Jerooboam's sins (cf. *7.3.2.1* above).

are told of these successors of Jehu that the king 'did not turn from the sins of Jeroboam . . . '; sometimes more fully that he 'went after the sins of Jeroboam . . . , and did not turn . . .'. Shallum, however, who reigned only one month after assassinating Zechariah before he himself was assassinated by Menahem, receives no evaluation.

7.3.2.7 The final surprise comes when we find the somewhat irregular pattern broken – in more than one sense – with Hoshea, the last king of Israel, who 'did evil in Yahweh's eyes, but not like the kings of Israel who were before him' (2Kgs 17: 2), and yet lost his throne to the Assyrians.

7.3.3 I suspect in fact that this writer in Kings knew next to nothing about many of those ancient kings of the north. Even the little content offered about Ahab's predecessors that is not actually formulaic is rather repetitive, as report after report on the early kings moves between the short-term capital Tirzah and the Israelite camp against the Philistines at Gibbethon. Indeed his source for Baasha's campaign against the south may well have been the Asa section of our shared text (see p. 108-09 above).[1] The whole house of Omri was judged the worst ever in Israel, because they were the dynasty associated with the Baal. That too was already remarked on in the Shared Text. The detail of the editorial evaluation of northern Israel provided in 2Kgs 17 is in striking contrast to the brevity we have noted in many of the individual reports. After a short report on the Assyrian invasion and its immediate aftermath (17: 3–6), the largest part of that long chapter is made up of a series of meditations on this crisis, its causes, and its results. A sketch treatment of the opening verses will illustrate the eclectic flavour of the whole, and demonstrate that the language is far from typically 'Deuteronomistic'.

*7.3.3.*1 Verse 7 begins: 'It was because the people of Israel sinned against Yahweh their God . . . '. Outside 1Kgs 8, *ḥṭ'* [qal] is used

---

[1] Interestingly, it is only in connection with the earlier Kings of Israel – Jeroboam himself, these six, and Ahab's son Ahaziah – that the 'provocation' formula is used (see also *7.4.3* below). Afterwards in Kings it appears only withint eh final peroration on the fall of the north in 2Kgs 17: 11, 17, apart of course from its use towards the end of Judah's story already discussed (*4.2.5* above).

in Kings in 1Kgs 14: 16, 22; 15: 30; 16: 13, 19; 18: 9; 2Kgs 18: 14; 21: 17[1] – but always absolutely, never as here with the preposition *l-* marking the person sinned against.[2]

7.3.3.2 The following description of Yahweh as the one 'who brought them up from the land of Egypt from under the hand of Pharaoh king of Egypt' is unique. 'From under the *burdens* of Egypt' is used in Ex 6: 6, 7 with the verb 'bring out'; and 'from under the hand of *Egypt*' with the verb 'deliver' in Ex 18: 10. The shared text in 2Kgs 8: 20, 22 // 2Chr 21: 8, 10 talks of Edom rebelling 'from under the hand of Judah'; and a deliverer helped Israel (2Kgs 13: 5) to 'come out from under the hand of Aram'. But what is actually said in 2Kgs 17: 7 is nowhere else said.

7.3.3.3 'and walked in the customs of [the nations]' in v. 8 can be parallelled only in Lev 20: 23; 1Kgs 3: 3; 2Kgs 17: 19; and Ezek 33: 15. The closest parallel is the first: ' . . . of the nation[s] which I am sending forth before you'.[3]

7.3.3.4 The opening verb in v. 9, *wyḥp'w* is unique here in the Bible.

7.3.3.5 bmwt ('high places') are 'built' (verse 9) by Manasseh only within the Shared Text (2Kgs 21: 3//2Chr 33: 3) and only once more in Chronicles, in the obviously dependent 2Chr 33: 19. However, this idiom is also found in other Kings pluses, 1Kgs 11: 7; 14: 23; and in Jer 7: 31; 19: 5; 32: 35.

7.3.3.6 The exact expression at the end of v. 9, 'from watchtower to fortified city', is found also in 18:8; but nothing resembling it is found elsewhere.

7.3.3.7 The cognate hiphil *hṣyb* ('set up') is used with *mṣbh* ('pillar') in v. 10, and otherwise only in Gn 35: 14, 20 and 2Sam 18: 18.

---

[1] We noted in our earlier discussion of Manasseh (*4.2.5* above) that 2Kgs 21: 17 and 2Chr 33: 19 share the noun 'sin', but only Kings attaches the cognate verb in the manner of most of these references from the Israel story. Has an earlier Manasseh report provided the language for the northern story? Or has his report in Kings been harmonised with that story? Or are both perhaps true?

[2] The hiphil theme, 'cause to sin', is of course more frequent in Kings: 20x with Jeroboam as subject; and of Baasha in 1Kgs 16: 2; of Ahab in 21: 22; and of Manasseh in 2Kgs 21: 11, 16.

[3] V. 8b may be a late plus in its entirety – it is absent from the Syriac.

7.3.3.8 hglh in v. 11a (RSV's 'carried away' is less specific than the normal rendering 'carried into exile/exiled') belongs largely to Kings pluses and to Jeremiah. Half of the dozen instances in Kings are in this chapter;[1] there are a similar number (13) in Jeremiah. The expression here in 2Kgs 17: 11 appears equivalent to the commoner 'drove out', also construed with 'before' (*mpny*), in 17: 8 above. In fact Yahweh is only rarely the subject of the verb 'exiled': only in 17: 11 and in Jer 29: 4, 7, 14.

7.3.3.9 Only in v. 11b is it said that *dbrym*, presumably here 'things' rather than 'words', are 'done' (*'sh*); and only here are *dbrym* (plural) qualified as *r'ym*, 'wicked'. However, this expression ('they did wicked things') is reminiscent of two verses in Deuteronomy: 'will not continue to do *like* this wicked *dbr* among you' (13: 12; 19: 20).

7.3.3.10 Further, at the end of v. 12, 'you (plural) shall not do this thing (*dbr*)', though apparently unremarkable, is an idiom unique within the Bible.

7.3.3.11 The one verse replete with 'Deuteronomistic' expressions is v. 13; yet here too there are untypical features: the hiphil *h'd* ('adjure/admonish') is found elsewhere with Yahweh as subject, but not, apart from the following v. 15, in Deuteronomy or the Former Prophets – the other instances are Ex 19: 23; Jer 11: 7; 42: 19; Ps 50: 7; 81: 9; and Neh 9: 26, 29, 30.

7.3.3.12 The absolute 'they did not hearken' (v. 14a) is used also in 2Kgs 17: 40; 18: 12; 21: 9; Is 64: 3; Jer 7: 24; 11: 8; 13: 11; 17: 23; 35: 17; 44: 5; and Neh 9: 29 (cf. immediately below).

7.3.3.13 '[They] stiffened their neck' in v. 14b occurs nowhere else in Kings: the biblical comparators are in Jer 7: 26; 17: 23; 19: 15 and Neh 9: 16, 17, 29.

7.3.3.14 Finally, at the end of that verse, talk of their fathers not 'believing in Yahweh their God' is again without parallel in Kings. We may rather compare 2Chr 20: 20; 32: 15 or, within the Pentateuch, Gn 15: 6; Ex 14: 31; Nu14: 11; 20: 12; Dt 1: 32.

---

[1] 2Kgs 15: 29; 16: 9; 17: 6, 11, 26, 27, 28, 33; 18: 11; 24: 14, 15; 25: 11. On 16: 9, see footnote 2 to the translation on p. 119 above.

7.3.4 Divine intermediaries are much more prominent in the northern story than ever in the shared account of Judah. It may be helpful to correlate our remarks with the three stages in the Israel story identified in *7.3.1* above.

7.3.4.1 Elijah and Elisha dominate the second stage: it is they who are Yahweh's earthly protagonists in his conflict with Baal and the house of Omri. And even the two chapters within 1Kgs 17– 2Kgs 10 which do not name the one or the other still have prophets in their cast: 1Kgs 20 with 'a prophet' and 'one of the prophets', and 1Kgs 22 with Micaiah, Zedekiah, and some four hundred prophets of Yahweh.

7.3.4.2 The final section, culminating in Samaria's fall, is the sparest in its references: 2Kgs 13: 14–21 associates an acted sign involving arrows and a revivification miracle with Elisha's final illness and death. Jonah son of Amittai is cited in 2Kgs 14: 25; and the following two verses appear to insist that a bleak reading of Amos would be a mistake – though Amos is not cited by name. And, finally, 2Kgs 15: 12 refers, anonymously again, to a divine guarantee to King Jehu of a stay of execution on his royal line.

7.3.4.3 The opening section features the largest number of named divine intermediaries: Ahijah from Shiloh (at least 1Kgs 12: 15 and 15: 29), Shemaiah (12: 22–24), the man of God from Judah and the prophet of Bethel (13: 1–34), and Jehu son of Hanani (16: 1–4, 7, 12–13). The references in 1Kgs 12 to Ahijah and Shemaiah (vv. 15, 22–24) are preserved also in Chronicles (2Chr 10: 15; 11: 2–4). Ahijah is in fact much more prominent in Kings than the two verses just cited suggest. However, there is considerable divergence between MT and LXX over the portrayal of his role. But that topic is better handled as an element of our next section on the transition in Kings MT and LXX from Solomon to Jeroboam and Rehoboam.

7.3.4.4 This prominence of 'prophetic' activity in the portrayal of northern Israel is often evaluated in a straightforward – or is it naive? – historical manner. It is understood as an indicator of how things really were in the society of that area in the tenth to eighth centuries BCE. It is widely assumed, for example, that 'prophets' did play a larger role in the Israel of that period than in contemporary Judah. It is appropriate, however, to examine first of all in more cautious terms the history of the actual books we are studying, and their development. In our Shared Text, divine intermediaries are important (Nathan, Solomon, Huldah). But they are few, rather far between, and very strategically placed. The much greater frequency of 'prophetic' appearances in these Israel supplements we have been discussing should be correlated with two further features of Kings and Chronicles. The first is the expansion of the quite short shared text on Isaiah and Hezekiah to the lengthy narrative preserved in two forms in Isaiah and Kings. The second is the addition of many 'prophetic' stories as part of the Chronicler's expansion of the Shared Text on Judah. In as far as such features should be evaluated historically at all, they should be viewed as distinct but related samples of the interest taken at the time of the 'Second Temple' in the topic of divine intermediation within the 'First Temple' story. The Chronicler and the Deuteronomist both breathed the same post-exilic air. And their interests in prophets as actors, doers, healers, and intercessors, overlap with the concerns of these who developed the (strictly) prophetic books. The prose narratives of Jeremiah are replete with precisely these concerns – and were written in a similar period.[1]

7.3.5 We are now in a position to offer some proposals relating to one of the remaining portions of Kings that seems at first difficult

---

[1] If this approach commends itself, some restatement will be required of the far-from-naive account by Seeligmann of attitudes to prophecy among the Deuteronomists, in Jeremiah, and in the Chronicler. He notes (1978: 264) that the prophets in Kings till the time of Isaiah were from northern Israel, and addressed kings and not the people; commends Herrmann's description of such northern Israelite prophets as 'king-makers'; and insists on the difference between such (king-breaking) revolutionaries and their counterparts in southern Judah. Yet he does note in passing that the role of prophet as kingmaker is also found earlier in Samuel, Nathan, and Ahijah of Shiloh. Seen from our perspective, it rather distorts the evidence to say that the prophets in Kings till Isaiah are from the north: Nathan has a prominent role at the beginning of Kings (though in a Kings plus) in making Solomon king, and has a vital part to play in the Shared Text (2Sam 7//1Chr 17) in establishing the legitimacy of David himself. It is the example of Nathan and Ahijah (the Nathan and Ahijah of the shared text, even if not also of history) that is followed by all the king makers – and breakers – of the subsequent Israel story.

to square with our thesis. This concerns the transition from Solomon to Rehoboam and Jeroboam. The issues were ventilated by Trebolle (1980) at length in Spanish, and briefly summarised by him in English (1982). McKenzie added a somewhat sympathetic critique (1991); and Willis (1991) offered a detailed, if difficult, discussion of the issues in one of the key problem areas (1Kgs 11: 43–12: 3) already handled by Trebolle and McKenzie.

7.3.5.1 The Chronicler offers a much briefer account than the main text in 1 Kings, whether MT or LXX. However, the Shared Text of its most extended element (1Kgs 12: 1–16, 18–19//2Chr 10: 1–16, 18–19) is even one verse shorter (as was noted at the beginning of chapter 5 above: Solomon died; Rehoboam 'reigned in his stead'; Rehoboam went north to Shechem to be made king by all Israel; the discussions between him and an Israel led by Jeroboam failed, and Rehoboam had to hurry back to Jerusalem on his chariot; once there, he mustered Judah and Benjamin against Israel, but was advised against such a campaign by Shemaiah the man of God). 2Chr 10: 17 and 1Kgs 12: 17 (MT), add to this a note about 'the people of Israel living in the cities of Judah'. If this verse is an independent sentence, it has to be translated more emphatically than normal in English versions: 'As for the people of Israel living in the cities of Judah – over them did Rehoboam rule as king.' With such a *casus pendens* construction, Burney (1903: 176) compares 1Kgs 9:21. I find the Hebrew there, in the context of a much longer and more complex sentence, much less difficult than here; and suspect with many that this verse is a careless addition, hung on to the Shared Text in v. 16. Kings has more to say about Jeroboam, but – in LXX at least – preserves two quite different accounts of its additional information.

7.3.5.2 In chapter 11, the 'main' text of LXX offers a text broadly parallel to MT though somewhat shorter in vv. 1–8 and lacking vv. 23–24 and 39. LXX also talks of Solomon retaining two 'sceptres' after the kingdom has been torn from his hand and ten have been given to Jeroboam (vv. 31–32). The subject-matter of the prophetic tale in chapter 13 is irrelevant to this discussion; and it is all the more interesting that the differences there between the texts in MT and LXX are almost entirely stylistic.

1 Kgs 14: 1–20 (MT) about Jeroboam's sick child and his mother's consultation of the prophet Ahijah is wholly lacking from LXX at this point. And, lastly, the differences in chapter 12 are minimal where MT and LXX are running in parallel; the main discrepancy is that 12: 2 (MT) appears a little earlier in LXX, within 11:43 (LXX).

7.3.5.3 After 12:24, LXX offers an alternative account.

– This opens (12:24a) by recording in a manner typical of the remainder of Kings, and indeed of the Shared Text, the death of Solomon and the transfer of royal power to Rehoboam his son. Yet, though this opening information is typical of the Shared Text elsewhere, its elements are separately preserved in both other versions of this material – in 1 Kgs 11: 43; 14: 21–22 (MT and LXX) and 2 Chr 9: 31; 12: 13–14.

– Jeroboam's origins (12: 24b) are then recounted in a manner not unlike 1 Kgs 11: 26–28, and then his flight from Solomon to Egypt (12: 24c) like 11: 40.

– His period in Egypt, his marriage, his request to return home on Solomon's death, his return to Sareira and his fortification of that town (12: 24d–f) is a story quite different from the 'main text', though elements overlap with what is told in 1K 11: 14–25 of other refugees under Pharaoh's protection.

– The account in 12: 24g–n of his time in his home town, the illness of his child, his wife's consultation of the prophet is a mostly shorter version of the report in 14: 1–20 (MT only).

– The next episode (12: 24o) locates the story of the rending of the prophet's new mantle, not before Jeroboam's flight to Egypt (11: 29–31), but after both he and Rehoboam have arrived in Shechem for the assembly. The prophet in this alternative account is named Shemaiah, not Ahijah.

– The negotiations at the assembly (12: 24p–s) are a somewhat less repetitive version of 12: 3–13.

– The whole people's rejection of Rehoboam (12: 24t) follows as stated in 12:16, but without the editorial remark reported in 12: 15 about Yahweh fulfilling his prediction made through Ahijah.

– Rehoboam's ride to Jerusalem with Judah and Benjamin in his train (12: 24u) simply follows this rejection, and is not explained (as in 12: 18) by the stoning of his taskmaster Adoram.

– The closing portion (12: 24x–z) is a shorter version of 12: 21–24.

7.3.5.4 This alternative version shares one important feature with 2Chr 10 – that Jeroboam is not introduced to the story till after Solomon's death has been reported. However it goes beyond Chronicles in ascribing blame to Rehoboam as king (end of 12: 24a) before mentioning Jeroboam at all (beginning of 12:24b). It is also true that the alternative version is closest to the 'main text' of Kings precisely where that shares text with Chronicles as well – that is, in 24a (11: 43//9: 31; 14: 21–22//12: 13–14) and in 24p–z (12: 1–24//10: 1–11: 4). In fact our reconstructed Shared Text (in chapter 5 above) would lose little if it were shortened to take account of this alternative version within 1Kgs 12: 24a–z (LXX). If the alternative version was – like all the 'main' versions – expanded from the 'original' Shared Text, then we should have to reckon with the possibility that it was ignorant of almost all the material in 1Kgs 11 according to the 'main text' represented by MT and LXX. The 'promise to David' theme in 1Kgs 11: 1–13, 29–39 is very repetitive. Our earlier discussion of it (p.133-34 above) identified portions in the Shared Text about later monarchs from which its building blocks could have been quarried. This 'alternative' account of Jeroboam may offer an objective criterion for identifying this whole amalgam of promise to David within critique of Solomon as secondary to the original introduction of Jeroboam. There the rending of the kingdom had been 'simply' stated – 'simply', though not necessarily 'innocently' (readers might have been expected to know of the rending of the kingdom away from Saul to David in 1Sam 15: 28, and to contrast that with this rending back to the north).

7.3.5.5 Our preference throughout this whole study has been to regard a shorter text as more likely to be more original. That inevitably predisposes us here to accept the testimony of this distinctive and shorter alternative. But, if we do that, we have to recognise that both Chronicles and the main text of Kings LXX have been adjusted towards the consistently different version whose best example is Kings MT. Yet the sort of development for which it gives vital evidence would square with other features of our study. The development of Kings from its origins in the

Shared Text on Judah required that Jeroboam should be more fully introduced than he is, for example, in Chronicles. The short version in 1 Kgs 12: 24a–z is without internal problem as a first draft of the introduction to the first king of northern Israel – I simply fail to see the problems detected by McKenzie (1991: 27–40); but then, of course, I no longer expect to find 'Deuteronomistic' hands responsible for the earliest drafts of Kings, nor Kings to be always prior to Chronicles. Jeroboam's rivalry with Solomon leads to exile from that king's presence. There are resonances with the stories of Solomon and David: marriage with a daughter of Pharaoh, and the death of a firstborn – as in the case of David and Bathsheba's child. Two prophetic words are reported, one after the other: first the ultimately more potent negative one about Jeroboam's descendants;[1] and then the positive one symbolised by the ten pieces given him from the mantle torn in twelve. Subsequent expansive drafts within Kings would spell out what the first draft only hinted at, or did not even hint at: that ten parts of the prophet's mantle for Jeroboam meant only one (MT) or two (LXX) for the house of David (11: 32); that Solomon was culpable for what happened after him (11: 1–13, 31, 33); that Jeroboam will be given an opportunity as rich as that offered David and Solomon (11: 37–38; 14: 7–8). And it certainly overlaps with our general thesis that prophetic figures play a larger role in the longer Kings texts than in the shorter text of the Chronicler. And it comes as no surprise, given the piecemeal development just sketched, that 'main text' and 'alternative text' in 1 Kgs 11–14 present Ahijah and Shemaiah so differently.

7.4 'Jeremiah Wrote the Book of Kings'

There are two briefer yet analogous statements in the biblical writings about Judah being warned by the fate of the northern kingdom. The one is the extended poetic 'parable' of Psalm 78 – it is actually termed *mashal* in the Hebrew of v. 1. In that song we find documented the failure, despite several fresh starts, of a

---

[1] His descendants, and not his 'dynasty' as McKenzie strangely states (1991: 29) and then ties himself up further when he objects to his dynasty being mentioned before ever he is king.

people known variously as Jacob, Israel, Joseph, or Ephraim; a further fresh start with David and the 'staff' of Judah is mentioned at the end, and the hearer or reader is left to ponder whether they will do any better. And the other is the book of Jeremiah, which supplies useful clues as to the origins and development of the Books of Kings.

7.4.1 At several points, the book of Jeremiah juxtaposes the situation of Judah and Israel, using Israel's story to probe Judah's fate. The first and perhaps classic example is Jer 3: 1–4: 4. In what is itself a heavily reworked passage, Jeremiah adapts the image of divorce by Yahweh of Israel, on grounds of her adultery with other gods, to explain Israel's forcible removal from the ancestral home. Jeremiah cites the law that prohibits the reconstitution of a marriage once dissolved by divorce, where one of the parties has subsequently remarried. The legal facts are undisputed – but the questions then suggested and opened up are more interesting, and more troubling in Jerusalem, than the facts: Will the people's 'divorce' from Yahweh be as irrevocable as any human divorce would have to be? Is Judah heading for the same fate as Israel?

7.4.2 Beyond this shared concern of Kings and Jeremiah we should next note their common interest in 'prophecy' and 'the word of the Lord'. The terms 'prophet' and 'prophesy' are commoner in Kings and Jeremiah than anywhere else in the Hebrew Scriptures; and *dbr yhwh* occurs quite the most frequently in these two books and in Ezekiel. Not only so: the overwhelming proportion of instances in Kings of *nby'* (prophet) and *dbr yhwh* (the word of Yahweh) are located within our strata (c)and (d) as identified in *7.2.1* above: those best candidates for identification with the 'Deuteronomists' who gave the Books of Kings their distinctive shape.

7.4.3 Then there is a great deal of language shared between Jeremiah and Kings. This fact has been given repeated scholarly attention, without convergent results being achieved. There are two frequently cited monographs. The one (Weippert 1973) argues against the view that the prose speeches of Jeremiah were Deuteronomistic creations, and the other (Thiel 1972, 1982) attempts to demonstrate that the book of Jeremiah was edited by the Deuteronomists. This discussion has been reviewed in the recent commentaries on Jeremiah (very fully in McKane 1986: xli–l); and I suspect it will have to be reviewed anew in the light of our fresh questions about the origins of the books of Kings.

7.4.3.1 Typical of the many links between the book of Jeremiah and the books of Kings is their shared blame of Manasseh (with Jer 15: 1–4 compare 2Kgs 24: 3–4), discussed also by Seeligmann (1978: 281–2).

7.4.3.2 The other book in which the verb 'provoke' is at all commonly used is Jeremiah – in its later layers. Only Jer 8: 19 could deserve serious consideration as being early since it appears in a poetic context, while the other five contexts (7: 18, 19; 11: 17; 25: 6, 7; 32: 29, 30, 32; and 44: 3, 8) are part of the developed prose – in fact 25: 7 and 32: 30 are MT pluses, not represented in the Greek. McKane's doubts, however, are to be taken very seriously: he does not even print Jer 8:19 in his translation (1986: 193) and holds that this mention of provocation has been copied secondarily from 7: 18–19.

7.4.4 Given the many similarities of language between the two books, and given our case that the beginnings of Israel's story as told in Kings cannot be earlier than the core of the book of Jeremiah, it seems not unreasonable to see in Jeremiah the vital impulses towards the composition of Kings. In recent scholarship, it has been their shared language and the explanatory motifs common to Kings and Jeremiah that have been cited to explain the ancient tradition found both among the early rabbis and in the early church fathers that 'Jeremiah wrote his own book and . . . the book of Kings'. Indeed that may suffice to explain such an attribution in a period when it was customary to explain the sacredness of certain texts by naming an inspired and revered figure as the authority behind them. Yet, beyond this and with no suggestion that what I am proposing was intended by those for whom the tradition was important, I am of the opinion that Jeremiah, or at least his book, may have had some influence on the books of Kings.

7.4.5 There is a danger that our fumbling for a new approach and a new terminology consists of too many riddles. I have simply been drawing attention to the possible connectedness of a few strands: the Books of Jeremiah and Kings are well known as having several close links; the origins of the Book of Jeremiah are no earlier than the very end of Judah's monarchy; the origins of the Books of Kings are no earlier than the collapse of that monarchy, for our Shared Text on which they depend itself tells the story of that collapse. Given these relationships, it may make more sense to argue from Jeremiah to Kings, rather than the other way round, especially when issues relating to prophecy are a prominent concern of those who turned the Shared Text into the prototype of Kings. At the very least, we should become more cautious (if not yet quite to the point of silence) about using the term 'Deuteronomistic', as defined by (Deuteronomy-)Kings, in analyses of the Book of Jeremiah.

7.5 Judah's Kings and Judah's Collapse

The Books of Kings invite their readers to view Israel's fate as a model for, as an explanation of, the similar fate that befell Judah. But Israel is not blamed for the southern kingdom's fate. That dishonour belongs to David's line. The writers of Kings inherited from their major source the summary verdicts on each king who had 'done right/evil in Yahweh's eyes'. The Chronicler moved in the direction of offering even a notorious sinner like Manasseh an opportunity for repentance. But Kings was resolutely unforgiving to David's line: when it in turn wanted an illustration of the surprising quality of divine mercy, it chose Ahab of Israel rather than Manasseh of Judah. Early kings about whom its authors had learned little beyond their reputation for having done right are now blamed anachronistically for their attitude to the 'high places'. Added narratives about David and Solomon exhibit a darker wisdom than had formerly been attributed to the founding fathers of the dynasty. And even Hezekiah and Josiah are unable to alter the collective fate of the royal line, despite acting according to the best standards of Moses and David combined. The demands made of David by Nathan and of Solomon directly in a divine vision are clearly remembered. The privileges of divine choice are reduced to zero.

8

Casting Off

8.0 Introduction

Endings and beginnings are closely entwined. Accordingly, it seems suitable to gather my few remaining remarks under a tolerant rubric. 'Casting off' can convey the completion of a woollen garment, by detaching it from the needles on which it has been knitted. It can convey the inauguration of a new voyage when a boat's mooring ropes are thrown aboard. And, because 'cast-offs' are also thrown out when no longer serviceable, our rubric could equally presage the fate of a presumptuous colleague rusticated from orderly scholarly society – quite as menacing as the dangers attending a boat leaving safe haven!

We took our cue from two details in the Solomon story: his vision at Gibeon and the end of his dedicatory prayer in the Jerusalem temple. From these worked examples we looked back through a more original image of Solomon towards an earlier form of the whole story of David's royal line. And, with that still imperfectly focussed story as our pattern, we then looked forwards and plotted some of the radical shifts of perception introduced in various re-tellings of the story in Kings no less than in Chronicles. Just as the Books of Kings became more critical of the kings of Judah than their source had been, just as in its pages these kings lost some of their privilege (and none of them more than Solomon), so these Books of Kings – and not least their traditional Hebrew text – must lose their pride of place as our best source for the history of the period they describe. And that conclusion alone must make the end of this book the beginning of several others.

8.1 Joshua, Judges, and Samuel

Where has the argument been leading in terms of reading the other 'Former Prophets'? Having pledged myself to prepare a large-scale commentary on Joshua, I will shortly find out what sort of trap I have dug for myself in publishing this study. If it was the addition of the northern story with its prophetic critique – originally intended, Jeremiah-like, as a mirror in which the south might view itself and shudder – that signalled the fresh creation of the Books of Kings out of the Common Text, this new work in its new geographical dimensions soon took on a life of its own. Remarkably few of the stories of David and Solomon that Samuel-Kings and Chronicles share are actually played out in northern territory. David makes war widely in Philistia and Aram, and in much of what we call Transjordan. But hardly a domestic place-name is mentioned outside Judah: and the prominent exceptions, Geba and Jericho, are just inside neighbouring Benjamin. Similarly, Solomon's first vision is at Benjaminite Gibeon, itself only a short walk from Jerusalem; and the only other clear reference to northern Israelite territory concerns the Galilee towns at issue between Solomon and Hiram. Yet David and Solomon, originally kings of Judah, were available as monarchs of 'all Israel'. They were easily re-presented as belonging to, presiding over – as even having constituted – that ideal time before the division. In the case of Solomon, the addition of a list of officers in northern Israel responsible for his provisions month by month (1 Kgs 4: 7–19) and strategic Kings pluses mentioning 'Judah and Israel' (4: 20; 5: 5) were sufficiently suggestive to discourage serious probing by later readers of his 'all Israel' credentials.

8.1.1 This 'larger Israel' is the geopolitical entity whose prehistory is sketched in Joshua, Judges, and Samuel. The Saul stories are largely set north of Judah, yet not very far north. Many northern stories in Judges appear secondary to elements of northern stories in Samuel and Kings. Gideon or Jerubbaal, for example, anticipates aspects of the Jeroboam story: their Hebrew names are even more alike than appears in English dress – *yrb-b'l* and *yrb-'m*; and both are associated with Zeredah (or Zererah).[1] Again

[1] Judg 7: 22 and 1 Kgs 11: 26

Jeroboam's new cultic arrangements in Bethel and Dan (1 Kgs 12: 25–33)are anticipated – and mocked in advance – in the accounts in Jg 8: 24–28 of Gideon's false cult and in Jg 17–18 of the establishment by Danites in the north of a cult stolen from further south. Then there are several unflattering anticipations of Saul in Jg 19–21 (Auld 1989: 267).

8.1.2 Much of the literary stratification practised over twenty years on elements of Joshua-Kings, or Deuteronomy-Kings, remains valid. It is important that my earlier remarks (*7.2.3* above) about Dtr 1 and Dtr 2, and Dtr H/P/N should not be read as dismissing much of the valid argumentation behind these proposals. The present books of Kings and Chronicles were developed in stages from the Shared Text; and doubtless that Shared Text had also been developed in stages. But, just as I learned – excitingly – from my first experience of pre-historic archaeology, the relative stratigraphic interpretation of individual portions of a site may be fully understood, at the same time as the picture across the whole site is in serious need of adjustment.

8.2 Deuteronomy

The course we have taken may have dragged the anchor which has linked the Book of Deuteronomy historically, since the time of de Wette at least, to the reform of Josiah. Dragged the anchor, but not cut its cable: even the story of Josiah in our Shared Text talks of a book found in the temple – and Huldah's response to the king's emissaries has some 'Deuteronomic' features. But once we concede that most of the specific reform measures listed in 2 Kgs 23: 4–20 are Kings pluses to a base text which itself is post-monarchic, then many of the claimed links between Deuteronomy and a historical Josiah have been removed. On the other side, we would want to go beyond our earlier discussion that questioned whether Nathan's oracle and Solomon's prayer and visions were really prime examples of Deuteronomistic composition (*7.2* above). We suggested then that these texts were influenced as a whole by the poetic tradition which has also given us the royal psalms. We would now also want to claim that elements in them influenced portions of Deuteronomy, rather than the other way round. One good example is the strange phrase *šmr hbryt whḥsd*. In 1Kgs 8: 23 // 2Chr 6: 14, as in all occurrences of the phrase and its close relatives, it is used within prayer. In line with the principle that 'how you pray is how you believe' (*lex orandi lex credendi*), it appears that what had long been prayed became part of official 'teaching' (*torah*) in Dt 7: 9, 12. Not only so, such a development provides a further example of a promise originally understood as belonging to the Davidic line being 'democratised' in favour of the nation Israel.

8.3 History-Writing and Sources

John Van Seters opened a recent discussion of 'Historiography in the Deuteronomistic History'[1] by contrasting positions taken up by Halpern and Garbini. Halpern (1988) he cites as holding 'that Dtr H "concocts" nothing but is dependent upon received data for all of his "facts". His ideology is only the logical interpretation of his material . . . ' On the other hand, Garbini (1988) 'asserts that in Dtr H and in the OT generally ideology is everything and that historical documents could be manipulated freely in the service of that ideology.'

This book offers a measure of support to both rival positions. In terms of our discussion, the authors of Kings and of Chronicles are the historians whose work actually appears in the biblical text. We can compare their finished work with their major source. We find in both of them very substantial fidelity in transcribing the words of that source. And we also find in both of them many examples of the 'logical interpretation' of which Halpern writes. And yet at the very same time – witness only the great differences in ideological atmosphere between Kings and Chronicles – both the fidelity and the logic are operating in a wider hermeneutical context.

8.4 Newer Study of the Pentateuch

Some of the recent fresh discussion of Pentateuchal origins, of the

---

[1] I am grateful to Professor Van Seters for making available to me the text of his presentation to the Deuteronomistic History section of the Society of Biblical Literature at its meeting in San Francisco in November 1992.

development of and inter-relationships between, different strands of the Pentateuch, has appealed to the analogy of the known relationship between the Deuteronomistic and Chronistic Histories – or, more locally, between Kings and Chronicles (see especially Johnstone 1988). The relevance of such an analogy can be reaffirmed, though with some modification. We have found much evidence of substantial supplementation to older texts that permits, and even requires, reinterpretation of what was there before. But our observation of the development of the Books of Samuel-Kings and Chronicles should discourage us from citing the Chronicles' analogy in favour of any theory proposing major rewriting of the original words of a text by any editor who supplemented them.

8.5 The 'Real' and the 'Ideal'

One of the results of this study may be to encourage fresh scrutiny of the inter-relationships between more realistic and more idealised materials in the Hebrew Bible. It is often assumed that more realistic reports are earlier, and closer to what they describe. We have argued, especially in the case of David and Solomon, that the more ideal portrayals found in the Shared Text – and to an extent still in Chronicles as well – existed prior to the critical realism of Kings. Very likely it was only after the institution of the monarchy no longer wielded power, in fact was no longer there at all, that it could be criticised as openly as it was in Samuel and Kings. It is with the help of Chronicles that we have recovered the story of Judah which Kings also rewrote. It is with the help of Chronicles that we have recovered the ideology of Judah's kings which the Books of Kings called in question – that privileged position which the kings had enjoyed, but which in Kings' eyes they had deservedly forfeited.

Bibliography

Ackroyd, P. R.
1982   'Isaiah 36–39: Structure and Function', in W. C.
        Delsman et al. (eds), *Von Kanaan bis Kerala:*
        Festschrift für J. P. M.van der Ploeg O.P. (AOAT
        211), 3–21

Auld, A. G.
1983a   'Prophets Through the Looking Glass: Between
        Writings and Moses', *JSOT* 27, 3–23
1983b   'Prophets through the Looking Glass: A
        Response', *JSOT* 27, 41–44
1984   'Prophets and Prophecy in Jeremiah and Kings',
        ZAW 96, 66–82
1986   *Kings* (DSB)
1989   'Gideon: Hacking at the heart of the Old
        Testament', *VT* 39, 257–67
1992   'Salomo und die Deuteronomisten: Vision einer
        neuen Zukunft?', *ThZ* 48, 343–55
1993   'Solomon at Gibeon: History Glimpsed', *FS*
        Malamat (EI 23)

Auld, A. G. and Ho, Craig Y. S.
1992   'The Making of David and Goliath', *JSOT* 56, 19–
        39

Auld, A. G. and Steiner, M.
1994   *Jerusalem* (Cities of the Biblical World),
        Cambridge: Lutterworth,

Barnes, W. H.
1991   *Studies in the Chronology of the Divided Monarchy of Israel* (HSM 48)

Barr, J.
1989   *Spelling in the Hebrew Bible* (Schweich Lectures), Oxford: OUP, for the British Academy

Ben Zvi, E.
1991   'The Account of the Reign of Manasseh in II Reg 21, 1–18 and the Redactional History of the Book of Kings', *ZAW* 103, 355–74

Braun, R.L.
1986   *1 Chronicles* (WBC 14)

Brekelmans, C. H. W.
1982   'Solomon at Gibeon', in *Von Kanaan bis Kerala*, Festschrift für Professor J.P.M. van der Ploeg (AOAT 211), 53–59

Brettler, M.
1991a   'The Structure of 1 Kings 1–11', *JSOT* 49, 87–97
1991b   '2 Kings 24: 13–14 as History', *CBQ* 53, 541–52

Burney, C. F.
1903   *Notes on the Hebrew Text of the Book of Kings*, Oxford: Clarendon

Chamaza, G. W. V.
1988   *Hizkijjahu Rey de Judá. Interpretación y reconstrucción de las narraciones de Ezequías* (Institución San Jerónimo, 20), Valencia

Childs, B. S.
1967   *Isaiah and the Assyrian Crisis* (SBT 3)

Clements, R. E.
1980   *Isaiah and the Deliverance of Jerusalem: A study of the*

interpretation of prophecy in the Old Testament
(JSOTS 13)

1991   'The Prophecies of Isaiah to Hezekiah
        concerning Sennacherib: 2 Kings 19.21–34 //
        Isaiah 37.22–35', in R. Liwak and S. Wagner
        (eds), *Prophetie und geschichtliche
        Wirklichkeit im alten Israel*, Stuttgart:
        Kohlhammer, 65-78

Cogan, M. and Tadmor, H.
1988   *II Kings* (Anchor Bible)

Cross, F. M.
1973   *Canaanite Myth and Hebrew Epic*, Cambridge:
        Harvard University Press,

De Vries, S. J.
1985   *1 Kings* (WBC 12)

Dietrich, W.
1972   *Prophetie und Geschichte* (FRLANT 108)

Eslinger, L.
1986   'Josiah and the Torah Book: Comparison of 2
        Kgs 22: 1–23: 28 and 2 Chr 34: 1–35: 19', *HAR*
        10, 37–62

Fishbane, M.
1985   *Biblical Interpretation in Ancient Israel*, Oxford:
        Clarendon

Floss, J. P.
1989   *David und Jerusalem. Ziele und Folgen des
        Stadteroberungsberichts 2 Sam 5,6-9
        literaturwissenschaftlich betrachtet* (ATSAT 30)

Frisch, A.
1991a   'Structure and its Significance: The Narrative of
        Solomon's Reign (1 Kings 1–12: 24)', *JSOT* 51, 3–
        14

1991b   'The Narrative of Solomon's Reign: A Rejoinder',
           JSOT 51, 22–24

Garbini, G.
   1988   *History and Ideology in Ancient Israel*, London:
           SCM

Gelander, S.
   1991   *David and his God. Religious Ideas as reflected in
           Biblical Historiography and Literature* (Jerusalem
           Biblical Studies 5), Jerusalem: Simor

Gonçalves, F. J.
   1986   *L'Expédition de Sennachérib en Palestine dans la
           Littérature Hébraïque Ancienne* (Études Bibliques,
           NS 7), Paris: Gabalda,

Haag, H.
   1951   'La Campagne de Sennachérib contre Jérusalem
           en 701', *RB* 58, 348–59

Halpern, B.
   1988   *The First Historians: The Hebrew Bible and History*,
           San Francisco: Harper and Row,

Halpern, B. and Vanderhooft, D. S.
   1991   'The Editions of Kings in the 7th–6th Centuries
           B.C.E.', *HUCA* 62, 179–244

Hardmeier, C.
   1990   *Prophetie im Streit vor dem Untergang Judas* (BZAW
           187)

Hobbs, T. R.
   1985   *2 Kings* (WBC 13)

Hoffmann, H.-D.
   1980   *Reform und Reformen: Untersuchungen zu einem
           Grundthema der deuteronomistischen*

Geschichtsschreibung (AThANT 66)

Hurvitz, A.
1974   'The Evidence of Language in Dating the Priestly
        Code: A linguistic study in technical idioms and
        terminology', *RB* 81, 24–56

Japhet, S.
1989   *The Ideology of the Book of Chronicles and its Place in
        Biblical Thought* (BEATAJ 9)

Jobling, D.
1991   '"Forced Labour": Solomon's Golden Age and
        the Question of Literary Representation', in
        Poststructuralism as Exegesis, *Semeia* 54, 57–76

Johnstone, W.
1987   'Reactivating the Chronicles Analogy in
        Pentateuchal Studies with Special Reference to
        the Sinai Pericope in Exodus', *ZAW* 99, 16–37

Jones, G. H.
1984   *1 and 2 Kings* (NCB)

Joosten, J.
1992   'Biblical Hebrew *weqatal* and Syriac *hwa qatel*
        Expressing Repetition in the Past', *ZAH* 5, 1–14

Konkel, A. H.
1993   'The Source of the Hezekiah Story in Isaiah', *VT*
        43, 462–482

Koopmans, W. T.
1991   'The Testament of David in 1 Kings ii 1–10', *VT*
        41, 429–49

Lowery, R. H.
1991   *The Reforming Kings: Cult and Society in First
        Temple Judah* (JSOTS 120)

McConville, J. G.
1989 'Narrative and Meaning in the Books of Kings',
Bib 70, 31–49

McKane, W.
1986 *Jeremiah 1–20* (ICC)

McKenzie, S. L.
1985 *The Chronicler's Use of the Deuteronomistic History*
(HSM 33)
1991 *The Trouble with Kings* (SVT 42)

Le Moyne, J.
1957 'Les deux Ambassades de Sennachérib à
Jérusalem', *Mélanges Bibliques redigés en l'honneur
de Andre Robert* (Travaux de l'Institut Catholique
de Paris, 4), Paris, 149–153

Nelson, R. D.
1981 *The Double Redaction of the Deuteronomistic History*
(JSOTS 18)
1986 'The Altar of Ahaz: A Revisionist View', *HAR* 10,
267–76

Noth, M.
1943 *Überlieferungsgeschichtliche Studien*. EngTr *The
Deuteronomistic History* (1981; JSOTS 15); *The
Chronicler's History* (1987; JSOTS 50)

O'Brien, M. A.
1989 *The Deuteronomistic History Hypothesis : A
Reassessment* (OBO 92)

O'Neill, J. C.
1991 'The Lost Written Records of Jesus' Words and
Deeds behind our Records', *JTS* (NS) 42, 483–
504

Parker, K. I.
  1988   'Repetition as a Structuring Device in 1 Kings 1–
           11', *JSOT* 42, 19–27
  1991   'The Limits to Solomon's Reign: A response to
           Amos Frisch', *JSOT* 51, 15–21
  1992   'Solomon as Philosopher King? The Nexus of
           Law and Wisdom in 1 Kings 1–11', *JSOT* 53, 75–
           91

Provan, I. W.
  1988   *Hezekiah and the Books of Kings* (BZAW 172)

Rofé, A.
  1988   *The Prophetical Stories. The Narratives about the
           Prophets in the Hebrew Bible: Their Literary Types
           and History*, Jerusalem: Magnes

Schniedewind, W. M.
  1991   'The Source Citations of Manasseh: King
           Manasseh in History and Homily', *VT* 41, 450–61

Seeligmann, I. L.
  1978   'Die Auffassung von der Prophetie in der
           deuteronomistischen und chronistischen
           Geschichtsschreibung (mit einem Exkurs über
           das Buch Jeremia)', *Congress Volume Göttingen
           1977* (SVT 29), 254–84

Seitz, C. R.
  1991   *Zion's Final Destiny. The Development of the Book of
           Isaiah: A Reassessment of Isaiah 36–39*,
           Minneapolis: Fortress

Shaver, J. R.
  1990   'Passover Legislation and the Identity of the
           Chronicler's Law Book', *Society and Literature in
           Analysis* (New Perspectives on Ancient Judaism
           5), 135–49

Smelik, K. A. D.
1986 'Distortion of Old Testament Prophecy. The Purpose of Isaiah xxxvi and xxxvii', in A. S. van der Woude (ed.), *Crises and Perspectives* (OTS 24), 70–93
1992a 'Hezekiah Advocates True Prophecy. Remarks on Isaiah xxxvi and xxxvii // II Kings xviii and xix', in *Converting the Past: Studies in Ancient Israelite and Moabite Historiography* (OTS 28), 93–128
1992b 'The Portrayal of King Manasseh. A literary analysis of II Kings xxi and II Chronicles xxxiii', in *Converting the Past: Studies in Ancient Israelite and Moabite Historiography* (OTS 28), 129–189

Smend, R.
1978 *Die Entstehung des Alten Testaments* (ThW 1)

Strübind, K.
1991 *Tradition als Interpretation in der Chronik* (BZAW 201)

Thiel, W.
1973 *Die deuteronomistische Redaktion von Jeremia 1–25* (WMANT 41)
1981 *Die deuteronomistische Redaktion von Jeremia 26–52* (WMANT 52)

Throntveit, M. A.
1988 'Hezekiah in the Books of Chronicles' (SBL 1988 Seminar Papers), 302–11

Trebolle-Barrera, J.
1980 *Salomón y Jeroboán. Historia de la recensión y redacción de I Reyes 2–12; 14* (Bibliotheca Salamaticensis. Dissertationes 3), Salamanca
1982 'Redaction, Recension, and Midrash in the Books of Kings', *BIOSCS* 15, 12–35
1984 *Jehú y Joás* (Institución San Jerónimo 17), Valencia

in press　'Histoire du Texte des Livres Historiques et Histoire de la Composition et de la Rédaction Deutéronomistes. Avec une Publication Préliminaire de 4Q481a, "Apocryphe d'Élisée"', *Congress Volume Paris 1992* (SVT)

Van Seters, J.
1992　'Historiography in the Deuteronomistic History', unpublished paper read to the Deuteronomistic History section of the SBL Meeting in San Francisco

Veijola, T.
1977　*Das Königtum in der Beurteilung des deuteronomistischen Historiographie* (AASF 198)

Verheij, A. C. J.
1990　*Verbs and Numbers* (Studia Semitica Neerlandica 28)
1992　'Die hebräischen Synopsen als Hilfsmittel beim sprachlichen Vergleich paralleler Text', *VT* 42, 90–102

Weinfeld, M.
1972　*Deuteronomy and the Deuteronomic School*, Oxford: Oxford University Press

Weippert, H.
1973　*Die Prosareden des Jeremiabuches* (BZAW 132)

Wellhausen, J.
1889　*Die Composition des Hexateuchs und der historischen Bücher des Alten Testaments*, Berlin

Welten, P.
1973　*Geschichte und Geschichtsdarstellung in den Chronikbüchern* (WMANT 48)

de Wette, W. L. M.
1806/7   *Beiträge zur Einleitung in das Alte Testament*

Willi, T.
1972   *Die Chronik als Auslegung*, Göttingen:
          Vandenhoeck & Rupprecht

Williamson, H. G. M.
1977   *Israel in the Books of Chronicles*, Cambridge:
          Cambridge University Press
1982   *1 and 2 Chronicles* (NCB)
1983   'A Response to A. G. Auld', *JSOT* 27, 33–9

Willis, T. M.
1991   'The Text of 1 Kings 11: 43–12: 3', *CBQ* 53, 37–
          44

Index of Authors

Parker, K. I. 31–4
Provan, I. W. viii, 5, 97

Rofé, A. 112

Schniedewind, W. M. 83
Seeligmann, 163, 169
Seitz, C. R. 98–100
Shaver, J. R. 131–2
Smelik, K. A. D 73, 98–100,
102
Smend, R. 153
Steiner, M. 24
Strübind, K. 95

Thiel, W. 168
Throntveit, M. A. 139
Trebolle-Barrera, J. v, 6–8,
22, 25, 79, 144–5, 151,
164

Van Seters, J. 174
Veijola, T. 153
Verheij, A. C. J. 9, 11

Weinfeld, M. 119
Weippert, H. 168
Wellhausen, J. 4, 8
Welten, P. 4
de Wette, W. L. M. 3, 8
Willi, T. 4, 64
Williamson, H. G. M. 4, 8,
40, 64, 125, 131
Willis, T. M. 164

Index of Biblical References